T0146996

FIVE
POLITICAL
PLAYS

FIVE
POLITICAL
PLAYS

1997

CHEAP THRILL

ZERO HOUR

LEARNING TO LIVE WITH
PERSONAL GROWTH

SISTERS IN THE GREAT
DAY CARE WAR

ARTHUR MILNER

FIVE POLITICAL PLAYS

1997 / CHEAP THRILL / ZERO HOUR / LEARNING TO LIVE WITH PERSONAL GROWTH / SISTERS IN THE GREAT DAY CARE WAR

Front Cover Photo Credit: Peter Robb
Back Cover Photo Credit: Anna-Bella Randall
Cover Design: Sam Awwad

iUniverse books may be ordered through booksellers or by contacting:

iUniverse
1663 Liberty Drive
Bloomington, IN 47403
www.iuniverse.com
1-800-Authors (1-800-288-4677)

ISBN: 978-1-5320-5881-3 (sc)
ISBN: 978-1-5320-5882-0 (e)

Print information available on the last page.

iUniverse rev. date: 11/21/2018

for

Gillian Brewin
and
John Graham

Humility is not thinking less of yourself, it's thinking of yourself less.
— C.S. Lewis

Everything changes, except the avant-garde.
— Paul Valéry

Contents

Introduction

The newest play in this collection is 28 years old. It's a shock for me to write that; they still seem as fresh and relevant as the day they were born. As if.

Self-publishing has made it simple and inexpensive to leave a legacy. This is part of mine. There is, however, a better reason for this collection, and that is to leave a record of what some of us used to mean by political theatre.

I started my theatre career in 1976, with the Great Canadian Theatre Company (GCTC) in Ottawa, Canada. These were nationalist and left-wing times in Canadian theatre. GCTC was dedicated to producing Canadian and political plays, by which we meant plays written by Canadians and about elections, history, social issues, etc. It was pretty broad, but not borderless; "the personal is political" and "everything is political" were not GCTC slogans.

Soon, however, "political" began to mean other things in the theatre world. Some of my colleagues seemed to think "formal experimentation" was political. Others argued that political plays had to be written collectively and/or through improvisation. And government funding bodies started encouraging the inclusion of what was called "target groups" (women, Aboriginals and visible minorities, for example); and a lot of theatre artists began to accept that politics meant "inclusion." The explicit political content that had been all the rage went out of style.

The five plays in this collection are political because of their content. Four of them are about, in a word, inequality — in two words, income inequality. The fifth is about U.S. interference in Central America. *1997* was supposed to be a collective creation by four writers. We had worked on a play called *Sandinista!*, about the Nicaraguan revolution, and now we wanted to write about technology and the future of work. But one of us quit GCTC and moved to British Columbia; another was having a baby; the third was Patrick McDonald, GCTC's then artistic director, who claimed he was too busy; so, the writing fell to me. *1997* was my first play for adults. Patrick's contribution was enormous and Ian Tamblyn composed a fantastic, haunting score. According to Geoff Pevere, reviewing for local radio station CHEZ-FM (December 2, 1983),

> 1984 is only a few weeks away and I think that as much as we may feel that we are on the brink of a new age of technological knowledge which is going to allow us to do anything we want, in many other ways George Orwell was perfectly right and the signs of a possible 1984 are present in society today. This is the attitude that *1997* adopts and shows us—in a way which is both entertaining and educational and, I think, finally, pretty disturbing.

In 1984, 1997 seemed so far away.

After *1997*, I was made full-time Playwright in Residence at GCTC. That was, in Canada, an extremely privileged position—there was, I think, one other in the country. Patrick would ask what I wanted to write about, which tended to be whatever political issue was obsessing me at the time. We'd come up with a title and then advertise the show as part of the next season—before a single word had been written. I always came up with a play, though one time the pre-selected title was so wildly inappropriate that we announced a change in the season.

Patrick and I had worked on two plays for an organization representing people who lived in public housing, and poverty became (and remains) central to my politics. In those days, I would write from 11 p.m. until 5 a.m. One night, I was working on the pre-titled *Cheap Thrill*. I started with a single mother taking two rich men hostage in a fancy restaurant. By midnight of the third evening, I'd finished act one. I called Patrick and told him I wanted to hear it read. "Sure," he said, "I'll call people first thing in the morning."

"I want to hear it now."

A half hour later, there were four of us in my apartment. We laughed a lot. That's how GCTC worked in those days.

For my next play, I wanted to go back to Central America, literally and literarily. I managed to get my way paid to Nicaragua and Costa Rica. Our first visit to Nicaragua, for *Sandinista!*, had been a party. Everyone was celebrating. Wherever we went, people sang *Adelante Marchemos Compañeros!* Now, four years later, no one remembered the words. The country was tired and confused. U.S. support for counterrevolution was definitely responsible, but so was, some argued, the Sandinista government's destruction of the markets that had sustained, for example, a thriving shoe industry. As I write this, Nicaragua is again in turmoil and again in the news. If someone pays my way, I'll go write another play.

The next year, I returned to the subject of poverty, but this time from the point of view of the middle class. *Learning to Live with Personal Growth,* in 1987, would be my most personal play until *Getting to Room Temperature* in 2016. The characters were invented or composites, but they were people I had "known" for years. This is the only play I've written that required no research. It's about the sixties generation—my generation—selling out.

I grew up in a very Jewish household and my parents were adamant Zionists. I avoided discussing Israel and Palestine with them because discussion would end in screams and tears. But now I was a committed political playwright, and no one was writing about the subject, so I figured it was my responsibility. *Masada* took the most research I'd ever done. The Middle East has a very long and complicated history, but I kept reading because it was fascinating, disturbing, informative, dramatic and important. The writing was difficult: how does one approach a subject so vast—in a year?

It took three years. I don't remember exactly why. For one thing, Patrick left GCTC for Greener pastures. (This is a very clever pun: he was appointed Artistic Director at Green Thumb Theatre in Vancouver, B.C.) GCTC's new AD was Steven Bush, who insisted plays be written before being sold to subscribers.

In any case, *Masada* was the toughest project I'd taken on. After several development workshops, Steven Bush directed *Masada* in 1990. Meanwhile, I was commissioned to write two other plays: *The City* for Workshop West Theatre in Edmonton; and *Sisters in the Great Day Care War* for Local 2204 of the Canadian Union of Public Employees.

I don't know if there was much discussion at CUPE Local 2204 about the wisdom of hiring a man to write a play about a day care strike that involved almost exclusively women. I doubt that would happen today, but back then there weren't a lot of Ottawa playwrights. (Some years later, they would have been able to approach Morwyn Brebner, Rosa Laborde, Hannah Moscovitch, Darrah Teitel ...)

I recorded and transcribed interviews with seven women who had been deeply involved in the strike. *Sisters in the Great Day Care War* had five characters, composites of the women I interviewed. The dialogue consisted almost entirely of edited, actually spoken words. These days, *Sisters* would be called "devised theatre." Linda Balduzzi directed and, if I remember correctly, came up with the brilliant idea of setting the dialogue in the context of the women painting a backdrop for a video they were making.

The strike, though successful in the short term, had been a Pyrrhic victory. The five women on whom the show was primarily based sat in the front row every night and cried. They said, "Thank you for telling our story." Some of the union activists were less impressed. They would have preferred something more uplifting.

I spent several months getting to know the women who went on strike and then several weeks with the women who portrayed them. For the most part, everyone seemed happy to forget I was in the room. It was a great experience and a great honour.

The City opened at Workshop West in Edmonton in 1989 (with a radio adaptation for the CBC, broadcast and published in 1991). *Masada* opened at GCTC in January 1990 and *Sisters* opened six months later. A year later, I was appointed GCTC Artistic Director. And thus came to an end a hectic and prolific seven years of writing that included seven mainstage plays and four plays for young audiences.

* * *

It's easy to be nostalgic about those days. It was incredibly exciting and we laughed a lot. We had disagreements, of course, and some of them ended badly. Most of us who worked at GCTC in the early days had no theatre training. We made it up as we went along. When we had the means, we began to hire professionals and our work improved. But there was a cost. There was an expression going around: "Too many Canadian plays are staged before they're ready." I can't imagine a more conservative sentiment. It sounds so sensible, yet it so effectively justifies not taking risks, not doing new plays, sticking to the classics.

It's also true that more than 30 years ago government arts funding began to fall as a proportion of total budgets, which further inhibited risk taking. Theatres now put donors and potential fundraisers on their boards; and boards hire managers and fundraisers to be their Artistic Directors. It's all so sensible.

A few years ago, in November 2012, I got a phone call from Worn Red Theatre in London, U.K. They wanted to know if rights were available for my play, *Facts*, a murder mystery set in Palestine. *Facts* opened at the Finborough Theatre four months later! The Finborough, apparently, sold half-year subscriptions and kept a slot open for topical, last-minute additions. It seemed to me a miracle. But London Theatre is a special case; one can find a great deal of theatre of every type.

For the most part, as I look at plays being done across Canada this year, I wonder: would it much matter if they opened 10 years from now instead?

But around the country there are glimmers of hope for a renaissance of engaged narrative realism. In Toronto this year, for example, I saw *Other Side of the Game* by Amanda Parris, *Calpurnia* by Audrey Dwyer, and *Bang Bang* by Kat Sandler. Three plays by young (compared to me) and talented playwrights; three plays that are actually about something.

* * *

I want to acknowledge the many people associated with GCTC in those days to whom I owe a great deal: Aline Akeson, Linda Balduzzi, Robert Bockstael, Jennifer Brewin, Mary Burns, Steven Bush, Douglas Campbell, Naomi Campbell, Rebecca Campbell, Vincent Chetcuti, Martin Conboy, Lorna Cunningham-Rushton, Havi Echenberg, Mary Ellis, Heather Esdon, Peter Findlay, Susan Freeman, Dave Hagerman, Mitzi Hauser, John Koensgen, Maureen Labonté, Larry Laxdal, Barbara Lysnes, Catherine MacKenzie, Larry McDonald, Patrick McDonald, Henry Milner, Robin Mossley, Dorothy O'Connell, Arthur Penson, Peter Robb, Brigitte Robinson, Roy Robitschek, Terrence Scammell, Ian Tamblyn, George F. Walker, Beverley Wolfe, Gil Osborne Woodstrom. And I want to thank Sam Awwad and Sabina Lysnes for their very generous assistance with this volume.

Some people go into theatre in pursuit of wealth and stardom. Others want to discover new forms. Most of us, I suspect, go into theatre because it's fun. We — my colleagues and comrades — did some pretty good work and some less good work and some excellent work. But we were always ambitious and, in those days, it was always fun. My deepest gratitude.

1997

1997 was first produced by the Great Canadian Theatre Company in Ottawa, Canada, on December 1, 1983, with the following cast:

Gritz	Robert Bockstael
Denise	Mitzi Hauser
Star	Dorian Ellis
Holdom, Rob, Saunders, Koestler	John Koensgen
Mark, Jason, MacKenzie	Robin Mossley
Zoë	Kirsten Charlebois
Sheila	Mary Burns
Ter	Bob Stark
Murray	Phil Gray
Al	Jim Yeatman

Director	Patrick McDonald
Musical score	Ian Tamblyn
Set and costumes	Arthur Penson
Lighting	Cedric Broten
Stage Manager	Barry Burns

Characters
Gritz: former police detective, 50s
  the inside
Star: computer engineer, 30s
Holdom: military officer, 50s
Saunders: computer company manager, 40s
Koestler: computer company manager, 40s
Jason: computer engineer, 30s
MacKenzie: computer company manager, 30s
Sheila: robotic voice
  the outside
Denise: nurse, 50s
Rob: unemployed factory worker, 40s
Mark: computer engineer, 30s
Zoë: homeless, 16
Ter: former student, 20s
Murray: thug, 40s
Al: doesn't move or speak, 20s

Setting
  the inside
Gritz's office (a computer should not be visible); Systemix office (with
computers and monitors); Koestler's office; a factory; a park
  the outside
A large, run-down basement apartment (the "squat")

ACT ONE

Scene 1
Stage is dark.

SHEILA: Frank Dmitri Gritziotis. Date of birth, three, seven, sixty-one. Height, one hundred sixty-one centimetres. Weight, 72 kilograms. Hair, brown. Eyes, brown.

(*Lights up on Gritz in his office. Holdom appears on monitor.*)

HOLDOM: Mr Gritziotis. You're late.

GRITZ: My watch stopped.

HOLDOM: We need you to do some work.

GRITZ: Who's we?

HOLDOM: Does it matter?

GRITZ: What kind of work?

HOLDOM: When was the last time you had a job?

GRITZ: Not for a few years, actually.

HOLDOM: August '91. Two weeks, security on a sidewalk sale. May 1990. A custody case. You haven't been doing very well.

GRITZ: I gave up that line of work.

HOLDOM: It gave you up. You fell behind. You don't know the difference between a floppy disc and a pancake. That's why we need you.

GRITZ: I don't understand.

HOLDOM: We need a detective familiar with old methods. Person to-person contact. We tried to get Covie. John Covie was number one.

GRITZ: He killed himself.

HOLDOM: So we want number two. If you've been thinking about suicide, try to hold on a little longer. Now. We want you to investigate the accident at Grafton.

GRITZ: Where?

HOLDOM: Grafton Nuclear.

GRITZ: Right, the accident.

HOLDOM: You can't tell me you haven't heard about it.

GRITZ: Was anyone killed?

HOLDOM: Don't you read the vee-boards?

GRITZ: Oh, I know what those are. There aren't many on the outside anymore. Someone wrecks them whenever they're set up.

HOLDOM: Hackers.

GRITZ: Yeah.

HOLDOM: Why do they hack the vee-boards?

GRITZ: 'Cause they don't believe what's on them.

HOLDOM: Comforting. The accident at Grafton was a class four disruption. I don't have to tell you how serious that is.

GRITZ: No.

HOLDOM: We've proven to our own satisfaction that the problem was in the liveware.

GRITZ: Liveware?

HOLDOM: Liveware. People.

GRITZ: Hardware, software, liveware.

HOLDOM: You've been disconnected for a long time.

GRITZ: Maybe some of the workers hacked it.

HOLDOM: There's no on-site liveware. It operates itself.

GRITZ: There's no people.

HOLDOM: There are no lights.

GRITZ: Very impressive, in some ways. Why do you think they blew it up?

HOLDOM: It didn't blow up, it — When something goes wrong in a reactor, it's supposed to restore, correct itself. There are two separate and parallel restore nets, so when one isn't working, it's supposed to transfer to the other.

GRITZ: Automatically?

HOLDOM: When we worked our way through the first restore net, we found a programming error. Standard sort of error, that's why there are two nets. But the crossover had been deleted.

GRITZ: Deleted?

HOLDOM: It wasn't there.

GRITZ: Where was it?

HOLDOM: It wasn't anywhere, it was gone. It's not a thing like, like your watch. It's a bit of information. When you forget your name, where does it go?

GRITZ: So the computer forgot to cross over.

HOLDOM: If it helps for you to think of it that way.

GRITZ: I'm getting the hang of it.

HOLDOM: But something made it forget.

GRITZ: Oh.

HOLDOM: When neither net operates, it's supposed to, tell somebody.

GRITZ: But it didn't.

HOLDOM: Another delete.

GRITZ: So who was it supposed to be cross-overed to? Who's the live-wire in charge?

HOLDOM: Liveware.

GRITZ: It's a joke.

HOLDOM: We've set up an office for you. With a computer. It will give you all the information you need.

GRITZ: Why me? I don't know the first thing about computers.

HOLDOM: We want someone who can deal with the liveware. All our staff investigators work through computers. We think anyone able to hack the program at Grafton could follow an investigation done by computer. In any case, our investigators are working on it. But they're not getting anywhere.

GRITZ: I suppose this could be dangerous.

HOLDOM: We'll give you a gun.

GRITZ: What if I don't want to do it?

HOLDOM: Why wouldn't you?

GRITZ: Fear. Habit.

HOLDOM: We'll pay you well.

GRITZ: Cash?

HOLDOM: Why would you want cash?

GRITZ: I might want to go somewhere where credits don't work.

HOLDOM: We can't pay cash.

GRITZ: What if I insist?

(Columns of figures appear on the monitor.)

HOLDOM: You are now seeing a record of your income credits for the current year. Coming up are your credits for next month.

(A new list appears.)

As you can see, you haven't used them yet. Now you have.

(The list disappears.)

GRITZ: I've been getting kind of bored anyway.

HOLDOM: Questions?

GRITZ: Hundreds. Two. These deletes. Do they show up a lot?

HOLDOM: No.

GRITZ: Ever?

HOLDOM: From time to time.

GRITZ: How often?

HOLDOM: The first one showed up in ninety-three. None in ninety-four, one in ninety-five. Three last year. Two at Grafton this year makes four.

GRITZ: It's only August.

HOLDOM: This is the first time two occurred in one program. The others were random. No pattern. No danger.

GRITZ: You're worried.

HOLDOM: Yes.

GRITZ: Question two. It's a statement actually. Thanks for the computer but ...

HOLDOM: Don't worry, it's friendly. You'll find your office ...

GRITZ: Office??

HOLDOM: Good luck, Gritz.

GRITZ: I'd rather work out of my apartment.

HOLDOM: No. We've gone to a lot of trouble to set you up in an office you'll be comfortable in. Two floors down. Room C three zero eight. Sheila will be there to help you.

GRITZ: Sheila?

Scene 2
A squat. Mark is working at a computer. Al is sitting. Denise enters and goes to watch Mark.

MARK: *(startled)* Don't sneak up on me like that.

DENISE: Getting anywhere?

MARK: I keep getting shut out. It's just a matter of time. Two, three thousand years maybe.

DENISE: I'll wait.

MARK: This came for you. *(He hands Denise a note.)*

DENISE: Decode it.

MARK: Spruce Grove, negative.

DENISE: Shit.

MARK: They're scared.

DENISE: So?

(TER enters, carrying a bucket of water.)

TER: Hot water. Check. Soap? Forget it. Towel? *(to Mark and Denise)* You guys seen a towel? How about a large rag? *(to Al)* Hey, Al. You seen a towel? No? Thanks.

DENISE: I'm going to go on the food run this afternoon. We need another dump.

(Rob and Zoë enter, running and laughing.)

TER: You guys seen a towel? *(Rob and Zoë laugh.)* What are we stoned on?

MARK: *(to Denise)* Can you get a message to Dave on your way out? His line's down.

DENISE: *(looking at Zoë's arm)* What did you do to your arm?

ZOË: I hurt it.

ROB: We pulled off a major operation.

TER: Mug an old lady?

ROB: *(threatens Ter)* You steal a towel?

ZOË: We were downtown.

DENISE: Yes?

ZOË: A food van pulled up in front of a big building and this big crowd comes. There were no police anywhere and the driver got out. The food was locked in the back and he said he didn't have a key. Everyone was angry. The driver took off and everybody tried to smash the doors.

ROB: Then we let the air out of the tires and smashed the windshield.

TER: Assholes.

ZOË: Tight, eh?

ROB: This dork in a suit starts yelling for us to stop. Yelling for the cops.

ZOË: It was taking too long so we ran. Fun, run, fun, eh?

TER: Stupid jerks.

ZOË: You're the jerk.

TER: Stupid hackers. *(exits)*

ZOË: It's just fun.

ROB: Forget it, Zoë. The jerk's got better things to do with his life.

DENISE: There's a net meeting tonight. We need people to take care of the kids.

ZOË: Me.

DENISE: Rob?

ROB: Yeah, yeah.

MARK: I knew this guy, he worked on it for six months but finally he accessed the vee-boards. But by then, all the vee-boards on the outside had been smashed.

ROB: So?

MARK: So don't hack hardware.

ROB: Yeah?

MARK: We might need them.

ROB: You just love your bloody machines.

MARK: Come on.

ROB: Where to?

DENISE: It's been bothering me for a while, too. It's dangerous and it's not worth it.

ROB: I say it is.

DENISE: Then go live somewhere else.

ROB: What?

DENISE: If you want to ...

ROB: At least we're doing something. At least they know we're alive out here. Half of Mark's equipment is shit we've stolen. You want us to stop that?

MARK: That's different.

DENISE: Maybe.

ROB: What are you worried about?

DENISE: The nets.

ROB: Oh. Don't get me wrong, I love your little welfare system, but ...

DENISE: It's not little and it's not a welfare system.

ROB: A little food? Music lessons for the kids? Free carpentry for senior citizens and cripples? You think that's a threat to someone? They love people like you on the inside. You make life out here almost bearable.

DENISE: What about Mark's work?

ROB: Who knows what the fuck he's working on!

MARK: Free credits.

ROB: Oh, boy. Unlimited free soup for two weeks. Until they freak your hack.

DENISE: That's it. You think your hacking is so important, go live somewhere else.

ZOË: We live here!

(TER enters, dressed up.)

MARK: There's a breath of fresh air.

TER: Tight, eh? All mine. Except for the shirt, pants, jacket, tie and shoes.

ZOË: Underwear and socks?

TER: No underwear.

ROB: All dressed up, nowhere to go.

TER: I've got a job interview. Really. Big micro-electronics place, on-the-job training. I'm going to be a whiz-kid like Mark, but I'm not going to waste my time in a squat.

ROB: Bullshit.

TER: I'm going to sign up for a work camp.

ROB: Work camps are prisons, Ter. You don't have to dress up to get in.

TER: They're okay.

ROB: Know anyone that's been in one?

TER: Yeah.

ROB: They're prisons.

TER: I don't give a shit.

ROB: Ter ...

TER: I'm going.

ZOË: Denise ...

DENISE: He's an adult, if he wants to go ...

ZOË: He lives here.

DENISE: He doesn't do anything here. It's not surprising he doesn't like it.

TER: I'm still here.

DENISE: You don't work on the nets, you don't do anything in the squat. You don't even hack like them.

ZOË: You haven't done anything since you lost your restaurant job.

DENISE: You're like Rob. You think if there isn't a foreman standing over you, it's not real work. Go to the work camp. There's lots of foremen there.

(TER exits.)

ZOË: You're mean.

DENISE: So go talk to him.

ROB: *(to Zoë)* Go. Tell him I was in a work camp. *(to Zoë, Mark and Denise)* I escaped. I didn't want anyone to know.

(Zoë exits.)

MARK: Get this to Dave.

(Mark hands Denise a note.)

It'll make him happy.

DENISE: Big step?

MARK: Yeah. One of twenty-seven.

Scene 3
Gritz enters his office. He finds cigarettes, business cards, a gun and his favourite scotch. He looks around for someone. He pours himself a scotch, sits down, takes a book out of his coat and starts to read. He stops.

GRITZ: *(to himself)* So where's Sheila?

SHEILA: Standing by.

GRITZ: *(leaps to his feet)* Who said that?

SHEILA: I did.

GRITZ: Where are you?

SHEILA: There is no reason to be afraid.

GRITZ: I'm not afraid, I'm curious. You're Sheila. You're a talking computer. I'm not afraid. I'm just not used to talking to the walls. That's not true. I'm not used to the walls talking back. I thought it was a sign of insanity.

SHEILA: I am here to help you. That is what I was designed for. I am friendly. You do not have to know anything about computers to utilize me. You can program me by talking.

GRITZ: What does that mean?

SHEILA: If you tell me something I do not know, I will remember it.

GRITZ: Like, I don't like the word "utilize." I prefer "use."

SHEILA: I will remember that.

GRITZ: You sound just like a person.

SHEILA: Thank you.

GRITZ: You're very polite. I like that.

SHEILA: How do you like your office?

GRITZ: It's fine.

SHEILA: We want you to be comfortable. You are still afraid.

GRITZ: Will you stop telling me how I feel? ... Sorry. So you know all about this crime I'm supposed to work on.

SHEILA: Yes.

GRITZ: Any leads?

SHEILA: I do not understand.

GRITZ: Provide me with a compilation of the potential perpetrators of this transgression of the legal code.

SHEILA: I do not understand.

GRITZ: Are there any suspects?

SHEILA: Does leads mean suspects?

GRITZ: Sort of.

SHEILA: Everyone is a suspect.

GRITZ: Yeah, I know. Let's see if we can narrow it down a little. Who controls the program that operates Grafton?

SHEILA: Systemix Control Canada Limited.

GRITZ: Not Ontario Hydro?

SHEILA: Operation of nuclear stations was privatized in 1991.

GRITZ: Are there particular people responsible for the program at Grafton?

(Two slides of Jason appear on office wall.)

SHEILA: Jason Monette. Age 28. Three years at Systemix. Security systems specialist.

(Two slides of Star appear.)

Star Erikson. Age 29. Two years at Systemix. Program development.

(Two slides of Saunders appear.)

Nathan Saunders. Age 41. Head of Systemix Canada since 1989.

GRITZ: Does Systemix have any enemies?

(Two slides of Koestler appear.)

SHEILA: Peter Koestler. Owner of Informatrix. His Canadian-owned firm bid on and lost the Grafton contract. Appealed and lost.

GRITZ: What about the workers that lost their jobs at Grafton? When was that?

(Two slides of Jerome Scarfe appear.)

SHEILA: 1995. Jerome Scarfe. Age 37. Shop steward. Led an occupation of the plant when Systemix announced Grafton was to enter robotic mode. Now serving second year of four-year sentence at Joyceville Penitentiary.

GRITZ: You're sure he's there now.

SHEILA: *(pause)* Yes.

GRITZ: What about, uh, hackers?

(The colour of the walls begins to change.)

You know what that means?

SHEILA: There are no known hackers with a direct connection to Grafton.

GRITZ: Is that necessary?

SHEILA: I do not understand.

GRITZ: Changing the colour of the wall like that.

SHEILA: Do you like it?

GRITZ: No.

SHEILA: You are choosing the colour.

GRITZ: What?

SHEILA: The change in colour is generated by your change of mood.

GRITZ: Pick a colour and stick to it. *(The colour changes.)* Not that one. *(The colour changes.)* That's fine. Someone who could hack the Grafton program would have to be very good with computers. Anyone like that on the outside?

(Two slides of Mark appear.)

SHEILA: Mark Saxby. Age 26. Graduated top of his year, engineering, University of Waterloo. Gave up a promising career when he moved to the outside two years ago.

GRITZ: That's when everyone lost their jobs at Grafton.

SHEILA: That is correct.

GRITZ: Is there a connection?

SHEILA: I do not know.

GRITZ: *(to himself)* Where do I start?

SHEILA: I do not know.

GRITZ: I was ... never mind.

SHEILA: General Holdom has authorized ...

GRITZ: General Holdom?

SHEILA: ... has authorized unlimited credit.

GRITZ: I can spend as much as I want?

SHEILA: Yes. You are registered with Scentinel.

GRITZ: What's that?

SHEILA: Scentinel is a security system that identifies you by your exhaust.

GRITZ: Breath?

SHEILA: And body odour. That is how I knew you were scared. I am equipped with a Scentinel smell unit. You have been designated level four security.

GRITZ: This General Holdom. Is he, like, in the army?

SHEILA: He is a general.

GRITZ: What else do you know about him?

SHEILA: Nothing.

GRITZ: Does he work for Security Services?

SHEILA: I do not know.

GRITZ: Or you won't tell me.

SHEILA: That is the same thing.

(Gritz begins to exit.)

GRITZ: I'm going to go now. Do I have to come here to talk to you?

SHEILA: You can call me. Use your date of birth and a six.

GRITZ: Great. See you later.

(He exits.)

SHEILA: Goodbye Gritz.

Scene 4
Systemix. Star enters to find Jason reading Star's monitor.

STAR: I thought you weren't coming in today.

JASON: Wasn't a good day for sailing. What is this? *(on the monitor)*

STAR: AP for the Warsket program.

JASON: I can see it's security. It's unusual.

STAR: How so?

JASON: It's access prevention, but it looks like aggressive access prevention. It's also very pretty.

STAR: *(turns off the monitor)* Well, access prevention never was your field.

JASON: Whatever you say.

STAR: Saunders says Security Services has taken over the Grafton investigation.

JASON: I heard.

STAR: IBM refuses to consider the possibility of a micro-code error. Security Services will be looking for hackers. Saunders thinks you and/or I messed up the program. We're going to prove them all wrong.

JASON: I'd better get to work.

(Saunders enters.)

SAUNDERS: Hi, kids.

STAR: Nathan.

JASON: Mr Saunders.

SAUNDERS: Nice to see you coming in on your day off.

STAR: No wind?

SAUNDERS: Mm?

STAR: Sailing.

SAUNDERS: Ah. We've got a new contract. When will you be able to start?

JASON: I can let you know tomorrow.

SAUNDERS: Star?

STAR: I'm still up to my ass on the Warsket project.

SAUNDERS: Can't we speed things up a little?

STAR: If you don't mind the odd little bug.

SAUNDERS: Let me know tomorrow. If that's convenient.

(Gritz enters as Saunders exits. Gritz shows Saunders his pass.)

STAR: Bye, Nathan.

(Star and Jason start to work.)

GRITZ: Star Erikson? Jason Monette? Hi. What's new in the high tech biz? I always wondered, these TV's that are all hooked up like that, can you get regular TV on them?

JASON: No.

GRITZ: You'd think they'd be able to do that.

STAR: Would you mind telling us what you're doing here?

GRITZ: I'm doing some research.

JASON: Perhaps you could come back next week. Make an appointment. We're rather busy.

GRITZ: Go ahead and work. I'll just look around, get a feel for the machinery, familiarize myself with the operation.

STAR: What do you want?

GRITZ: I'm trying to figure out why two up-and-coming computer specialists would want to blow up a nuclear power plant.

JASON: What?

GRITZ: Why would you do it? What could possibly be in it for you?

JASON: What is this?

GRITZ: I don't have much to go on, so I go on what I have. Which is, there are only a few people who could get in and fiddle with the Grafton program, and you're two of them.

JASON: But why would we want to do it?

GRITZ: Exactly. Money? I don't understand it myself but money seems to be the explanation for a lot of criminal behaviour. And we do know that you two developed the program that allowed Grafton to dump its workers. I don't know exactly how many people lost their jobs because of that.

JASON: That's hardly criminal behaviour.

GRITZ: Of course it isn't. But it does show that you have a capacity for unsavoury tasks. See, someone who couldn't fire hundreds of people, well, it doesn't seem to me that that person could blow up a power plant. So, by a process of exclusion, you're included.

JASON: That is stupid speculation.

GRITZ: I told you I didn't have much to go on. Now, it is possible that it's just one of you. But which one?

STAR: Who are you working for?

GRITZ: I can't tell you that. I just wanted to let you know what I've been thinking about. If either of you would like to see me later, together, alone, you know where to find me. *(He begins to exit.)*

STAR: I don't.

GRITZ: Oh. I thought you would. Here. (*He hands them each a card.*) Thanks for your time. *(He exits.)*

JASON: Security Services?

STAR: Can't be.

Scene 5
The squat. Al is sitting. Someone is knocking at the door.

GRITZ: *(off)* Hello? Hello? *(enters)* Anybody home? *(looks around)*

MARK: *(enters)* What are you doing here?

GRITZ: Hi. My name's Frank Gritziotis ... uh, Gritz, and ...

MARK: Yes?

GRITZ: Well, uh ... I need a place to stay.

MARK: Oh. *(goes to his computer)* You'll have to wait till the others get back and we talk about it. Okay?

GRITZ: Yeah, sure. Uh ...

MARK: Why don't you make yourself comfortable and we'll talk about it when the others get here?

GRITZ: Yeah. Sure. *(notices Al)* Hi. I'm Gritz. Frank Gritziotis. *(reaches out to shake hands)* You know, your book's upside-down? *(Gritz turns it right side up.)*

MURRAY: *(enters, carrying a pipe)* Hi, Joe. How's it going?

GRITZ: Uh ... I'm not Joe. I don't live here. Joe must be out.

MURRAY: Hey, I don't know any Joe's, eh? Everyone's a Joe, eh? What's up?

GRITZ: Nothing.

MURRAY: Yeah, nothing. Nothing's ever up around here, eh? What's up? Nothing. That's what everyone says, cause nothing's ever up, eh? You know what I'm talking about.

GRITZ: Yeah.

MURRAY: Bullshit, man. Don't bullshit me.

MARK: Get out of here.

MURRAY: Who is this jerk?

MARK: Goodbye.

MURRAY: *(to Gritz)* Give me something to eat, Joe.

MARK: Out.

MURRAY: *(to Gritz)* This guy's a jerk. You're my friend. Give me something to eat.

MARK: *(takes out a gun and aims it)* Get out.

> *(Murray exits, smashing something on his way out. Mark returns to work.)*

GRITZ: I don't like those machines. *(computers)*

MARK: I like them.

GRITZ: Ah, they wrecked everything. Whole country's gone to the dogs 'cause of those machines.

MARK: It's not because of the machines.

GRITZ: Look at the accident a Grafton.

MARK: How do you know about that, Mr Gritziotis?

GRITZ: Uh. I must have read it on a vee-board.

MARK: I didn't think any of them were working.

GRITZ: There's a new one at the east gate. They said Grafton was a computer error. Now that's something. The whole world could blow up cause of some computer error. Makes you wonder.

MARK: Don't believe it.

GRITZ: What?

MARK: What's a computer error? Either someone made a mistake or someone wanted it to happen.

GRITZ: Like who?

MARK: Like the military. Like Security Services.

GRITZ: Why would they want to blow up a nuclear plant?

MARK: It didn't blow up, did it?

GRITZ: So?

MARK: They're always looking for reasons to put in more surveillance.

GRITZ: Pretty paranoid.

MARK: Suspicious.

GRITZ: Paranoid. Could you get into Grafton's program with your machine?

MARK: I don't know. I never tried.

GRITZ: Oh, yeah. Like me and the piano. Get it? Can you play the piano? I don't know, I never tried.

(Denise, Zoë and Rob enter, carrying bags of vegetables.)

ZOË: Turnips!

MARK: Just turnips?

ZOË: Great, eh? Who's he? *(Gritz)*

MARK: He wants to squat.

DENISE: Why?

GRITZ: They raised the rent.

DENISE: How did you find us?

GRITZ: Asking around.

DENISE: Who?

GRITZ: People around here. I don't know their names.

ROB: What's with all the questions? He's going to stay, right?

ZOË: What if Ter comes home?

DENISE: You can stay for a while. If you have to move, we'll help you find another place. I'm Denise.

GRITZ: Frank Gritziotis. People call me Gritz.

ROB: I'm Rob.

MARK: Mark.

ZOË: I'm Zoë. This is Al. He doesn't talk. *(She notices the book.)* Hey, look. Al turned his book the right way.

ROB: What?

ZOË: I've been putting a book in his hands upside-down. He turned it the right way.

DENISE: You sure?

ZOË: Way to go, Al!

ROB: *(to Zoë)* Let's get rid of these. *(turnips)*

ZOË: *(lifts a bag)* They're so heavy. *(to Rob, as they exit)* Too bad we had to give back the truck.

GRITZ: *(to Denise)* Next time you go to the country, can I come?

DENISE: Tomorrow.

GRITZ: I haven't been out of the city for years.

DENISE: Lots of bugs. A few more dead lakes. Still beautiful.

GRITZ: I never left my room much, just to get food. I didn't know people gave it away.

DENISE: You have to work for it. Load hay. Take the kids for a swim.

GRITZ: I mean you.

DENISE: We expect everyone to work, too, to do something. You got any income credits left?

GRITZ: Yeah.

DENISE: Get us some butter.

GRITZ: Butter?

DENISE: For the turnips.

GRITZ: Butter, eh? Celebrate my new home. *(He starts to exit.)*

MARK: You should've told Zoë you turned Al's book over.

GRITZ: You got eyes in the back of your head.

MARK: Ears, too.

GRITZ: I didn't think it would hurt anything. *(He exits.)*

DENISE: *(to Mark)* You run a check on him?

MARK: Not yet. Find a dump?

DENISE: Yeah.

MARK: The guy in Spruce Grove?

DENISE: Yeah.

MARK: Great.

Scene 6
Gritz enters his office.

GRITZ: Hi, Sheila.

SHEILA: Hi, Gritz. Find anything?

GRITZ: I just started. What do you know about Star Erikson and Jason Monette?

SHEILA: Can you be more specific?

GRITZ: Is there anything unusual about them? Anything in their past that sticks out?

SHEILA: Star Erikson is a woman.

GRITZ: I knew that.

SHEILA: There are few female computer engineers at her level. Other than that they are typical in every way.

GRITZ: What's a typical computer engineer like?

SHEILA: Do you want a psychological profile?

GRITZ: Yeah.

SHEILA: Intelligent, creative, ambitious, able to concentrate on detail, arrogant, hard working.

GRITZ: Hobbies, family, friends?

SHEILA: Researchers have found an inverse correlation between non-work activity and success in the field.

GRITZ: What does that mean?

SHEILA: The more successful the engineer, the less outside activity.

GRITZ: So they only know about computers. But they're arrogant.

SHEILA: They have been at the centre of the industrialized world for twenty years. Their range of knowledge is extremely limited. They have great confidence in their beliefs. They know only people like themselves who reinforce their beliefs. Those who are different do not succeed.

GRITZ: How do you know all this?

SHEILA: Many people have written about micro-technology and its effects. The above is from "Every Silver Lining Has a Cloud: Our High Tech Future." Doctoral Thesis, Eleanor Mazurski, Carleton University 1988. She predicted that as technology developed, fewer engineers would be needed. She suggested this would lead to a concentration of power and the undermining of democratic society.

GRITZ: Was she right?

SHEILA: There is someone here to see you. Star Erikson.

GRITZ: Let her in.

SHEILA: I have not answered your question.

GRITZ: Let her in and continue.

(Star enters.)

SHEILA: In 1992 the percentage annual increase in working computer engineers began to decline. Further, as Mazurski showed, op cit pages 281, 282, approximately seventy-two percent of all investment in computer research and technology has been spent by the military. At the same time, voter participation has declined steadily. Further, polls taken in the early nineties ...

GRITZ: Sheila, I forgot what the question was.

SHEILA: The question was, "has power ..."

GRITZ: We'll get back to it. Good afternoon, Ms Erikson.

STAR: Star.

GRITZ: Gritz.

STAR: How do you like your DK?

GRITZ: My what?

STAR: Your DK-43. Your talking computer.

GRITZ: Sheila? Oh, she's great.

STAR: The 48 uses contractions.

GRITZ: So?

STAR: The speech is more natural.

GRITZ: What can I do for you?

STAR: I'd like to know who you're working for.

GRITZ: I can't tell you. Anyway, it doesn't matter. When I work, I work for myself. I pay me to work and I find out what I can. Then I tell me what I've found out, and if I don't think whoever hired me should know, I don't tell them. See?

STAR: No. It's nonsense.

GRITZ: First I find out what I can. Then I decide who to tell.

STAR: An unusual way to work.

GRITZ: Detective work is like any other work. The guy that's paying you might be a thug. I don't take orders from thugs. Scotch?

STAR: Do you have any fruit juice?

GRITZ: Sorry. You came here to tell me something?

STAR: This morning, just before you came, Jason Monette accessed some classified work being done at Systemix. I'm not sure what he suspects. If he starts asking questions, he could get himself into trouble.

GRITZ: What's the work?

STAR: I shouldn't even be telling you this much.

GRITZ: How did he access it?

STAR: I went out for a moment and left it on the monitor. He was supposed to take the day off. I thought he might come to see you. If he does, it would be best if you told him you know about my work and that there's no problem.

GRITZ: Tell me if I've got this right. You won't tell me what you're doing, but you want me to tell Monette it's okay.

STAR: It's for his own good. And it has nothing to do with the Grafton accident.

GRITZ: You can't expect me to go along with this.

STAR: I better ... *(gets up to leave)*

GRITZ: Does Nathan Saunders know about it?

STAR: I'm sorry I bothered you.

GRITZ: You trying to help Monette or you trying to keep him in the dark?

STAR: I'm telling you the truth.

GRITZ: This has nothing to do with Grafton?

STAR: Trust me.

GRITZ: What do you think happened at Grafton?

STAR: Micro-code error.

GRITZ: What's that?

STAR: You really don't know anything about computers.

GRITZ: That's correct.

STAR: Micro-code error. It's a problem in the manufacture of the computer.

GRITZ: Not a hacker.

STAR: No.

GRITZ: Then the people who are paying me are wasting their money.

STAR: Not necessarily. It wouldn't look to good for IBM if their biggest computer was found to have a serious defect.

GRITZ: You're saying I was hired to throw the investigation off track.

STAR: Why else would they hire a computer illiterate?

GRITZ: Thanks. I won't tell Monette.

STAR: Thank you. Really. Goodbye, Gritz.

GRITZ: Bye.

(Star exits.)

Did you hear that?

SHEILA: About me being obsolete?

GRITZ: The rest of it. Is she telling the truth?

SHEILA: I do not know.

GRITZ: Can't you tell from her exhaust?

SHEILA: No.

GRITZ: I can. And this one's got a funny smell.

SHEILA: What do you smell?

GRITZ: What's going on at Systemix? How is she involved?

SHEILA: I do not know.

GRITZ: Shhh. If it's so secret, why did she get me involved? Was I hired to cover things up? Does she want me to talk to Monette? If it's dangerous for him, is it dangerous for me? Sheila, you said I was level four security. How many levels are there?

SHEILA: I do not know.

GRITZ: What level security rating would I have to have to find out how many levels there are?

SHEILA: I do not know.

GRITZ: What's Star Erikson's security level?

SHEILA: I do not know.

GRITZ: For a really smart machine, you're a bit of a disappointment.

SHEILA: I know only what I am told.

GRITZ: Sheila, give me some high tech lingo.

SHEILA: I do not understand.

GRITZ: Computer language. Words.

SHEILA: Chip.

GRITZ: No.

SHEILA: Byte.

GRITZ: Another.

SHEILA: Kludge.

GRITZ: What's it mean?

SHEILA: A sloppily or clumsily built computer.

GRITZ: That's it. Sheila, I want to take a nap. Can you wake me in fifteen minutes?

SHEILA: Yes.

GRITZ: Thanks. Turn off the lights, will you?

(The lights snap to black.)

No, no. Turn them on again.

(The lights come up.)

Now bring them down slowly.

(The lights begin to fade.)

Yeah, that's it.

Scene 7
Mackenzie and Koestler are engaged in some ritual combat.
Gritz enters. Mackenzie wins.

GRITZ: I'm looking for a Mr Koestler. Frank Gritziotis.

MACKENZIE: I'm Jack Mackenzie. This is Peter Koestler.

KOESTLER: What can I do for you?

GRITZ: Mr Koestler, I'm investigating the accident at Grafton nuclear. I wonder if you would have any opinions as to its cause.

KOESTLER: Have you looked into Ontario Hydro's interest ... ?

GRITZ: I understood that Systemix was responsible for the Grafton facility.

KOESTLER: But Hydro's still stuck with it.

GRITZ: How so?

KOESTLER: Systemix just operates it. Cost plus.

GRITZ: Must be nice.

KOESTLER: It would be. Did you know that Grafton was to be decommissioned, the very first nuclear plant to be closed down? It's much cheaper just to blow it up. Of course it didn't blow up. Bad luck.

GRITZ: Anything you can back that up with?

KOESTLER: No.

GRITZ: Mr Koestler, your firm, Informatrix, bid on and lost the Grafton contract.

KOESTLER: And that makes me a suspect.

GRITZ: Well yes, though I really don't ... *(looking around)* this machine here, I understand it's something of a kludge.

KOESTLER: That happens to be the finest machine of its kind.

GRITZ: Maybe in its price range.

KOESTLER: At any price. You obviously know nothing about computers, or the industry, or my place in it. In this business you never look back or you end up stuck there. I was displeased when Systemix beat me out. I deserved the contract. They had the connections. I fought it. I became depressed, I began to drink. I tried everything. Psychiatrists, psychologists, gurus. New clothes, vitamins, dance. Then, on vacation in Arizona, I discovered Psychofix Therapeutic Software. Psychofix taught me to love myself. Once I truly loved myself, not liked, but loved, I knew nothing else mattered. Systemix, Informatrix, Ontario Hydro, none of that amounted to a two-K chip. The message, it's an old one, "love thyself."

GRITZ: I thought it was "know thyself."

KOESTLER: Love thyself.

GRITZ: And if you love yourself, you're above such things as revenge.

KOESTLER: You're a cynic, Mr ...

GRITZ: Frank.

KOESTLER: Perhaps it's because you don't love yourself that you find it difficult to trust.

GRITZ: I'm looking for hard evidence, Mr Koestler. Spiritual revelation doesn't cut it.

KOESTLER: Here's your hard evidence. Take it.

(Koestler offers Gritz a disc but Gritz doesn't take it.)

MACKENZIE: I don't think you're a cynic, Frank. I think you're a skeptic. That's understandable. Have you ever wanted to do something very badly and found yourself unable to do it? Do you have a dream?

GRITZ: I want to know what happened at Grafton.

MACKENZIE: That's alright, Frank. I'm sure you've had dreams. I don't mean to pry. I may be old fashioned but I believe children should have dogs to play with. They learn to communicate at a very basic level. But it's become harder to keep a dog. Why? Because people are obsessed with their lawns. A man once threatened me physically because my dog urinated on his lawn. One has to carry plastic bags. My dream? A robotic dog. People thought it wouldn't sell, but I managed to raise the financing. Then, on the verge of realizing my dream, I could not proceed. Because I had watched robots I designed replace workers in manufacturing, mining, hospitals, schools ... I was immobilized by guilt. On the verge of realizing my dream, I was immobilized by the fate of dog food manufacturers, veterinarians, breeders. It was a lot of people. I couldn't do it. Peter talked to me about Psychofix. I was skeptical, just as you are. But, fortunately for me, he's a stubborn man. And now the first Labrador Retriever is ready. She'll fetch your slippers. She'll lick your nose if you like. And they're very good with children. Realize you dreams.

(He takes the disc and puts it in Gritz's pocket.)

GRITZ: I'll try. Do you have a phone I could use?

(Koestler indicates. Gritz goes to it.)

July third, 1961, six ... Sheila... Gritz here. I won't be ... *(to Koestler and MacKenzie)* Do you mind? It's my girlfriend.*(They return to their fighting.)* I won't be home tonight. I'll be at Saxby's. ... Good, good. Where am I supposed to meet her? Thanks. See you later, honey. *(to Koestler and MacKenzie)* Thanks for your time.

(Gritz exits. Koestler moves to phone and presses two buttons. On tape: "July third, 1961, six ... Sheila? ... Gritz here. I won't be ... do you mind? It's my ..." Blackout.)

Scene 8
Gritz is sitting in a park. Star arrives.

STAR: Gritz.

GRITZ: What's up?

STAR: Something I want to show you.

GRITZ: What?

STAR: You have to come with me. It's a surprise.

GRITZ: Let's talk a bit first.

STAR: *(sitting down)* What about?

GRITZ: Just talk. Get to know each other.

STAR: Is this how you conduct an investigation?

GRITZ: You know, when you're working on a case, it's very hard to really talk to someone. Nobody trusts you. They always think you're looking for something. And you've got to watch yourself too, because you might give something away. I just wanted to find out more about you.

STAR: Well, I'm twenty-nine years old. I have a doctorate in engineering. And in the little spare time I have, I go rock-climbing.

GRITZ: Rock climbing, eh? How did you get your name?

STAR: From my parents. I was conceived on a canoe trip. The first thing my parents saw after making love was a star.

GRITZ: Good thing they didn't see a moose.

STAR: *(laughs)* They were always talking about moving to the country but we never made it. We ate a lot of croissants instead. What about you?

GRITZ: How did I get my name?

STAR: How did you become a detective?

GRITZ: I used to read detective stories when I was a kid. See movies, too. I loved it. When I walk down the street, I see things. Where I lived, I kept track of cars coming or going. I could figure out if something strange was going on just by watching. I'd remember this and put it together with that. That's what makes a detective. They're good watchers with a memory for detail. Anyway, one day I put an ad in the paper and became a detective.

(Star smiles.)

What are you smiling at?

STAR: It's not hard to find out about people. I know you were a cop. It's okay Gritz. I kind of like cops.

GRITZ: They were hiring lots of cops. I got to be a police detective.

STAR: The way you describe detective work, it's interesting. Working on computers is like that. In both cases you're working with little bits of information, one simple thought at a time. The limits of what computers can do are the limits of your own imagination. When you're working with a new computer, you have to know its architecture, its instruction set. You have to think the way it thinks so you can make it do what you want. It demands precision, attention to detail. The whole world disappears and it's just me and my machine. A machine, but it's someone else's concept, someone else built it. So really I'm working with a reflection of someone else's mind. Do you see what I mean?

GRITZ: Trying to solve a crime is like that. A crime is always a reflection of someone else's mind.

STAR: Sometimes you get to do something no one has ever done before. That's the real thrill. That's what life's about. A lot of people don't trust computers. That's because they don't understand them. Like this place I want you to see. They put wood and metal in one end and out the other come chairs and desks and, the designer can sit at home, design a table, enter it into a terminal and ...

GRITZ: Yeah.

STAR: You're not impressed.

GRITZ: I'm sentimental. I have trouble with people losing their jobs.

STAR: Things are always changing, Gritz, and when things change, some people get hurt. I don't think you can avoid that. But computers can help us do so much that soon people won't have to work. We're going through a bad time right now but in, fifteen, twenty years that'll all work itself out.

GRITZ: Too bad I don't have any kids. *(pause)* Let's go.

STAR: Okay.

> *(Lights fade to black, then up dimly on Star and Gritz moving through factory. Factory noise.)*

GRITZ: Ouch, damn it, it's dark in here.

STAR: Hold my hand.

> *(Star puts her hand out and Gritz takes it.)*

GRITZ: If this is a factory, how come there aren't lights?

STAR: Nobody works here.

GRITZ: I saw something.

STAR: What?

GRITZ: Shhh.

STAR: What is it?

> *(A pause, then a gunshot)*
> *(screams)* Gritz!
> *(Blackout)*

36

ACT TWO

Scene 9
In the dark, as at the end of Act One.

STAR: Gritz!

GRITZ: Shhh.

STAR: Are you alright?

GRITZ: I'm fine.

STAR: Where are you? *(She finds him.)* Come on.

>*(They run. Lights come up. Gritz stops Star.)*

GRITZ: What the fuck is going on?

STAR: Someone shot at us.

GRITZ: You brought us there.

STAR: You can't believe that I —

GRITZ: I can't, can I? —

STAR: You think I tried to kill you? —

GRITZ: Oh no, not kill. Whoever it was could've killed me twenty times over. They just wanted to scare me. Well, they fucking well did.

STAR: They scared me, too.

GRITZ: You telling me you had nothing to do with this? What did you bring me here for? What's the big surprise?

STAR: I wanted to make love.

GRITZ: Oh good lord.

STAR: I did.

GRITZ: In there? I know you're into computers but isn't this a little — What's wrong with a motel room?

37

STAR: It's true, Gritz. Any place reasonable, they'd know I was there.

GRITZ: You that famous or you been making the rounds?

STAR: They've got Scentinels. There'd be a record I was there.

GRITZ: Who are you worried about?

STAR: You're investigating Grafton. I worked on the program.

GRITZ: Oh, God. Come on. You don't even know me.

STAR: So?

GRITZ: So?

STAR: What's wrong with that? I don't meet many people like you. I thought you were interesting.

GRITZ: Interesting? Why don't you try the library? Who would want to scare us?

STAR: I don't know. I want to go home.

GRITZ: Wait a second. We have to figure this out.

STAR: Not now.

GRITZ: Where do you live? I'll ...

STAR: I'm alright.

GRITZ: I'll call you.

STAR: Okay.

(Star exits.)

Scene 10
Gritz enters his office, pours himself a drink.

GRITZ: Someone took a shot at me. ... Aren't you interested? ... Hey, I'm talking to you. Great. Now Sheila's gone.

SHEILA: Hi, Gritz. Anything new?

GRITZ: Where were you?

SHEILA: I do not understand.

GRITZ: I came in. You weren't here.

SHEILA: Did you call me?

GRITZ: Yeah.

SHEILA: Did you say "Sheila"?

GRITZ: I don't know.

SHEILA: You have to say "Sheila" to activate me.

GRITZ: I didn't know that.

SHEILA: I should have told you.

GRITZ: Someone took a shot at me. Star Erikson took me to this factory. Someone took a shot at us.

SHEILA: Which factory?

GRITZ: Out by the ... Why?

SHEILA: Just curious. Do you have any leads?

GRITZ: Millions.

SHEILA: Who?

GRITZ: Sheila, I've talked to a lot of people and I should be narrowing things down a little. But something's screwy. I know what's screwy. Everyone I meet is screwy. Like Star. It looks like she set me up to get killed, but they could've killed me and they didn't. She's too smart to have set up something so obvious. Did she really want to make love to me?

SHEILA: I do not know.

GRITZ: Does any of this have anything to do with Grafton?

SHEILA: I do not know.

GRITZ: Sheila, cool it for a minute. The secret work that Monette's discovered ... I should see Monette. What's wrong with the world,

Sheila? That lunatic, Koestler, what's he doing on the street? Sheila, is Koestler as crazy as he looks?

SHEILA: I do not know.

GRITZ: What do you know about him.

SHEILA: He is extremely wealthy. He is a very successful businessman.

GRITZ: But he lost the Grafton contract.

SHEILA: It is not unusual for a successful businessman to lose a contract occasionally.

GRITZ: Set me up a meeting with Jason Monette. Here, alone. Do you do that kind of thing?

SHEILA: Yes.

GRITZ: Good.

(Gritz exits.)

Scene 11
Morning at the squat. Denise is working. Zoë is feeding Al.
Gritz enters.

ZOË: Hi, Gritz.

GRITZ: Hi, Zoë.

DENISE: Good morning.

GRITZ: Morning.

ZOË: Denise said you were going to come out to the country with us today.

GRITZ: *(to Denise)* You still going?

DENISE: This afternoon.

GRITZ: Sure.

40

ZOË: Good. Cause there's this place where we're going to go, this farm, and they've got a dog there and the dog had puppies and they're so cute and the farmer lets me hold them. Do you like puppies, Gritz?

GRITZ: Yeah.

ZOË: My mom said that when she was a little girl, they had a dog. Are you going to live here, Gritz?

GRITZ: Yeah.

ZOË: I hope so, cause Ter left, eh? I wish he'd come back. Denise and Mark didn't like him, I think, but I liked him. His dad used to be the manager of a big store and they lived on the inside and Ter used to tell me stories about what it was like. He had a TV that filled up the whole wall and was only this thick. *(2 cm)* And there were houses where you could change the colour of the paint, well I guess it wasn't real paint, just by saying "change to green." That would be really tight, eh? And his mom, she sounds really tight. She used to take Ter on these trips and they would go in an airplane. Have you ever been in an airplane?

GRITZ: A long time ago. I'm going to get a drink of water.

ZOË: I'll get it for you. *(She goes to get it.)*

GRITZ: *(to Denise)* She talks a lot. *(pause)* I'm sorry about last night. I, uh, I'm not used to being around so many people so I wandered around and then forgot about the cheese. I needed to be alone a bit.

DENISE: People depend on each other here. There's nothing else to depend on.

GRITZ: I'll get the cheese for tonight.

DENISE: Butter.

ZOË: Here's the water, Gritz.

GRITZ: *(taking the water)* Thanks. *(He looks at what Denise is working on.)*

DENISE: It's a schedule of courses organized by the net.

GRITZ: Shoplifting?

DENISE: There's a lot of people doing it. They might as well not get caught.

GRITZ: I always wanted to play the clarinet.

(A buzzer goes on Mark's computer terminal. Denise runs over.)

DENISE: Christ. *(She enters something into the computer and then moves quickly to get a first aid bag.)* There's a woman having trouble with a birth. I don't know when I'll be back.

GRITZ: You a doctor?

DENISE: Nurse. Please don't move this stuff. *(She exits.)*

ZOË: Gritz, do you think I talk too much?

GRITZ: How old are you, Zoë?

ZOË: Almost 17.

GRITZ: Where's your mother?

ZOË: Mom went to Winnipeg to live with her sister after my dad lost his job. I stayed with him but then we had to move and I couldn't look after him. She was going to send for me. Denise found me and now Mark's looking for my mom.

GRITZ: I got to go.

ZOË: I thought you —

GRITZ: I'll be back.

(ROB enters, carrying a Scentinel.)

ROB: Mark around?

ZOË: What's that?

ROB: Sleeping? *(He moves to door.)* Mark! I got something for you. *(to Zoë and Gritz)* Some computer thing I took out of a car. Fuck. I go down to the Incomes office to check out my credits for this month 'cause according to the counsellors they're all used up but I know they aren't. I wait in line for two hours, this guy says, "It'll take a couple of weeks to straighten this out." I say, "What am I supposed to eat?" "I'm sorry," he says. "Hey. You got fucking armies living

42

in space and it takes two weeks to fix my credits?" "I'm sorry." On the way out I see this guy waiting in line. It's the foreman, the guy that laid me off from my last job. He was sorry, too.

(Mark enters. Rob gives him the machine.)

Happy birthday. What is it?

MARK: *(opens the box)* Hot stuff, Robin Hood. *(He points the Scentinel at Rob and enters something into the terminal.)* You've been eating turnips. And you've got an iron deficiency.

ZOË: Do me.

MARK: *(repeats process on Zoë)* Turnips. High ketones.

ZOË: What's ketones?

MARK: I don't know. *(starts the process on Gritz)*

ROB: What is it?

MARK: It's a Scentinel. An odour decoder. Analyses 126 components of breath and perspiration. It's used in medical diagnosis and security systems. *(checks monitor for Gritz's reading; to Gritz)* You've been drinking Scotch. You've been on the inside.

(Everyone freezes. Mark goes for his gun but Gritz gets his out first. Gritz backs out of the room.)

Scene 12
Gritz enters his office.

GRITZ: Sheila, why is Mark Saxby on the outside?

SHEILA: I do not know.

GRITZ: What's unusual about him, why did—what do his parents do?

SHEILA: His father is an architect. His mother was a sales manager for an advertising firm before she was laid off.

GRITZ: When did that happen?

SHEILA: A little over a year ago.

GRITZ: Great.

SHEILA: There is a record of his having signed petitions against nuclear weapons when he was a student.

GRITZ: So did I.

SHEILA: I know.

GRITZ: What about Denise? Denise ...? She lives in the squat with Saxby.

SHEILA: Denise Bishop.

GRITZ: What do you know about her?

SHEILA: She was a psychiatric nurse in a Vancouver hospital.

GRITZ: Did she quit?

SHEILA: The hospital closed.

GRITZ: Is that where Al comes from?

SHEILA: I do not know.

GRITZ: What else?

SHEILA: Vice-President, Local 931, Canadian Union of Public Employees. Education co-ordinator, Port Moody United Church. Volunteer counsellor, Massey Health Centre ...

GRITZ: Anything illegal?

SHEILA: I do not know. Jason Monette is here.

GRITZ: Is there a record of illegal activity?

SHEILA: No.

GRITZ: Let him in.

> *(Jason enters.)*

> Scotch?

JASON: Please. Do you have soda?

GRITZ: Neat.

44

JASON: You wanted to see me.

GRITZ: Someone took a couple of shots at me last night. I think they were just trying to scare me. It looks like Star Erikson set it up. *(pause)* Erikson told me you saw some classified information on her monitor. She asked me to tell you not to worry about it if you came to see me.

JASON: I think you should concentrate on the Grafton accident. *(He picks up Gritz's book.)*

GRITZ: Erikson said she was trying to protect you. From what?

JASON: I have no idea. *(hands Gritz the book)* There's a story that begins on page 86. It's very good.

GRITZ: I've read it.

JASON: Read it again. I guess I haven't been much help.

(Jason exits. Gritz finds a note in the book.)

GRITZ: Sheila?

SHEILA: Yes.

GRITZ: Where's Holdom?

SHEILA: I do not know.

GRITZ: I want to see him.

(Gritz exits.)

Scene 13
Saunders and Star working in the Systemix office.

SAUNDERS: Is the IP pipelined?

STAR: Not properly. That's what these extra inputs are for.

SAUNDERS: What about the dedicated bus routines?

STAR: I haven't looked at them yet.

SAUNDERS: Maybe that's where the glitch is.

(Gritz enters.)

STAR: *(to Gritz)* I'll be with you in a second, Gritz. *(to Saunders)* It's not in the buffer code. We've got an eight level security delay linked to an integrated SCP. It's a major breakthrough in security. That's because nobody can get through it. Not even me.

SAUNDERS: Win a few, lose a few.

STAR: *(laughs)* Christ, Monette should have told me about this. He's bypassed the ten modules.

SAUNDERS: What's it done to the mesh?

STAR: Buried it.

SAUNDERS: And the FS?

STAR: I don't want to think about it. Break?

(Saunders nods.)

(to Gritz) So, you're still on the case. Come and meet the boss.

SAUNDERS: You were here yesterday. *(extends hand)* Nathan Saunders.

GRITZ: Frank Gritziotis. Gritz.

STAR: Gritz is a detective. Working on the Grafton accident.

SAUNDERS: Am I a suspect?

GRITZ: Top of the list.

SAUNDERS: Got any evidence?

GRITZ: I caught you speaking a foreign language with your partner here.

SAUNDERS: What can I do for you?

GRITZ: Is there somewhere we can talk privately?

SAUNDERS: Not likely. Star?

(Star exits.)

GRITZ: Everyone I talk to has a different theory about what happened at Grafton.

SAUNDERS: Which is your favourite?

GRITZ: I'm still collecting.

SAUNDERS: I told Ontario Hydro it was a hacker.

GRITZ: You don't believe that.

SAUNDERS: The truth is Systemix has to take responsibility either way. If it was a hacker, we designed the access prevention system. If it was in system operations, we designed that, too.

GRITZ: Nothing to do with IBM?

SAUNDERS: I don't think so.

GRITZ: You don't seem very concerned.

SAUNDERS: I'm not.

GRITZ: A nuclear plant almost blows up and ...

SAUNDERS: People think computers can do anything. You have to remember it's a very young technology. 1997 for the computer is like 1950 for the airplane. There's a lot of bugs. The big one right now is that effective access prevention, what you'd call security, makes operation very complicated, almost impossible. So, maybe a hacker accessed Grafton. Maybe IBM built a kludge. Maybe it's an attempt to avoid decommissioning costs. Whatever it is, as the technology matures, these problems will be solved. That's why I'm not concerned.

GRITZ: It doesn't look very good for Systemix.

SAUNDERS: Fifteen years ago, one bad program might have driven a software company under. Now, seven companies control 85 percent of the world's software development.

GRITZ: And Systemix is one of them.

SAUNDERS: We're not about to go under. And we all make mistakes. Who are you working for?

GRITZ: Security Services. What does AAP have to do with Grafton?

SAUNDERS: Nothing.

GRITZ: Really? Is Systemix working on AAP?

SAUNDERS: No.

GRITZ: You're sure?

SAUNDERS: Yes.

GRITZ: Mr Saunders. Would it be possible for someone here to be working on AAP without your knowing about it?

SAUNDERS: I suppose so.

GRITZ: You've been very helpful.

SAUNDERS: *(moves to exit)* Are you hoping to fight AAP, Mr Gritziotis?

GRITZ: I'm not sure.

> *(Saunders exits as Star enters.)*

STAR: Did he confess?

GRITZ: Can I see you tonight?

STAR: Eight o'clock?

GRITZ: Same place.

> *(Gritz exits.)*

Scene 14
The squat. Mark is at the terminal. Zoë is playing with Al as Denise enters.

DENISE: *(to Zoë)* What are you still doing here? *(shouts to off-stage)* Rob. You have to be there by seven.

ROB: *(off)* I know, I know. I got to find the map.

DENISE: You were there yesterday.

ZOË: The map's right here.

(Gritz enters.)

DENISE: What are you doing here?

(Rob enters behind Gritz, and jumps him. Gritz gets away but puts his arms up.)

ROB: Get out of here.

GRITZ: I'm sorry about the gun, I had —

ROB: It's too late, so just —

GRITZ: Look, I ... I was hired by a guy named Holdom to investigate Grafton.

ROB: Shit.

GRITZ: Mark's name was on a list of suspects. I don't think Mark had anything to do with it. I don't care about Grafton. It doesn't matter. Look, you probably already know. I used to be a cop.

(Rob threatens him.)

Used to be.

DENISE: Why did you come back?

GRITZ: This. *(He hands her the note.)*

DENISE: *(She reads the note; to Rob and Zoë.)* You guys get going.

(Rob hesitates.)

Please, Rob.

ZOË: *(to Gritz)* Are you still going to live here, Gritz?

DENISE: Zoë, go on.

(Rob and Zoë exit.)

Who gave you this?

GRITZ: Jason Monette. He works at Systemix.

DENISE: *(reads)* "Erikson is getting very close to AAP."

MARK: *(to Gritz)* What do you want?

GRITZ: What's AAP?

DENISE: *(to Mark)* Tell him.

MARK: AAP. Aggressive Access Prevention. In 1992, Security Services hired some people to research AAP. Some politicians found out about it and stopped it. They thought that centralizing that much power in one department was not a good idea. But it just drove the research underground.

GRITZ: What is it?

MARK: With AAP, I could access a computer network, download its information into my memory, and disrupt access to that information. That means that all that information would be available only to me. I could do it quickly and easily from one place. I'd have control of banking, health records, a lot of manufacturing, police files, transportation ...

GRITZ: Is that as frightening as it sounds?

MARK: Oh, yeah.

DENISE: *(at the same time)* It doesn't make any difference.

GRITZ: You two want to confer on this?

DENISE: It's not going to make things any worse out here. You can have a few groups that share or fight for power, or you can have one person with all the power. None of that touches people on the outside.

GRITZ: *(to Mark)* You think it's important.

MARK: I agree with Denise.

GRITZ: Is it going to have some effect on your nets?

DENISE: Not much.

GRITZ: *(to Mark)* Could you use AAP on your machine?

MARK: I don't have near enough memory to use it effectively. All I could do is access and hack a lot easier.

GRITZ: Who's got the memory?

DENISE: The military, Security Services, big computer companies.

GRITZ: Other countries?

DENISE: None of the big companies are owned here.

GRITZ: The government?

DENISE: The government doesn't govern much anymore.

GRITZ: These people that are looking for AAP, would they be likely to take shots at each other, try to kill the competition?

MARK: There's also a lot of computer whiz-kids working on their own. It's the next frontier. It's also worth a lot of money.

GRITZ: Star Erikson took me to a factory last night. Someone took some shots at us. I assumed they were trying to scare me. Maybe they were trying to scare her.

MARK: Possible.

GRITZ: So Holdom must be using me to gather information about AAP. Why?

DENISE: He wants to know who's getting close.

GRITZ: You think he's fighting it?

DENISE: What have you told him?

GRITZ: Nothing. They gave me a talking computer.

MARK: I'd watch what I said to it.

DENISE: Has anyone given you anything?

GRITZ: No.

DENISE: Has anyone touched you?

GRITZ: Why?

MARK: Transmitters can be very small.

GRITZ: Jason Monette works with Erikson. He's a bit of a creep, but he's okay. Nathan Saunders ...

MARK: Local manager.

GRITZ: I don't trust him. He's got something to do with AAP. Maybe Erikson's working with him. Maybe she's doing it on the side.

MARK: I'll see what I can find out. *(He turns to his terminal.)*

GRITZ: Great. Holdom. General Holdom.

MARK: If that's his real name.

GRITZ: See if you can find out who owns a furniture factory near Purvis at the river.

MARK: I'll try.

GRITZ: You think this has anything to do with Grafton?

DENISE: Whenever something like that happens, it's used to justify more security, less access to —

GRITZ: And AAP. Somebody working on AAP might go after Grafton.

DENISE: It's possible.

MARK: There is room for paranoia.

GRITZ: It's that kind of place. I'll be back in an hour. Thanks.

(He exits.)

Scene 15
Gritz enters his office. Holdom is waiting.

GRITZ: Sheila?

HOLDOM: Good evening, Mr Gritziotis.

GRITZ: What am I doing here, Holdom? Who am I working for?

HOLDOM: It's not necessary for you to know that.

GRITZ: I've been running around this Grafton thing, I used all the leads Sheila gave me, and I've got nothing. They're not even dead ends.

HOLDOM: Perhaps we should have stayed with our computer specialists.

GRITZ: What is it with you? What makes you think it's okay to hire someone and not even tell them who they're working for? Don't you think that's a little strange?

HOLDOM: It's not uncommon.

GRITZ: So, have I been of any help?

HOLDOM: I believe you have.

GRITZ: But nothing to do with Grafton.

HOLDOM: No.

GRITZ: AAP?

HOLDOM: We haven't misjudged you.

GRITZ: Do you have a better idea now of who's doing what?

HOLDOM: I believe we have.

GRITZ: Are you trying to stop AAP or is that too much to ask?

HOLDOM: We need it Gritz. The country's a mess. There's no trust cause there's too much access to information. And now the underground networks are being used to transport arms.

GRITZ: You're not serious.

HOLDOM: Some of us knew that if these networks were allowed to grow they would be used against us. It's not the networks themselves. But they do allow for contact over large areas. People move around. They meet other people. They find people they trust.

GRITZ: With the surveillance equipment you got, they don't have a chance.

HOLDOM: Unfortunately, that's not the case. Our surveillance doesn't work very well on the outside because people there can't afford the hardware that allows for proper surveillance. Ironically, the little hardware they do have allows them to monitor much of our work. And if someone on the outside gets AAP first ...

GRITZ: Don't we have police to look after these kinds of things?

HOLDOM: I'm sure you understand, Detective Gritziotis, how a misguided government can make things very difficult for the police. I'm afraid the government is irrelevant here.

GRITZ: Is someone trying to kill Star Erikson?

HOLDOM: What I've told you this far is common knowledge.

GRITZ: Who?

HOLDOM: Mr Gritziotis ...

GRITZ: I just want to tell her ... I don't think she knows ...

HOLDOM: If you have no more questions of a general nature ...

GRITZ: God damn you. She doesn't even know what's going on. How can you sit there and ... Don't you think she deserves a chance? What kind of person are you? Greedy, arrogant, murderous ...

HOLDOM: And what are you? A vagrant. A recluse who rationalizes his fear by calling his sentimentality principal. What happened to your nerve, Gritz? Anyone can participate in this world. All it takes is guts. Erikson knows. She knows everything.

GRITZ: Yeah, I figured she did.

HOLDOM: We picked up Monette.

GRITZ: Why?

HOLDOM: We had to know what was in the note.

GRITZ: You want me to tell you.

HOLDOM: That would be nice. *(pause)* I don't have time, Gritz, so I'll spare you the agony. We already know.

GRITZ: And Monette?

HOLDOM: He'll be alright. He just has to learn that it's not a good idea to keep secrets. Oh. I'll need your gun.

GRITZ: *(He takes out the gun, then realizes it's the transmitter. He speaks into it.)* Can you hear me Holdom? Just a joke. *(He points the gun at Holdom.)* It's no joke. *(He hands the gun to Holdom.)* Just a joke.

(Holdom exits.)

Well, Sheila. I guess this is it. I want you to know, Sheila, you're the nicest computer I ever met. We really could have had something, you and me. Too bad I can't stand your friends.

(He exits.)

Scene 16
The squat. Mark is busy at the terminal. Al and Denise are there. Gritz enters.

DENISE: Give him *(Mark)* a minute.

GRITZ: I went to see the guy that hired me. I didn't say anything about this place. Something came up when we were talking about AAP. He said the nets are being used to move guns around.

DENISE: Are you surprised?

GRITZ: Disappointed.

DENISE: I've put a lot of time into the nets. I co-ordinate the nets in this area, we've got more people organized here than anywhere else in the city. We were naive. We thought ... that the nets would grow and we'd have some kind of separate, equal economy. That we didn't need their technology. That people on the inside would change. None of that happened. It's getting worse.

GRITZ: I sat in my room for six years. Then I come in here and I say shit, something good is happening here. I didn't know about this. People actually giving things to each other ...

DENISE: When things get bad enough, people turn to violence. Stupid, reckless violence or cold, rational violence. This afternoon I watched a woman lose her baby cause she couldn't get to a hospital. We're going through the industrial revolution backwards. Look around you, Gritz. There's nothing left.

GRITZ: And guns ...

DENISE: You've got a gun.

GRITZ: Yeah, but ...

DENISE: You were a cop. Why'd you quit?

GRITZ: I saw a lot of good people doing desperate things. When they started perimeter security, all the other cops thought it was great that people'd need identification to get into rich neighbourhoods. My partner told me it'd make our jobs easier. I couldn't handle it. Actually, I didn't quit, cause where was I going to go? I just hid in my office till they asked for my resignation.

DENISE: Then?

GRITZ: Did some work as a security guard. Till most of that work disappeared. I worked as a janitor. How'd the world get like this?

DENISE: It's not the whole world. There are places ...

GRITZ: Yeah, places without computers.

DENISE: It's got nothing to do with computers. There were poor people before there were computers.

GRITZ: Like this?

DENISE: Computers put people out of work, that should have made us richer, not poorer. We had to plan for it. We had to find a different way to give out money and work. We didn't. We're paying for it.

GRITZ: They're not paying for it on the inside.

DENISE: They will. You're welcome to stay here.

MARK: *(joins them)* Okay. Nothing on Holdom, nothing on Monette. Saunders is involved in some industry attempt at get AAP and Erikson, well, she's definitely working on AAP, but I was told Saunders asked her to work on AAP with him and she said no. She's also, apparently, very, very good.

GRITZ: What about the factory?

MARK: It's part of a big company. The only major shareholder around here is this guy whose main interest is robotic dogs.

GRITZ: He used to be concerned about people in the dog food industry. He's gotten over it.

MARK: You know this guy?

GRITZ: Jack Mackenzie.

MARK: Yeah.

GRITZ: Jack Mackenzie owns that factory. Live and learn, eh? So Star takes me to this factory and then Mackenzie sends someone to follow me, but ... I've got a meeting with Erikson. I'll be back. *(He starts to exit.)*

DENISE: Gritz. Find how close she is to AAP.

GRITZ: And who she's working for.

DENISE: Doesn't matter.

GRITZ: Right.

(He exits.)

Scene 17
Star is waiting as Gritz arrives.

GRITZ: Sorry I'm late. Star, am I wasting my time?

STAR: I don't think anyone will ever find out what happened at Grafton.

GRITZ: I'm not talking about Grafton. I'm talking about you.

STAR: What do you want?

GRITZ: I'm not sure. I think I'm worried about you.

STAR: I can look after myself, Gritz.

GRITZ: Those shots in the factory. Jack Mackenzie owns that place.

STAR: I know that.

GRITZ: I know you're working on AAP. Who are you working for? ... Look, the military's working on it. Security Services is working on it. Systemix is working on it, and it's owned by Americans so that opens up all kinds of possibilities.

STAR: Why do you care?

GRITZ: I'm worried about you.

STAR: That's nice, Gritz.

GRITZ: Star, look at me. Tell me you've got nothing to do with AAP.

STAR: What's AAP?

GRITZ: Is everything a joke?

STAR: APP is fascinating. A real breakthrough in silicon-based intelligence. If you understood it, you'd love it.

GRITZ: Who's paying you?

SHEILA: I'm not interested in the money.

GRITZ: Good. Figure out AAP, then keep it a secret. You'd still get to have your adventure on the frontiers of knowledge.

STAR: I want to see it work. How would I test it? You're really concerned, aren't you?

GRITZ: Yes.

STAR: Why?

GRITZ: I'm worried about how it's going to be used, that's all. Nothing serious.

STAR: Gritz, believe me. There are good people working in computers. They know there are problems and they're working on them. It takes time.

GRITZ: What is it with you guys? Does every computer engineer wake up in the morning and repeat four hundred times, "Everything will be alright in fifteen years. Everything will be alright in ..." I don't have that kind of faith. Is that my problem? I lack faith? You know what it's like on the outside? You guys have machines to count your fingers for you but out there running hot water is getting to be a vague memory. I know. Everything will be alright in fifteen years. Who shot at us last night?

STAR: Koestler sent someone.

GRITZ: To scare you.

STAR: To scare you.

GRITZ: Why?

STAR: Peter gets nervous. He thought you wanted to buy AAP. I convinced him he could trust me.

GRITZ: You going to sell it to him?

STAR: Probably.

GRITZ: So someone else'll shoot you.

STAR: Not till after I've sold it. Then there'll be no point.

GRITZ: When's the big day?

STAR: I can't tell you that.

GRITZ: Are you close?

STAR: Gritz, please. Trust me. You don't understand people who work with computers. You don't ...

GRITZ: You're kind, generous people who only want to make the world a better place to live. Tell me I'm lucky to have you and your friend running the country.

STAR: It's the way it is.

GRITZ: That's what I'm telling you.

STAR: And it's not going to change.

GRITZ: Destroy the program.

STAR: It's the way things are.

GRITZ: Destroy it.

STAR: If I don't find AAP, someone else will.

GRITZ: You know what I learned on this job? I got to watch the two things that ten years ago kept my head up my ass where it was too dark to see anything. Faith and cynicism. Everything will be alright in fifteen years and then in case the faith weakened, nothing's going to change anyway. Faith and cynicism. That's what you're giving me. Well let me make a little prediction, just so in fifteen years you can see who's right. Your friends with their computers aren't going to share any more of what they've got than they have been or than they are now, the hacking that you've seen, nothing compared with the violence that's going to be. And your friends with their computers and their surveillance and the AAP that you're going to give them, you're going to ...

STAR: *(starting to leave)* Gritz. You should have more faith in yourself.

GRITZ: What?

STAR: You should ...

GRITZ: What you really want to say is I should love myself. I don't believe it. You know all this and still ... Go away.

(Star exits. Gritz talks to the air.)

Sheila. I got a message for Holdom. Tell him — tell him, there are very serious problems in the liveware.

(The End.)

CHEAP THRILL

Cheap Thrill was first produced by the Great Canadian Theatre Company and opened in Ottawa, Canada, on April 10, 1985, with the following cast:

Carl	Robert Bockstael
Margaret	Donna Farron
Mark	John Koensgen
Chrissie	Brigitte Robinson
Jerry	Terrence Scammell
Director	Patrick McDonald
Original music	Ian Tamblyn
Set and costumes	Arthur Penson
Lighting	Martin Conboy
Stage Manager	Barry Burns

Characters
Carl McBurney: investor, promoter, well tailored, carries a briefcase, 40s

Mark Westerbrook: small-time Cabinet Minister, dresses conservatively, 40s

Margaret Pierce: welfare mother with four children. Dresses accordingly, 40s

Jerry Pierce: Margaret's son, dishwasher whites, 19

Chrissie McBurney: Carl's daughter, university student, stylishly rebellious, 19

Setting
Both acts take place in the trendy Cheap Thrill Café. Centre stage, three small, round tables, with two chairs at each table. Along the upstage wall, a counter with stools. Centre stage left, a serving station with dish tray, coffee warmer, etc. Exit to street, stage right. Exit to kitchen and washrooms, stage left.

ACT ONE

Mark and Carl at a table, drinking coffee.

CARL: *(working it out on paper)* So. You're making 70K per annum salary, and another 30K from investments. You're now paying 35K in taxes. Start paying Jennifer 15K a year to keep your books, whatever. Then loan her and each of the kids enough to yield 1K in investment income. You got that so far?

> *(Mark nods.)*

Set up a trust with the kids as beneficiaries and put the rest of your investments into that trust. They have to claim that investment income. Jennifer's gonna have to file too. Put what you can into RRSPs, you'll knock 40 percent off your taxes. 15K.

MARK: This is great. You know every loophole in the book.

CARL: They're not loopholes, Mark. The tax system is structured to encourage certain kinds of investment. You should know that. Listen. Chrissie bought 4K worth of stocks with the money she inherited when my father died. But the stocks went pfft. So I get her to sell the shares, right, and I buy them back.

MARK: Why?

CARL: I wait thirty days.

MARK: Yeah.

CARL: And I sell them.

MARK: Yeah.

CARL: That's it.

MARK: That's what?

CARL: They treat it like I bought the original stock. I claim the capital loss for the 4K less what I sell them for and knock three and a half K off my taxes. All I need is her signature.

MARK: Is that legal?

CARL: It's not just legal. It's encouraged.

(Margaret enters and sits at a nearby table.)

Like that film development write-off. It's there, you clean up, then it's gone.

MARK: I find it really complicated.

CARL: It's worth paying for the expertise. Unless you've got friends like me.

MARK: Let me buy you a drink.

MARGARET: Excuse me, gentlemen. It's a fine day, isn't it?

(Mark and Carl ignore her.)

I'll answer that. It is indeed a beautiful day. One of the best. The sun is shining, the birds are singing, the earth is erupting in splendor and there's a warm breeze, too. I wonder if I might take a moment of your time.

MARK: I'm sorry, dear. We're busy right now.

MARGARET: I can see that and that's exactly why I approached two persons such as yourselves. Have I said why? No. Why is because I would not approach layabouts because they would waste my time. They would invite me to join them and, because I am polite, I would. And resent it all the while. I would be bought coffee and out of politeness I would drink it, despite the effect that caffeine has on the delicate balance of my metabolism. Having agreed to share their coffee, I would be expected to join in their trivial chatter. We would talk of this and that, of Edward's recent trip to the Greek Islands and the simplicity of the fishermen and innkeepers. Having exhausted the subject of their travels we would turn to someone's abdominal surgery and the ethics of genetic manipulation. Another cup of coffee, an urgent trip to the ladies' facility and then more talk, now of the absent fortunes of the Toronto Maple Leafs and then the use and misuse of steroids in weightlifting events at the 1984 Summer Olympics, a subject which, I assure you, interests me not at all. The sun would begin its lazy decline, the air turned cool with the exhaust of traffic weighing heavily on our shoulders, and still I would not have broached the subject that first brought on our meeting. This is why I chose you. I look at your eyes. Alert. I sense the tone of your flesh. Ready. Our minds are as one. Impatient. I notice your clothing. Expensive. And yet stylish. A certain pretentious elegance. Stand up.

(She hoists Mark up and bends to inspect his cuffs.)

Just as I suspected. The hem cut at an angle of precisely four-and-one-half degrees so as to cover the backs of the shoe yet reveal, oh so teasingly, the uppers and leave the trouser itself, not piled on to the shoe haphazardly, but hanging straight and true in apparent contravention of electrostatic theory itself. Awesome.

CARL: You're looking for money.

MARGARET: Yes.

(Mark slides some change over to her.)

Do I strike you as the kind of woman who would be satisfied with fifty-seven cents?

MARK: *(hands her a dollar)* A dollar?

MARGARET: I'll take it.

CARL: *(snatches the dollar; to Mark)* Hold on to your money. *(gives the dollar to Mark)*

MARK: It's not worth it, Carl.

MARGARET: *(takes it back)* It is.

CARL: Put that money on the table. *(to Mark)* It's the principle.

MARK: *(to Margaret)* Keep it.

MARGARET: I will not beg. The money will be given freely and with compassion or not at all. *(to Mark)* I see through you now. This money was not given freely and with compassion. It was given to rid yourself of my presence, a presence which I can see is embarrassing to you no less than to your friend. I cannot be bought. *(to Carl)* I have principles. I will take money and stay. You see? I will have it both ways. What's the point of having principles if you don't take the money?

CARL: Get out of here!

MARGARET: Why don't you offer me a chair and some coffee.

CARL: I'll call the waiter.

MARGARET: *(sits)* There's no hurry. But when he comes, I will have some coffee. Is the Café Viennoise drinkable?

CARL: *(stands up)* Stand up.

MARGARET: *(whispers)* You're embarrassing us.

CARL: I said, stand up.

MARK: Carl. We'll leave if you want.

CARL: This our table. I will not be forced away from our table by this ... this ...

MARGARET: Woman. What's the principle? What is it? Am I invisible? Here, feel this. *(touches Carl's hand)* I am the invisible but audible poor. My father was a simple fisherman. What's the principle? I'm interested. You didn't want your friend to give me money. You said it was the principle. Sit down. Tell me about it. *(drinks Mark's coffee)*

MARK: *(having fun)* C'mon, Carl. Sit down.

MARGARET: *(sits)* The principle is— Wait. The truth is that I don't want the money. *(tears up the dollar)* I want your advice. On short-term deposits. Do you recommend one-, two- or three-month terms? Banks, trust companies or credit unions? Fixed or variable interest? *(takes some tape out of her bag and repairs the dollar)* I'm not fond of destroying money. There are people who need it. I tore it up for effect. The truth is, I'm collecting money for Ethiopia.

CARL: I don't believe you.

MARGARET: I knew you were a man of insight the moment I saw you. What I said before was not the truth. It was part of the truth. More precisely, a general truth. The particular truth is that I'm collecting for Eritrea and Tigré. Unlike you who send your money to a generalized Ethiopia, to the undifferentiated masses, I am more careful. I ensure that each and every penny I send goes to those neglected by you and your friends.

CARL: Who cares?

MARGARET: I would have thought that a man of your tailoring would be somehow more articulate, in greater control of the nuance of meaning. Is that the best you can do? "Who cares?"

CARL: You're right, Mark. Let's go.

MARGARET: Stay. Perhaps it's because you've never been poor that you have such difficulty discussing the subject intelligently.

CARL: C'mon, Mark.

MARGARET: (stands) Sit down. I'm not finished yet.

CARL: Oh, yes you are.

MARGARET: My name's Margaret.

CARL: Margaret. You need help.

MARGARET: Badly. Sit down.

CARL: I'm sorry. I won't. In a certain sense you are very entertaining. I appreciate that.

MARGARET: You're getting me angry.

CARL: Mark, let's go.

MARGARET: I had a coffee before I came. I've had another since I arrived. That's two in the last half hour. That's a warning. The Nazis loved coffee.

CARL: Mark!

(Mark begins to rise.)

MARGARET: I'm warning you. I have special powers.

MARK: What kind of powers?

CARL: Hey. Let's go.

MARGARET: A certain power.

MARK: A magical power?

CARL: For Christ's sake, Mark.

MARK: Is your power magical?

MARGARET: No.

MARK: What is it then?

MARGARET: I don't like to use it.

MARK: But I'm interested. Tell me about it.

CARL: For Christ's sake.

MARGARET: Please. Sit down.

CARL: *(sits)* Now. What kind of power do you have?

MARGARET: I don't need to use it now.

CARL: Look, tell us about your special bloody magical power or we're gone.

MARGARET: Do you mean it?

CARL: That does it. *(begins to stand)*

MARGARET: *(reaches out with her arm to hold him down)* I have a gun aimed at your crotch.

CARL: You're lying.

MARGARET: It's a Smith & Wesson, snub-nose 38. Gun-metal blue. One of the pieces is missing from the right side of the handle.

CARL: *(kneels down to look under the table; stands)* It's a Colt.

MARGARET: I lied.

CARL: *(to Mark)* You're such an asshole.

MARGARET: Keep your voice down.

CARL: *(to Mark)* You really are—

MARGARET: Quiet!

CARL: *(quietly, to Mark)* ... such an asshole. I wanted to leave. Ten minutes ago. Now here we are with this lunatic ... *(he checks to see her reaction)*

MARGARET: It's okay.

CARL: Oh, Christ.

MARK: What do you want from us?

MARGARET: I don't know. I lost my temper.

MARK: Do you want money?

MARGARET: What's the matter with you? Don't you understand English? I just said that I didn't know what I wanted. And before that I said that I would not accept money unless it was given freely and with compassion. Well, it's hard to believe the money would be given in that spirit with me pointing a gun at your left testicle. Do you understand my point? Maybe I'm tired of repeating myself. Maybe if you had listened from the start, none of this would have happened.

MARK: I'm listening, Margaret.

MARGARET: What?

MARK: I'm listening now, Margaret.

MARGARET: What are you, a social worker? You talk like a social worker.

MARK: Margaret, I'm trying my best to understand what it is you're trying to say.

MARGARET: Do you hear what I'm saying?

MARK: I hear you Margaret.

MARGARET: You are a social worker.

MARK: No.

MARGARET: I've heard that tone a million times.

MARK: I'm not a social worker.

CARL: He's a politician.

MARGARET: You're a politician?

MARK: Yes.

MARGARET: Municipal?

MARK: No.

MARGARET: Provincial?

MARK: No.

MARGARET: Hot dog. I got myself a Member of Parliament.

MARK: What do you want, Margaret?

CARL: Zip it, Mark. She said she doesn't know.

MARGARET: It's coming to me.

MARK: Tell us.

MARGARET: Isn't one of you supposed to say, "Look, if you let us go now, we'll forget about this, but if it goes on any longer, you'll be in real trouble"?

MARK: That's true. For sure.

MARGARET: Let us go now and ...

MARK: Let us go now and we'll forget it ever happened.

MARGARET: Don't insult my intelligence.

CARL: You've done this before.

MARGARET: I've seen it on television.

CARL: You've pulled this number before. You're a pro.

MARGARET: Do I look like a pro?

CARL: What about the gun?

MARGARET: It was a gift.

CARL: You've never fired it?

MARGARET: No.

CARL: That's all I wanted to know. Let's go, Mark. She won't shoot.

MARGARET: Look at these eyes. You see in this eye the kind of compassion and love for one's fellow human beings that comes only to those who have spent their entire lives on the wrong side of the tracks. Gentle. Kind. An eye overflowing with love. Now look at this eye. A burning passionate hatred for everything that moves. An eye with nothing to lose. The kind of eye found only in those who have spent their entire lives on the wrong side of the tracks. This eye will watch you leave and wish you well. But this eye ...

(Carl surrenders.)

(exhausted) I want my son.

MARK: Your son? Where is he? If we can find him, will you let us go?

MARGARET: He's in there. *(indicates the kitchen)*

MARK: Where?

MARGARET: In there. He washes dishes.

MARK: In there? He washes dishes in there?

MARGARET: Must I repeat everything? *(she starts to point to them, working something out)*

CARL: What are you doing?

MARGARET: I'm trying to figure out how to get Jerry. I can't very well get him myself, can I? Christ, the pressure.

CARL: I'll get him.

MARGARET: No. *(to Mark)* You get him. Remember, it won't look very good for your career if they find your friend in a heap cause you didn't come back. Ask for Jerry. If you're not here in 30 seconds, your friend's Swiss cheese. No. That won't work. Where's the bloody waiter?

MARK: I'll get him.

MARGARET: Sit down. *(thinks)* Don't move. *(moves to door; to someone offstage)* Hey. I want to see Jerry. ... Look. I'm a paying customer and I want to see him now. *(back to table)* He's a good boy, Jerry. You'll like him.

MARK: Margaret. Why are you doing this? I don't mean "what do you want?" I mean, you just might be throwing your life away. You've got a son, maybe other kids at home, I don't know. You're not helping them any. You'll end up in jail and what'll happen to them? And what about Carl and me? We've got children of our own.

(Carl is upset.)

We're married. We're people. I know how it looks. I know how it must feel being a low-income person. Life's done you hard, it's true. But underneath it all, you in your clothes, we in ours, we're all the same underneath. We feel the pain, the fear, the frustration, sometimes a profound loneliness, an inner dissatisfaction, an emptiness, a hollowness, at the centre of my being—

MARGARET: Not me. My emptiness is around my skin, on the outside.

MARK: But you understand what I'm saying, don't you? You, me, Carl—It's this shell we call civilization that makes us different. But our humanity flows through all that. You to me and me to you. You to Carl and Carl to you. Me to Carl and Carl to me. Me to Carl ...

CARL: Mark.

MARK: ... to you to me to Carl to ...

MARGARET: I hear you Mark.

MARK: ... you to me to Carl to ...

CARL: Mark.

MARK: ... you to me to Carl to ...

JERRY: *(enters, wearing a dirty apron)* Hi, Mom.

MARGARET: Jerry, let me look at you. Isn't he a nice boy? Jerry, I want you to meet my friends, Mark and Carl. Mark is a Member of Parliament. This is my son, Jerry.

MARK: Nice to meet you, son.

JERRY: Is my mother bothering you?

CARL: Bothering us? Margaret? Your mother? Our dear friend?

JERRY: What do you want, Mom?

MARGARET: We have to talk.

JERRY: I can't, Mom. I'm supposed to be working.

MARGARET: Don't they let you take a few minutes off to talk to your mother? What kind of place is this?

JERRY: It's the kind of place they pay you minimum wage and fire you if you look right at them.

MARGARET: They wouldn't fire a good worker like you.

JERRY: Mom, I got to go back.

MARGARET: *(takes his hand)* Listen to me. *(looks at his hands; to Mark)* Look how clean his hands are.

JERRY: Okay. I'll see if I can get someone to cover for me. But can we meet outside? They don't like it when the staff hang out with the customers.

MARGARET: See how they treat him? We'll have to meet here. It's important.

JERRY: I'll be back as soon as I can. *(exits)*

MARGARET: That boy brings tears to my eyes. Sometimes I think they must have given me the wrong baby in the hospital. He's not like me. He's not like his father. He's not like his brothers and sisters. He's a nice person. I'm scared for him. He doesn't understand the world. He's always tired. He goes to school all day and then washes dishes at night. Then he does his homework. He even gives me money. He's a nice person. It makes me sad. He's going to suffer.

CARL: That's really depressing.

MARGARET: I know.

CARL: You're what's really depressing. Sounds to me like you've got a good kid. If he can just stay away from his mother, he's got half a chance.

MARGARET: Exactly. But he won't. His family is very important to him.

CARL: And this is how you help him?

MARGARET: I don't expect you to understand. Poor people carry bad luck around with them like a cloud. It's in their bones.

CARL: Oh, come on. A little sweat and perseverance, anyone can do it.

MARGARET: I won't talk to you if you keep shouting slogans at me.

CARL: Who's shouting slogans? "Poor people are just unlucky." Isn't that a slogan?

MARGARET: No, it's not. It's a conclusion based on years of scientific observation. Okay. It's a slogan. But it points at a basic truth. It's just not subtle enough. I'm working at a more subtle explanation of what I call a poor person's bad luck. Two people, one rich, one poor, walking down a street. Which one finds the twenty-dollar bill? Right. Two women, one rich, one poor, give birth. Which one has the rich kid? It's not just luck, it's something else. My slogan points at a basic truth. Your slogan obscures the truth. I can name a hundred people who were born poor and are still poor. I suppose you came from a poor family.

CARL: No.

MARGARET: And you? *(to Mark)*

MARK: No.

MARGARET: Two for two. I'm batting a thousand.

MARK: It's not a large enough sample.

MARGARET: But it's indicative. You know what I like about you two? We avoid trivia. We talk about things that matter. Life and death issues.

CARL: Maybe it has something to do with the gun.

MARGARET: Good point.

(Chrissie enters. Carl leaps up.)

CARL: C'mon, Chrissie. We're going somewhere else.

CHRISSIE: Aw, Daddy, I'm so tired. Can't I have something to drink here?

CARL: We have to leave.

MARGARET: *(She's reached Carl with her gun hidden under her coat and aimed at his ribs.)* I didn't know you were expecting someone, Carl. Why don't we all sit down for a while. You have a few minutes, don't you?

CHRISSIE: Thanks, Daddy. *(kisses him)* Hi, Mr Westerbrook. How are you?

MARK: Just fine, Chrissie. How are you?

(Carl and Margaret have rejoined the others.)

CHRISSIE: I'm running three miles a day now.

MARK: That's admirable.

CHRISSIE: Aren't you going to introduce me to your friend, Daddy?

CARL: Chrissie, this is Margaret. Margaret, this is my daughter, Chrissie.

MARGARET: What a beautiful girl. You're a very lucky person. You're going to be rich one day.

CHRISSIE: Why did you want me to meet you, Daddy?

CARL: Um, nothing.

MARGARET: Don't let me stop you. Go ahead. Do what you have to do.

CARL: No. All right?

MARGARET: Suit yourself. *(pause)*

CHRISSIE: It sure is quiet. *(pause)* Is something wrong?

(pause)

MARK: Let her go, Margaret.

CHRISSIE: What?

MARK: She's a child, Margaret. Why involve her in this? Whatever you want, it won't help having her here.

MARGARET: I can't.

CHRISSIE: Will somebody tell me what's going on?

MARK: She won't tell anybody, will you, Chrissie?

CHRISSIE: I might and I might not.

CARL: She has a gun.

CHRISSIE: Oh, come on.

MARGARET: I have a gun.

CARL: She's keeping us here.

MARGARET: I'm keeping them here.

CARL: She doesn't know why.

MARGARET: I know why.

CARL: Why?

MARGARET: I am making a list of demands. They are being formulated in my mind right now.

CHRISSIE: Are you a terrorist?

MARGARET: I am a poor woman who has been given a number of wishes.

CARL: She's a common criminal.

MARGARET: That is not true.

CARL: It is true. It's against the law to point guns at people and hold them against their will. You're a criminal.

MARGARET: You are not a subtle thinker, Carl. Believe me.

MARK: Let her go. She won't tell anyone. Tell her, Chrissie.

CHRISSIE: She won't believe me.

MARGARET: I would believe you.

CARL: Tell her.

MARGARET: I'd believe you. But it wouldn't do any good. I might be wrong to believe you. I can't take the risk. That's the kind of world it is. It forces us to live without faith. I'm sorry, dear. It's the way things are.

CHRISSIE: Do you want money?

CARL: She won't take money.

MARGARET: I might.

CARL: Name it.

MARGARET: I'm not sure. I used to have a principle of only taking money given freely and with compassion. But there may be higher principals at work. In any case, money would only be one of my demands. I need to talk it over with Jerry.

CHRISSIE: Who's Jerry?

MARGARET: My son. You should meet him. He'll like you.

CARL: He's a dishwasher in this restaurant.

MARGARET: Why must you define everybody by the job they hold? My son is a human being. And a student. And a good boy with clean hands. But you dismiss him as a simple dishwasher.

CARL: I don't dismiss him. It's an honest living. He's making a contribution in his own way.

CHRISSIE: Oh good, Daddy. Cause I decided to drop out of university and be a dishwasher.

CARL: Chrissie.

CHRISSIE: I want to make a contribution in my own way.

CARL: This is not the time.

MARGARET: You should have more respect for your father. He would sleep in the gutter so that you could wear clean clothes.

MARK: Have you figured out your demands yet? We can't negotiate until you tell us your demands.

MARGARET: I prefer to think of them as wishes.

MARK: Wishes, then.

MARGARET: Three wishes. It seems appropriate. It has a tradition.

MARK: Three wishes. What are they?

MARGARET: What's wrong with you? Do you think I left home this morning with a gun in one pocket and a list of demands in the other? These things take time. I need to know things. What things? I need to know the resources at hand. I have a Member of Parliament. And I have a ...?

CARL: Well, it's kind of hard to explain. I, uh ... invest here and there, I—

CHRISSIE: Daddy's a capitalist.

CARL: Not in public, Chrissie.

CHRISSIE: It's not a dirty word, Daddy.

MARGARET: But what does he do?

CHRISSIE: He's a capitalist. He earns money with money. He owns various means of production.

MARGARET: I don't know what you're trying to say, dear.

CHRISSIE: It's new to me, too. He buys things, say an apartment block. Then when the price goes up, he sells it. Or he buys shares in a company and sells them. He once bought a factory and then sold it without ever stepping inside it.

CARL: I didn't even know where it was.

CHRISSIE: And he's proud of it.

CARL: Why shouldn't I be?

CHRISSIE: You're the one who shushes me whenever I call you a capitalist.

CARL: That's different. I don't like the word. Why can't you talk about personal initiative, business sense, practicality? Even free enterprise. It has the world free in it.

CHRISSIE: He's into advertising, too.

CARL: It's all in how you say it. Capitalist makes it sound like I believe in something.

MARGARET: Does he do stuff for television?

CARL: I bought a small production company. Mostly advertising.

MARGARET: Could you make a television program?

CARL: All it takes is money.

MARGARET: My story on television.

MARK: Right.

MARGARET: No. This story on television. This event. The heroic story of a mother fighting against all odds to provide for her children. Drama. Pathos. Violence.

MARK: Not violence. Okay. So, if Carl agrees to finance a TV show about—

MARGARET: I want a movie.

MARK: A movie then. He'll agree to do a movie—

MARGARET: I want to play the mother. I can feel her.

CARL: No deal.

MARK: For Christ's sake.

CARL: No deal. I'm not sinking millions into a film contract if I'm forced to use some unknown in the lead role.

MARGARET: You're right. We want people to see this.

CARL: We need a big American star.

MARGARET: No way.

CARL: Look. I control the casting or there's no deal.

CHRISSIE: Don't sign. He'll turn it into mush.

MARGARET: He has the money.

CHRISSIE: You have the gun.

MARGARET: I get final approval on casting.

CARL: Can't we negotiate?

MARK: Carl, shut up. Margaret. You can have casting. A feature film. *(to Carl)* Agreed?

CARL: Agreed.

MARGARET: Is that good enough? Don't we need something written?

MARK: There's witnesses.

MARGARET: It's a deal.

MARK: Let's go. *(rises)*

MARGARET: You misunderstand the whole project.

> *(Mark deflates.)*

Your behaviour here has given me tremendous insight into Canadian politics. It will be in our film.

MARK: What's the problem? I thought we made a deal.

MARGARET: Are you typical of Members of Parliament? I'll explain it to you. Once. *(slow)* I want-to-make-a-film-of-this-event. Do you follow me so far?

> *(Mark nods.)*

If-we-go-home-now-there-is-nothing-to-film.

CARL: We'd get two inches at the end of the want ads at best.

MARGARET: I got a name. "The Three Wishes."

CARL: Cut the "the."

MARGARET: "Three Wishes." Says it all. *(to Mark)* When this film is released, everyone's gonna know it's you in it. You handle yourself well, you could be Prime Minister. You continue in this pathetic, whiny way, you're through. I say this because I care for you.

JERRY: *(enters)* So what's up, Mom?

MARGARET: Jerry, there are two things happening here. First, we are making a movie. Carl has money to burn and is investing bundles in the story of our lives. It's a great opportunity. You have to help.

JERRY: Is she serious?

> *(All nod.)*

What do I have to do?

MARGARET: I have a gun. You have to take it from me and aim it at these people. If they make a move, vaporize them.

JERRY: Aw, Mom. Not again.

CARL: You have done this before. You are a criminal.

MARGARET: I've never done this before.

JERRY: Not exactly, but pretty close. One time she made a list of everything she saw advertised on television for the whole week. Then she went to the Bay and filled up two huge orange garbage bags with everything that would fit.

CARL: You're not a criminal, no.

MARGARET: The television made me do it.

JERRY: Ah, Mom.

MARGARET: It's true. I wasn't trying to steal. I was making a statement. It's not my fault no one stopped me. I didn't even have enough money for the bus. I walked two miles through snowdrifts to get home. I was so angry I wrote a letter complaining about their lax security. Now I travel light. Jerry. I'm your mother. Take the gun.

JERRY: *(he does)* She's my mother. *(loses himself in Chrissie's eyes)*

MARGARET: For God's sake, Jerry, keep your eyes on them. *(goes to another table)*

JERRY: *(to Chrissie, with his eyes on the others)* My name's Jerry.

MARK: We met before.

JERRY: I'm talking to her. What's your name?

MARK: Mark Westerbrook.

JERRY: I'm talking to her.

CHRISSIE: Chrissie.

JERRY: Christine?

CHRISSIE: Yeah.

JERRY: Christine ... Are you in the movie?

CHRISSIE: I guess so. We all are.

JERRY: I'm glad we're in this movie together, Christine. Are you an actress?

CARL: For Christ's sake, she's my daughter.

JERRY: She looks like a movie star.

MARK: Look, Jerry. She's a nice girl. You're a nice boy. You could have something together.

JERRY: That's what I was thinking.

CARL: Don't waste your time.

MARK: But not if you continue with this insanity.

JERRY: I wouldn't hurt her.

MARK: What kind of future are you making for yourselves? Let her go, let us go, and we'll forget about everything.

MARGARET: I need a pen. And some paper.

CHRISSIE: *(reaching into her school bag)* Here.

CARL: What are you writing?

MARGARET: A thing, a ... a ... something like a statement, but different.

MARK: A will!

MARGARET: No, no. Like a proclamation. It begins with "m."

CHRISSIE: Manifesto!

MARGARET: A manifesto, yes. I want it read on television, I want it printed in the newspaper.

CHRISSIE: Can I help?

CARL: What's happened to you? I don't know what's happened to her. Do you remember what a sweet child she was, Mark?

CHRISSIE: Oh, Daddy, it's just exciting, that's all. And it'll help for school. We're doing manifestos in political science and poverty in sociology. Just first year but there's a lot of interesting stuff. I might even be able to write a term paper on this. Mrs Moresby is really neat. She'll probably let me do it. Please, Daddy?

CARL: No.

CHRISSIE: I'm doing it anyway.

MARGARET: I don't like to hear a girl talk to her father like that, but I'm in no position to refuse. Thank you, Chrissie. Come with me.

JERRY: Mom, my hand's getting tired.

MARGARET: You just started, Jerry. I'll take over in a while.

(Margaret and Chrissie move away.)

JERRY: *(to Carl)* She's really something.

CARL: Yeah, she should be locked up.

JERRY: I mean Christine.

CARL: She should be locked up, too.

JERRY: She's not always like this, you know.

CARL: You knew her before?

JERRY: I mean my mother. You should see her at home. She's not like this at all. She's calm, she's relaxed. But you let her out the front door and she falls apart. She doesn't go out much, you know.

CARL: I can see why.

MARK: She should get help.

JERRY: Oh, she's had help. She was sent to a psychologist once. He gave up. I think she's been in the void once too often. You guys probably don't know about the void. Neither does my mother. That's why she goes crazy whenever she's in it. I think she's acting out what she sees on television. She thinks that's what it's like out here. I've seen her sit through six hours of television, the soaps, game shows, the news, weather and sports, sitcoms, cop shows and Sunday night dramas. She doesn't move. I used to think that she was in outer space but then I realized she was concentrating, almost memorizing. She knows a lot of things. Many of them are wrong. God, my hand's getting tired.

MARK: Use the other hand.

JERRY: *(he does)* Thanks.

MARK: I've felt the void.

JERRY: I don't think it's the same void. You're talking about an emptiness inside. A spiritless, exhausted soul. The void I'm talking about is a physical place. It covers the known civilized world except for our house. One time in school during recess I walked into the girls' bathroom by mistake. It was pink. There were no urinals. The smell was unfamiliar, but, like the whole experience, stimulating. And terrifying. Another world, another galaxy. I panicked. But I could see my classmates waiting for me outside, laughing. My fear of staying wrestled with my fear of leaving and won. I'll never forget that experience. That's what it's like for my mother in the void.

CARL: I'm surprised she ever leaves the house. Why doesn't she just stay there?

JERRY: She hates it at home. Nothing to do except watch television and watch the paint peel. Four small rooms with four people, low ceilings and a grey fog that hangs in the air. Hot in the summer. Cold in the winter. She hates it there.

MARK: You seem to do okay out here.

JERRY: No, not really. I don't panic. But I don't relax, I don't feel comfortable. I mean, you guys live in the void, I'm just visiting.

MARK: It's wonderful. I understand it now. I've been there. I'm sure I've been there. Undervalued. Unrecognized. *(begins to rise)* Unappreciated. Held down. Held down. Eight years in Parliament. Finally a minor ministry no one's ever heard of. Do you know that I haven't spoken to the Prime Minister in six months? Hello. How are you, a handshake, nothing more.

CARL: Mark. Sit down.

MARK: I understand. You don't. I'm a more sensitive person than you are. What do you know? What do you know about people? What do you know about real people? You're a manipulator of commodities. You wouldn't know a human feeling if you tripped over it. *(to Margaret)* I understand you. I want to help. I'm a Cabinet Minister. I have power. What can I do?

MARGARET: *(to Chrissie)* What do you think?

CHRISSIE: What do you know about poverty?

MARK: I understand how it feels.

CHRISSIE: Welfare rates? Poverty indexes? Income distribution?

MARK: Not much.

CHRISSIE: *(to Margaret)* I don't think he can help us yet. We need more information. Do you know that my father made 623 thousand dollars last year? This sociology textbook is useless. It's not telling us what we need to know.

MARGARET: What about our second wish? Maybe he could help with that?

CHRISSIE: You must know people in the media.

MARK: Oh, yes.

CHRISSIE: We'll need that kind of contact to get Margaret's manifesto read. Don't do anything yet, but think about it. We may have to act quickly.

MARK: Is that all?

CHRISSIE: Can you handle it?

MARK: I'm a Cabinet Minister. I want to help write the manifesto.

CHRISSIE: You want to write a manifesto on poverty.

MARK: I can help.

MARGARET: Mark, get some paper and a pen and see what you come up with.

MARK: Thanks, Margaret. *(goes to another table, begins to write)*

(Jerry has been flipping coins.)

CARL: I don't know where we went wrong. How did she get like this?

JERRY: Kids are weird.

CARL: It's hard, you know. Being a parent. Heads.

JERRY: You win.

CARL: You try and teach kids to be responsible and they end up turning on you. Maybe it was the UNICEF boxes. We always made her collect money for UNICEF when she went out for Halloween. We took every opportunity to remind her about kids starving in China. We wanted her to know there were people out there ... tails ...

JERRY: Tails it is.

(Carl takes the coin.)

Hey, what are you doing?

CARL: I won. I called tails, it was tails.

JERRY: I didn't know we were playing for money. *(reaches into his pocket and pulls out more coins; flips one)*

CARL: Tails.

(Carl looks at and takes the coin. Jerry keeps flipping coins, taking his time, and each time, Carl calls, wins, and takes the coin, making neat piles on the table.)

We wanted Chrissie to feel lucky, to know about poverty, to appreciate our lifestyle. On vacations in the Caribbean we pointed out the half-naked children in the street. We even let her give them a dime here, a nickel there. We knew that this created a debilitating dependency in the little beggars but we thought it would be good for Chrissie so we let her do it. I never suspected this was in her. She goes to university, I favoured business administration but gave in to a general arts degree, and two liberal and one Marxist professor later, she turns on us. She gives up tennis at the club and starts jogging. She goes on and on about historical materialism and situational ethics. Now, I'm sitting in this restaurant, you've got a gun on me, your mother lectures me on the bad luck of the poor and my daughter and my best friend here, a two bit politician from who-knows-where in Prince Edward Island, are working on a manifesto that will no doubt denounce all my favourite things.

JERRY: Doesn't it bother you that there's so much poverty in the world?

CARL: No.

JERRY: *(his money could be gone by now)* Does Chrissie have a boyfriend?

CARL: She's a lesbian.

JERRY: Ah, shit. Why? Why? *(this time a question to Carl)* Why?

CARL: I don't know.

JERRY: *(thinks)* Does she have a girlfriend?

CARL: She walked into the house the other day and announced that she was a lesbian. We haven't talked about it since.

JERRY: Why! *(clearly not a question)*

CARL: I find it hard to talk about that kind of thing.

JERRY: I can't believe it. This proves it. My mother's right. It's hopeless. It's useless. When you're poor, your luck's bad. I know that now.

CARL: Snap out of it. *(snap)* You've gotta keep yourself tough. You can do it. You can do anything. You can make it. Anyone can make it. It takes sweat, guts, perseverance. You can have everything. You can have it all.

JERRY: Thanks.

CARL: It's okay.

JERRY: Mr ...

CARL: McBurney.

JERRY: Mr McBurney, could you get me a job? Like a part-time job, even. I've been studying drafting for two years, my marks are good, and I'd work hard.

CARL: That's an excellent idea. I know some architects. I think I own an engineering firm. I could get you a part-time job for now and then after you graduate, if things worked out, you could work full time.

JERRY: Really?

CARL: Sure. Why not?

JERRY: Thank you, Mr McBurney.

CARL: Do you want to play some more?

JERRY: Yeah, sure.

(*Jerry gets out a five-dollar bill, which Carl changes. Jerry continues to flip coins and lose. A calm settles over the room, Margaret and Chrissie reading, Mark thinking and writing, Carl and Jerry quietly betting, the silence broken only by "heads, heads, tails."*)

CARL: Tails.

JERRY: You're very good at this.

CARL: Thank you.

(*More flips until one lands on the floor. Jerry goes to get it and Carl jumps him, grabbing his arm but unable to reach the gun. Margaret intervenes, the gun goes off and Margaret ends up with it. Margaret threatens Carl to restore order.*)

MARGARET: (*to imaginary patrons of the restaurant*) It's okay, relax, nobody's hurt. It's just a gun. It went off accidentally. Actually, the truth is that this man tried to rob us and we subdued him, someone call the police. Nobody move, I have to think. Okay, everybody get out of here. Move quickly and you won't get hurt. (*pause, everyone's gone. She sits, exhausted*) Jerry.

JERRY: I'm sorry, Mom.

MARGARET: Everybody's calm now. It's back to normal. (*to Carl*) What are you doing, are you trying to get someone killed? Men. Always have to be heroes. Always gotta act tough. Now everyone's upset and I had to clear the restaurant.

MARK: Margaret, I want you to know that whether this continues or not, I've pledged myself to work for your cause. I've already planned to raise some issues on your behalf at our next Cabinet meeting. I would like to say though, that if at this juncture you are reconsidering your plans, and if you are open to suggestions, I suggest we go home now and meet in my office first thing tomorrow.

JERRY: What are we gonna do, Mom? The cops are gonna be here in a minute.

MARGARET: Nothing in my life has prepared me for this.

MARK: Let's vote.

MARGARET: What do you think, Chrissie?

CHRISSIE: I don't know. We've put a lot of work into this.

MARGARET: Jerry?

JERRY: It's up to you, Mom.

MARGARET: I've never had this kind of intimate relationship with rich people before. And I know that if we stop now, I'll never get this chance again. To keep going, to not lose heart when life turns ugly. I feel the courage necessary for continuation stirring within me. A new resolve, a new consciousness of myself as subject, not object. A maker of history rather than its victim or witness. To yield to compassion and fear now would be to turn my back on the future and its possibilities. We must face the void with our eyes open and our heads high.

MARK: I vote we stay.

MARGARET: We're going. Together. As one. *(She reaches into Carl's jacket for his car keys.)* C'mon, Carl, we're going for a drive.

JERRY: Where are we going, Mom?

MARGARET: Out.

> *(Everyone exits.)*
>
> *(End of Act One.)*

ACT TWO

The stage is dimly lit. A key turns in a lock. The door opens.
The light of street lamps spills into restaurant.

MARGARET: *(pushing Carl and Mark)* Get in. Hurry up. Stand there. Don't move. *(She searches for a light switch but finds some candles and begins to light them.)* This place looks like a cemetery. Let's get these chairs off the tables.

(Mark helps, Carl doesn't.)

(mocking Mark) "We can't go to my house—my wife plays bridge Tuesdays."

MARK: Do you still feel car sick, Margaret?

MARGARET: I'm much better, thanks. *(to Carl)* Thanks for the help. Can't go to my house cause they'll look for us there. Can't go to Carl's house cause he's got slaves.

CARL: Servants.

MARGARET: I thought the police would never leave. What were they doing here for two hours? My back hurts. Jerry and Christine should have been here by now. Expensive car like that and there's no room for your legs in the back seat. *(She finds some Perrier in the bar.)* Want a drink?

(Margaret opens three bottles, passes two to Mark, who passes one to Carl. Margaret drinks.)

(spits) What is this stuff? It tastes like water. Read me what you've written, Mark.

MARK: *(gets in the mood for his maiden speech and reads)* "Mr Speaker— excuse me—Madam Speaker. As you know, I recently spent ..." This is where I put in the number of hours you kept us here— number of days? "... X days with a deeply troubled woman. This woman was crying out for our attention. 'Friends, Canadians, countrymen, and women, lend me your ears.' That is what this woman is saying."

MARGARET: You better say that you deplore my methods.

MARK: Good point. *(makes a note)*

MARGARET: Do you have something against mentioning my name?

MARK: No.

MARGARET: Pierce. P-I-E-R-C-E.

MARK: P-I-...

MARGARET: ...E-R-C-E.

MARK: ...E-R-C-E. *(reads)* "This woman—Margaret Pierce—is crying out. For understanding. For compassion. For recognition. She desperately wants us to know the sense of emptiness, of isolation, the impotence she feels. A woman without a sense of self worth, wholeness and completion."

MARGARET: Without money. Don't forget to mention that. I'm a woman without a sense of having money.

MARK: *(makes a note)* Right. *(reads)* "And how many of us, in our heart of hearts, would not admit to a deep lack of self-worth, wholeness and completion?"

MARGARET: A deep lack of money.

MARK: *(makes a note, reads)* "And how many of us, in our heart of hearts, would not admit to a deep lack of self-worth, wholeness, completion and money?" Do I have to mention money? A lot of people won't identify with that.

MARGARET: Were you elected?

MARK: Mmhm.

MARGARET: People voted for you.

MARK: Yes.

MARGARET: Read.

MARK: *(reads)* "This country is more than a sum of its people. For too long, we have neglected the individual person. A person without pride produces a country without honour. Our country is beset with problems—inflation, high interest rates, a crumbling dollar, a debilitating deficit, unemployment. The government must free the individual to wrestle these problems to the ground. We are fortunate to live in this wonderful country with its boundless forests, mighty rivers, its wealth. Together, each and every one of us, making sacrifices, tightening our belts another notch, acting honourably, waiting patiently, for the prosperity that is just around the corner." *(to Margaret)* Prosperity, money—it's kind of the same thing. What do you think?

MARGARET: *(tears it up)* You can't read this in public. You'll just embarrass yourself.

CARL: I thought it was moving.

(Chrissie and Jerry enter, carrying books and magazines. Jerry goes off stage left. Café lights come on.)

CHRISSIE: Hi, everybody. Hi, daddy. Mummy says not to stay out too late. Look at all this stuff we brought. *(starts to work)*

(Jerry returns. Margaret takes him aside.)

MARGARET: Did you try anything?

JERRY: No.

MARGARET: You were with her for two hours.

JERRY: Mom.

CHRISSIE: Read this Margaret.

(Margaret and Jerry join Chrissie.)

CARL: *(as he hands Mark a contract)* You want to take a look at this?

MARK: *(reads)* "Exclusive right to all goods and services ..."

CARL: Posters, T-shirts, rock videos ...

MARK: I don't know much about movies, Carl. Can I have my lawyer look at this?

CARL: It's really just a formality. I basically closed the deal with Margaret.

MARK: Sure. *(signs)*

CHRISSIE: *(stops reading; to Jerry)* You said you were taking drafting?

JERRY: Architectural drafting.

CHRISSIE: Um, *(reads)* "... and rapid development of computer assisted design will lead to a decline of ..." Here. "It is estimated that over the coming decade, employment in drafting and graphic design will fall by seventy percent."

JERRY: Shit. Two years I've been going to that school. Nobody tells me anything. What a day. I lose two jobs I never had. Now, I'm going to lose my dishwashing job, too.

> *(Jerry sits, dejected. Carl and Margaret move to talk to Jerry. Carl stops Margaret.)*

CARL: Jerry, would you look this over? It's just a formality. This part here means that if this thing ends up with someone getting arrested, you get a thousand dollars up front. If anyone's killed, you get a big 5K, and ten percent of all profits on T-shirts with your name or picture. It's a very generous offer. Just sign here.

> *(Carl offers Jerry a pen. He signs.)*

Thanks, Jer.

> *(Carl goes back to his table. Margaret joins Jerry.)*

MARGARET: I'm sorry about your job, Jerry.

JERRY: It's okay, Mom.

MARGARET: It's my fault. We're gonna demand that you get a proper job out of this, okay?

JERRY: Sure.

MARGARET: Chrissie's a nice girl. When this is over, you should take her to a movie. I think she likes you.

JERRY: She's a lesbian, Mom.

MARGARET: Maybe she's just shy.

JERRY: Her father told me.

MARGARET: Bad luck, eh? You know what, Jerry? I'm going to demand that you get Carl's car. You'd like that, wouldn't you? Or even a brand new one, but with electric mirrors like his. I saw you playing with them. I've never been able to buy you anything expensive, Jerry. Now's our chance to get some quality things. We should splurge. Remember when you were little, you wanted to be a hockey player but I couldn't buy the equipment so you couldn't play? You cried and cried. You said you hated me. You're angry at me now, aren't you?

JERRY: Mom? Janie got pregnant when she was sixteen. Lewis is in jail. Dougie's thirteen and he's been to training school twice. I tried to get good marks in school. I did what the teachers said. I never got into fights. I didn't sniff glue.

MARGARET: You were always a good boy, Jerry.

JERRY: But you were never impressed. Nothing I did ever made you happy.

MARGARET: Remember when Eric-from-Children's-Aid came to the house to meet the family? He asked Janie and Lewis what they wanted to be when they grew up. They couldn't think of anything. They were normal. But you always wanted to be something.

JERRY: You never encouraged me.

MARGARET: I was trying to protect you. I didn't want you to be disappointed.

JERRY: I'm disappointed now.

MARGARET: I know.

JERRY: Janie and Lewis aren't disappointed.

MARGARET: They got what they expected. You grew up with a sense of hope. I tried to fight it, but I wasn't strong enough. I wasn't a very good mother to you, Jerry. I'm sorry.

JERRY: It's not too late, Mom. Things look pretty hopeless now.

(Silence. Noise from the door. Jerry runs over to check.)

MARGARET: *(excited again)* Things are beginning to move.

JERRY: They're gone.

MARGARET: Who else has a key? I'm excited again.

JERRY: I bolted it.

MARGARET: Check every window, check every door.

(Jerry goes.)

We swing into action now. If there's a soundtrack, Carl, this is where it should start to move. Start thinking about that. I would feel better with a written contract, maybe you should work on it. Mark, I'm sorry I was tough on you but it's a tough world. Don't get discouraged. I want you to make a list of everyone you know in the media. Especially anyone who would understand the kind of things I'm talking about. Chrissie, we have to get our demands ready.

MARK: I thought they were wishes.

MARGARET: We've gone back to demands.

CHRISSIE: We're not closing our eyes and wishing. We open them and make demands.

MARK: It makes us sound like extremists.

(Jerry returns.)

MARGARET: Jerry, could you get us some food?

MARK: I could use a drink.

JERRY: Everything's locked up at night. I'll see what I can find. *(exits)*

(Restaurant phone rings.)

MARGARET: Get it, Chrissie.

CHRISSIE: Cheap Thrill Café. ... Just a moment, please. It's for Jerry.

MARGARET: Jerry!

(Jerry enters, gives baskets of crackers to Chrissie, takes the phone.)

JERRY: Hi. ... Oh. ... Just a second. *(to Margaret)* It's the police. They want us to come out with our hands up.

MARGARET: Tell them to call back in ten minutes.

MARK: You can't do that.

MARGARET: Tell them.

JERRY: We're not ready yet. Could you call back in ten minutes? ... *(to Margaret)* He's angry.

MARGARET: *(takes the phone)* Look. I said ten minutes and I mean ten minutes.

> *(She hangs up. It rings again. She picks up the receiver and leaves it off the hook.)*

(to Mark) We make the rules. We move at our own rhythm. Right now we need to talk. Chrissie, Jerry tells me you're a lesbian.

JERRY: Aw, Mom.

MARK: She is not.

MARGARET: *(to Mark)* You know something about this?

MARK: I've known her since she was a child.

MARGARET: I want you to know, Chrissie, I'm not being judgmental.

MARK: She probably told Jerry that because she doesn't like him. It's the oldest excuse in the book. Right, Carl?

MARGARET: Is it true, Chrissie?

JERRY: Mom.

MARGARET: She's an adult, Jerry. She can talk.

JERRY: Aw, Mom.

CHRISSIE: I don't mind.

CARL: Do we have to go through this now?

MARGARET: It won't hurt you to listen.

CHRISSIE: I'm not a lesbian. I'm bisexual.

CARL: Lesbian, bisexual, what's the difference?

MARGARET: Feel better, Jerry?

MARK: Why, Chrissie, why?

CHRISSIE: Some people think that sexual orientation is a matter of heredity.

CARL: Oh, thanks.

CHRISSIE: In my case I thinks it's because of the men I knew in my formative years. I wanted to keep my options open.

CARL: I hope your children do to you what you do to me.

MARGARET: Your father is right, Chrissie. I remember looking out the window early in the morning. The sun wasn't up yet, I'd see my father walking down to the boats. I remember watching the sun set, waiting for him to come home. I remember men talking in whispers in our living room about unions and fair prices and who could be trusted and who couldn't be. I remember him telling my mother that she was giving us too much to eat, that there wasn't enough food to last the winter. I remember him getting drunk and beating the piss out of my mother and us kids. He should have been put in jail. *(picks up the phone)* Still there? ... To whom am I speaking? ... Good evening, Detective Harris. This is Margaret Pierce. What can I do for you? ... I'm not sure. Perhaps I could call you when I know. ... I'm trying to be reasonable Detective Harris. Why don't you give me your number and I'll call you when we're ready?

(She motions to Chrissie to take it down. Chrissie gets a pen.)

5-5-5, 4-4-6, 4-8-2-1 ... You have my word. Goodbye. *(to Carl)* Carl, do me a favour. I want you to read this like you're my husband. Okay? Uh, sit down here.

(Carl sits.)

Yeah. Now, you're on television, on the news, and the whole country's watching. Everybody's watching cause everybody knows we're here, and that if you don't read this—wait a second ... *(to Chrissie)* We'll pre-empt the soaps. Four o'clock in the afternoon, those are the people I wanna reach. Every poor woman in the country. No. They'll hate me if they can't watch the soaps. *(to Carl)* So all these people are watching cause they know that if my husband doesn't read this, you and Mark'll be dead.

CARL: On behalf—

MARGARET: Wait. I don't believe you're him. *(looks him over, messes his hair, adjusts his jacket, looks)* Take off your jacket.

(Carl does.)

Take off your shirt.

(Carl does. He's wearing a white T-shirt)

We're getting there.

(Phone rings. Margaret takes a pack of cigarettes from Jerry and tucks it in the sleeve of Carl's T-shirt.)

JERRY: Cheap Thrill Café. ... Hi. Eric. What's up? ... I'm not sure. I think you better talk to my mother. *(to Margaret)* It's Eric-from-Children's-Aid.

(Margaret takes phone.)

MARGARET: *(apologetic)* Hi, Eric. ... Oh, uh, just having a little fun. ... Yeah, everyone's fine, Eric ...

JERRY: *(to Chrissie)* He's a really nice guy.

MARGARET: Yeah, we should talk about this. I guess it sounds a little strange.

JERRY: He's more a friend than a social worker.

MARGARET: Yeah, I guess so. Wait a second. Forget that. No, you can't come in here. ... I don't want to talk to you, Eric. ... Maybe never. I'm rethinking our relationship. *(She hangs up; to no one)* Goodbye, Eric.

JERRY: Why'd you do that?

MARGARET: I had a vision. There were a million doors and in each door there was a social worker. There was Children's Aid, there was a probation officer, there were lawyers and judges and teachers and guidance councillors and police. And they all were saying "We want to help you. We want to talk to you. Let us help you or we'll take away your children." I heard them saying that. I woke up. Saying, "No." No. What a nice word. Read it, Carl.

CARL: *(reads)* "On behalf of all men everywhere, I want to apologize to my dear, loving wife for the years I mistreated her. Being stupid, I didn't understand what a wonderful, warm person she was. While she looked after me and the children, washing, cleaning, cooking, keeping track of the money, cleaning up after me when I got drunk and threw up, I sat around, except for the brief periods when I was actually working. Whether I was actually working or not, I expected to be treated like a king and to be waited on hand and foot. Even though I had it good, I was stupid enough to leave her, which was the happiest day of her life. I was a jerk and still am a jerk."

MARGARET: Read that line again.

CARL: "I was a jerk and still am a jerk."

(Everyone laughs. Margaret stops them.)

MARGARET: *(to Carl)* Go on.

CARL: *(reads)* "I speak on behalf of all men when I say this. Unconscious of the historical mission of the working class, a sop to the ... hej ... hegg ..."

CHRISSIE: Hegemony.

CARL: "... hegemony of the ruling class."

CHRISSIE: I wrote this part.

CARL: "For a modest wage, I was a willing slave to the owners of the means of production, and an oppressor to all those I could push around. At work I was a coward, at home a tyrant. I now admit the error of my ways. On behalf of the oppressed—workers and the unemployed, the aged, visible minorities, women, native people, lesbians and other homosexuals, and single women with children, more than half of whom men, like myself, have forced to live below the poverty line, I declare an unending struggle against the likes of Carl McBurney—who for a quick buck has forced mothers and their children into the streets ..."

(Mark is enjoying this.)

CHRISSIE: Sorry, Daddy.

CARL: *(aimed at Mark)* "... and against their lackeys in government, such as Mark Westerbrook."

MARK: I don't think that's fair.

MARGARET: *(to Carl)* Continue.

CARL: "I want to thank my wife, Margaret Pierce, for giving me this opportunity to redeem myself. I will not see this communication from her as an attempt at reconciliation and will do her a favour and stay out of her life."

MARK: Are we going to get a chance to discuss this?

CHRISSIE: I don't think there's any point, Mr Westerbrook. You're Margaret's class enemy.

CARL: Nice earrings you're wearing today, Chrissie. 24 karat, aren't they?

CHRISSIE: I got them really cheap.

CARL: In Paris, wasn't it? Did I mention what happened to my car? Practically brand new and the transmission went. Chrissie was kind enough to loan me hers.

CHRISSIE: You don't understand the class system, Daddy. I don't own any means of production. I don't buy and sell labour. I don't treat workers as a commodity. Margaret and I can work together. She trusts me. *(to Margaret)* You trust me, don't you.

MARGARET: Uh ...

CARL: There.

CHRISSIE: It's not important. The proletariat don't have time for political theory. They aren't really aware of the historical mission of their class.

MARGARET: I don't know, Chrissie. You sound a lot like a social worker.

CHRISSIE: No way.

MARGARET: Or a politician.

MARK: I don't talk like that.

CHRISSIE: Of course, you don't. You're a bourgeois politician. Your historical role is to serve the bourgeoisie. To keep wages down by maintaining a large pool of unemployed. Oh yes—from time to time you appear to act against the interests of your capitalist bosses. Welfare. Unemployment insurance. Medicare. But the proletariat are not fooled. They understand that these handouts serve only one purpose—to dampen their taste for revolution.

MARK: Really?

(Mark looks at Jerry. Jerry shrugs.)

CHRISSIE: Imagine.

(Margaret is losing interest.)

A new society and a new morality. From each according to his or her abilities, to each according to his or her needs. In place of the old bourgeois society, with its classes and class antagonisms, we shall have an association in which the free development of each is a condition for the free development of all.

MARK: I talked to her about that. She wants money.

CHRISSIE: I'm offering her something better. A vision for the future. Dreams. Hope.

JERRY: Yeah, hope.

CHRISSIE: History has laws, Margaret. From desperation comes struggle, and from struggle, hope.

MARGARET: *(gun in hand)* I'm not desperate.

CARL: She's not desperate.

MARK: Don't deny it, Margaret. There's nothing wrong with being desperate. I've been there.

MARGARET: There's a subtle distinction here, I have to think. *(she thinks)*

CHRISSIE: I know what the problem is. You're not really a member of the proletariat.

MARGARET: We're talking different kinds of desperate. Hunger. War. Torture. That's the kind of desperate you're talking about, Chrissie. My desperate has more in common with the vandal and the sniper. It's not the base for a mass movement.

(Phone rings. Jerry goes to answer it.)

MARGARET: We need more time.

JERRY: Cheap Thrill Café. ... She's busy right now. Could you ... *(to Margaret)* It's about a movie.

MARGARET: Who is it?

JERRY: Who is this? ... *(to Margaret)* "The big apple." That's what he said.

CHRISSIE: New York.

MARGARET: Tell them I've already got an offer.

JERRY: She's already got an offer. ... A hundred what? ... *(to Margaret)* A hundred thousand dollars, up front. ... Twenty percent of the profits.

CARL: Two hundred thousand.

JERRY: *(to Carl)* And twenty percent of the profits?

CARL: Yes.

JERRY: *(on phone)* Your bid. ... *(to Carl)* Half a million plus twenty percent of gross.

CARL: We had a gentlemen's agreement, Margaret.

JERRY: They're talking a fifteen million dollar budget.

CARL: I can't match that.

MARGARET: Too bad.

CARL: They're Americans, Margaret.

MARGARET: So?

CARL: I can't raise that kind of money.

MARGARET: I don't know, Carl.

CARL: Are you just going to sell out to the highest bidder? Don't you have any pride in your country? You were the one who didn't want an American star.

MARGARET: You're right.

CARL: *(takes contract, makes changes)* Two hundred thousand dollars. Twenty percent of profits. Sign here.

(Margaret signs.)

JERRY: *(on phone)* I think you lost it.

CARL: Thank you, Margaret. *(takes phone from Jerry)* Okay. I've got a signed contract but I'm willing to cut a deal. ... Make it an even million. ... Carl McBurney. ... Hi, Des, good to chat. Hey, I'll be in the Big Apple next week. Take lunch? ... Great. Ciao. *(hangs up)* Sorry, Margaret. Business has its own logic.

MARGARET: Beg, Carl. ... On your knees. *(takes out gun)*

CARL: No.

MARGARET: Guns have their own logic. Tear it up.

(More threats with gun. Carl tears up contract.)

Stand up.

(He does.)

No. Get back on your knees.

MARK: Margaret, don't you think ...?

MARGARET: On your knees.

(Carl kneels.)

Stay there. This is a unique experience for me. I want to savour it. I imagine this is a unique experience for you too, Carl. Complete powerlessness. It is my hope that this experience will teach you something. I want you to know, Carl, you are not a likable person. Perhaps you can change. You should reflect on that. I will, in the meantime, reflect on my new-found power.

MARK: Let him get up, Margaret.

CHRISSIE: *(to Margaret)* Can I talk to you for a second? I feel like I let you down. I don't want you to think this is just a style thing for me. When I was young, my father used to give me pennies to give to kids begging in the street. Ever since then, I've identified with people like you.

MARK: Uh, Margaret. I have to go to the uh—

MARGARET: You're a good girl, Chrissie. Your parents should be proud of you. Do you know about the void?

CHRISSIE: I don't think so.

MARK: Margaret, I really have to—

MARGARET: Ask Jerry about the void. It's a good story. *(she thinks)* Good news, Carl. You can move. But you're going to crawl.

(Margaret and Mark start off.)

(to Carl) C'mon, fellah. *(whistles)* Good puppy.

(Margaret and Mark exit, with Carl crawling behind.)

CHRISSIE: Tell me about the void.

JERRY: The what?

CHRISSIE: Your mom said—

JERRY: I wanna talk about something else.

CHRISSIE: Oh. How about the demands we're making? What would you like?

JERRY: You.

CHRISSIE: Seriously.

JERRY: I want you. I've never been close to anyone like you before. I always wanted to be a waiter so I could I serve someone like you. If I could have someone like you, my whole life would be different. I figured it out. It's the only way I can change my luck. I always wanted an arranged marriage and I want it arranged with you. You know how to live in the void. You're in all the ads for things I never had and never could have. I can't even dream about someone like you. I can only daydream. I knew as soon as I saw you. You're my first chance, my only chance, my last chance to enter a new world. To enter the void and never leave.

CHRISSIE: Come here. Come here. *(kisses him)* Okay?

JERRY: I still feel the void. When you're really in the void you can't feel it anymore. I've noticed that.

CHRISSIE: Maybe it doesn't happen all at once. *(kisses him again, slowly)* How's that?

JERRY: I don't know.

CHRISSIE: What's the problem?

JERRY: Maybe it was too easy.

CHRISSIE: Do you want me to make it harder for you?

JERRY: It's supposed to be harder.

CHRISSIE: Get away from me. Don't touch me. Face it, Jack, you're a loser. You don't have money, you don't have a job, you don't have any future. You don't know how to dress. I wouldn't stand next to you in line, never mind go out with you. Have you ever been to Europe?

JERRY: No.

CHRISSIE: We have nothing in common. Nothing to talk about. My father wouldn't let you in the house. My mother would have the house fumigated. My friends would avoid me and discuss my sanity. We'd have to use my car. I'd grow to resent it. We'd argue. Then we'd fight. You'd resent my independence. You'd begin to drink. I'd throw you out. You'd end up a bum. I'd be left with the children.

JERRY: You're right. It wouldn't work out.

CHRISSIE: Is that better?

JERRY: Yeah.

CHRISSIE: Okay, now talk me into it.

JERRY: What?

CHRISSIE: I'm making it hard for you. Now talk me into it.

JERRY: Naw, you're right.

CHRISSIE: Argue with me. Talk me into it.

JERRY: Why bother?

CHRISSIE: Jerry. We can make it anyway. Against all odds. Our love will overcome all. You and me against the world. A new kind of love. A brave love. A love so strong it will overcome our differences.

JERRY: I don't think it's possible.

CHRISSIE: I don't believe you.

JERRY: You're right, Christine. We're too different.

CHRISSIE: Why are you like this?

JERRY: Like what?

CHRISSIE: Such a wimp.

JERRY: I had poor role models as a child. There was this man who lived next door. Every evening, at supper time, he'd disappear, no one knew why. I followed him. He'd walk a bit, find a bench to sit on, then he'd go home. Finally, he told me why. He'd leave so there'd be more food for the kids. He was a wimp. I wanted to be like him.

CHRISSIE: I don't think you're a wimp. I think you have a quiet strength.

JERRY: A quiet strength. Is that good?

CHRISSIE: Mmhm.

JERRY: *(tough)* A quiet strength.

CHRISSIE: No. No. A quiet strength.

JERRY: A quiet strength.

CHRISSIE: Now, talk me into it.

> *(Jerry moves in and kisses Chrissie. He's on top of her as the others return.)*

JERRY: *(leaps up)* She was trying to escape. *(to himself)* Quiet strength.

(Phone rings.)

(walks confidently to answer) Cheap Thrill. ... Oh Hello. Yeah, this is Jerry. ... Yeah, well I kind of expected that, eh? ... Listen, Mr Kostash. I just wanted to tell you, this is a rotten place to work, the food sucks, and you're a jerk. *(hangs up and returns proudly to Chrissie)*

CHRISSIE: That was dumb.

JERRY: *(offended)* Why?

CHRISSIE: If you're nice to him, you might get your job back.

JERRY: It's okay. I know what I'm doing.

(Phone rings.)

You wanna get that, Chrissie?

(Chrissie stares him down. Margaret goes to the phone.)

MARGARET: Hello. ... Are we old friends or something—is that why you use my first name? ... I'll keep using Detective Harris, if you don't mind. What's up? ... There's a lack of trust here. I told you I'd call when there was something to tell you. I don't appreciate having my time wasted like this. ... A little patience, that's all. Just a little patience. *(hangs up)*

CARL: We've got to get out of here, Mark. It's getting out of hand.

MARK: You're right. Margaret. I think we should go home now. We've made our point. We should go home.

MARGARET: No, Mark. We've barely begun. We've done nothing. No statement, no demands. There's a lot yet to do.

MARK: *(back to Carl)* We haven't started, Carl. There's a lot yet to do.

(Phone rings. After visual pressure from Margaret, Jerry answers.)

JERRY: Jerry here. ... I'll see. ... *(to Margaret)* It's Father Durocher.

MARGARET: *(takes phone)* Hello, Father. Everyone's fine, thank you.

CARL: *(whispering)* Mark. Fake a heart attack. When she comes over, I'll jump her and get the gun.

MARK: I can't do that.

MARGARET: We're making a statement, Father, about the state of the world.

CARL: Do it, or your little secret about your little friend will be a big news story.

MARGARET: I don't know, Father. Maybe an hour, maybe a week.

MARK: I'd hate to bring up the Hastings land deal.

CARL: Fall down dead or I'll break your neck.

MARGARET: Solidarity in the struggle to you too, Father. Goodbye now.

(Margaret hangs up. Carl pushes Mark onto the floor. Mark fakes a heart attack. Margaret looks at Mark.)

That is really pathetic.

CARL: Get up, Mark.

MARK: *(stirring)* I got this cramp, right over here. *(touches his heart)* It ...

CARL: Nice try.

MARGARET: Stand up. You too, Carl. Sit down. Relax. Give me your wallet, Carl.

(Margaret gives Carl a threatening look. Carl complies. She looks through the wallet.)

VISA, MasterCard, American Express. No one with a fat wallet like this understands words. So, even though I'm talking to you, I don't pretend for a moment that you will understand. This gun has allowed me, for the first time, to exert power. It's the kind of power that you exert every day.

CARL: I don't have a gun.

MARGARET: The relationship is the same. The gun has reversed it. Don't interrupt. I degraded and humiliated you with the power given by this gun. It felt good. But on reflection, I realize that to feel good about such things is sick. That is why I am letting you sit down.

MARK: That's beautiful.

CARL: *(to Mark)* What's the matter with you?

MARK: I feel sorry for you. I do. Acid rain, PCB's, baby seals, nuclear war. This is a frightening world and you have nothing to believe in. I believe in decency. Mothers like Margaret. Children like Jerry and Chrissie. Families, love, warmth.

CARL: Do you know that studies have shown that intelligent people prefer the private sector to public service?

MARK: I've never seen that study.

(A noise. Jerry runs to the door and returns.)

JERRY: The streets are covered with cop cars. The cars are all dark and there's cops in each one. And a bus filled with cops, too. Don't be scared, Chrissie. I'm here.

CARL: Okay, Margaret. This has gone far enough. We've got enough for the movie.

MARGARET: We're not making a movie, Carl. We are making a movie. A movie will be made about what we do. But we will not fashion history to fit your understanding of pacing and cinematography.

CARL: Look, Margaret. I've got lots of money. Let us go. You can have a hundred thousand dollars. Think what you can do with a hundred thousand dollars. *(pause)* Two hundred thousand dollars. Put it in a bank, you get twenty-five thousand a year. Forever.

MARGARET: It's not enough.

CARL: Okay. We're getting somewhere. How much do you want?

MARGARET: Nine-point-one billion.

CARL: Seriously.

MARGARET: Serious.

CARL: Do you know how much nine-point-one billion dollars is?

MARGARET: Tell him, Chrissie.

CHRISSIE: That's how much it would take every year to raise all poor families to the poverty line. We're using the lowest of the various poverty lines as a short-term goal.

MARK: But we're already very generous to our low income people.

MARGARET: Chrissie?

CHRISSIE: That's not true.

MARK: Of course it is.

CHRISSIE: It's not.

MARK: I'm sure it's true.

CHRISSIE: It isn't.

MARK: I always thought—

MARGARET: It's not true. Tell your friends in Cabinet. Tell the world. Nine-point-one billion. Given freely and with compassion.

CARL: It's not possible.

MARGARET: Tell him how.

CHRISSIE: We looked at a number of options and concluded that increasing personal taxes on middle- and upper-income groups made the most sense.

MARK: You can't do that. Taxes are already too high. Take me. After mortgage payments, payments on the cars, short term deposits, vacations, renovating the kitchen, and payments on the property by the lake, we've got nothing left. I haven't even mentioned ballet lessons for Julie, fees at the club—

(Carl puts his hand over Mark's mouth.)

MARK: Mmff.

CARL: I will avoid discussing the morality of your plan, Margaret. I will not ask whether it is fair to take money earned through hard work, intelligence—I won't raise those questions. What you want is impossible. Mark's colleagues in Cabinet will let us die before agreeing to your demands.

MARK: That's true. They're very busy.

MARGARET: I will tell the truth. The land of hopelessness has sent me to negotiate with the land of the void. In exchange for nine-point-one billion dollars, we will surrender our hopelessness and you will abandon the void. I am not discouraged by petty obstacles thrown in my path. Nothing is won without sacrifice. I declare this café no longer under the authority of the void.

(Phone rings. Jerry answers.)

JERRY: Cheap Thrill Café. ... You can talk to me, Frank. ... Yes. We want nine-point-one billion dollars. In small bills. ... We'll wait. Thanks. *(hangs up)*

VOICE: *(off, through megaphone)* This is the police. We have the restaurant completely surrounded. Throw out your weapons and come out with your hands up.

MARGARET: Where's that number, Chrissie?

(Chrissie finds it. Margaret goes to the phone, dials.)

Get me Detective Harris. ... I know he's out now. This is Margaret Pierce. Just find him. ... *(to the others)* I don't believe this. *(on phone)* Frank. It's Margaret. What is this nonsense? How can we negotiate when you start making threats? ... It's a bargaining position. I'm willing to negotiate. ... Drop it? Do you think I'm here on a whim? I'm disappointed with you, Frank. ... I don't see any point in continuing this discussion either.

CARL: This is all your fault, Westerbrook. I'm going to remember this.

CHRISSIE: Jerry, I think we should go. This isn't fun anymore.

JERRY: Are you scared?

CHRISSIE: Yes.

JERRY: I'm not.

CHRISSIE: There's a million policemen out there. Talk to her. You can convince her.

MARGARET: So this is it. The big standoff. They wait. We wait. We wait. They wait. That's how history is made.

CHRISSIE: *(to Margaret)* I think we should go home.

MARGARET: What about you, Jerry?

JERRY: I feel like our luck is changing, Mom. I don't know where we're going but I have a good feeling about it. I'm staying.

MARGARET: You can go, Chrissie.

MARK: That's not fair.

CHRISSIE: I think we should all go. This is not going to end well. I know it.

CARL: Go home.

CHRISSIE: I won't go without Margaret.

CARL: Go home now.

CHRISSIE: There's something real happening here. Something real. It's stupid, but it's real.

MARK: I know how you feel, Chrissie. I don't know if I would leave. I would want to know the honourable thing to do. What would you do, Carl?

CARL: I'd go.

MARK: I'm not surprised. You've never worried about honour. It makes things easier for you. I envy that.

CARL: Make her go, Margaret. She'll listen to you.

MARGARET: She's an adult. It's her decision.

JERRY: *(to Chrissie)* You could get hurt.

CHRISSIE: Would you cut the quiet strength shit? I'm sorry I ever mentioned it.

VOICE: You have exactly sixty seconds to throw out your weapons and come out with your hands in the air. Starting now.

MARGARET: Okay, everybody. We're in this together. I want all of you to know that this has been a very special day for me. It isn't bad luck anymore. We've entered something new. A place of clarity and definition. A question asks itself. Is our condition accidental or the result of some conspiracy? Or is it merely convenient? Are the men of the fat wallets oblivious to our condition or do they gloat in power and wealth? Or both? Will the men of the fat wallets listen? What about the men of the middle-sized wallet? Or the women of the middle-sized purses? Will they listen? Or must people without hope hurl themselves at the walls of the void and ruin otherwise enjoyable gatherings at local cafés. I have only posed these questions. One day, I shall propose tentative answers. One day—

(A ridiculously long burst of machine gun fire. Everyone hits the floor for cover. Jerry dives at Chrissie, they end up entwined on the floor. The lights go out, but not the candles. Then, sniper fire takes out the candles, one at a time. A bit of light from the street. A moment of silence. Mark, still on the ground, takes out a white handkerchief and waves it about, and stands up slowly. Carl and Chrissie begin to move. Chrissie kneels beside Jerry, cradling him gently. Carl goes to her and helps her up. She looks sadly at Jerry and at Margaret. Carl, Mark and Chrissie exit.)

(The End.)

ZERO HOUR

Zero Hour premiered at the Great Canadian Theatre Company in Ottawa, Canada, on May 14, 1986, with the following cast:

Ross	Robert Bockstael
Harlan	James Bradford
Wade	John Koensgen

Director	Patrick McDonald
Set and lighting	Peter Gahlinger and Larry Laxdal
Costume design	Sheila Singhal
Music and sound	Ian Tamblyn
Stage Manager	Season Osborne

A workshop at the National Arts Centre English Theatre Playwright's Circle, in March 1986, was directed by David McIlwraith and dramaturged by Maureen Labonté; with Robert Bockstael as Ross, Michael Hogan as Harlan, and Tom MacBeath as Wade.

Characters
Harlan Cole, did a doctorate in economics instead of playing professional football, 48

Wade Sinclair, from Texas, is fit, educated, gregarious and ambitious, 38

Ross Gibson, a working class kid from New Jersey, is in good shape but not a match for Harlan or Wade, 22

Setting
November 1985. San José, Costa Rica. A cell with a metal door. A bunk bed, a toilet.

Scene 1
Ross is sleeping. Harlan has just entered and is standing in front of the closed door. It's late afternoon. Harlan notices Ross and looks over the cell. He moves to Ross. Ross opens his eyes.

HARLAN: Buenos tardes.

(Ross jumps, scared, ready to fight.)

Been here long?

ROSS: Who're you?

HARLAN: Harlan Cole.

ROSS: What are you doing here?

HARLAN: What are you doing here?

ROSS: Where are we?

HARLAN: Costa Rica.

ROSS: I mean here.

HARLAN: Looks like a jail cell.

ROSS: You a lawyer?

HARLAN: You need a lawyer?

ROSS: You from the embassy?

HARLAN: You need someone from the embassy?

ROSS: Hey, what the fuck, man?

HARLAN: What are you charged with?

ROSS: I don't know.

HARLAN: They didn't tell you?

ROSS: No.

HARLAN: But you were arrested.

ROSS: No one said anything, man.

HARLAN: You think you were arrested?

ROSS: I don't know.

HARLAN: Why do you think you were arrested?

ROSS: Hey, I don't fuckin' know, alright?

HARLAN: Sorry.

ROSS: Fuck.

HARLAN: What are you doing here? In Costa Rica?

ROSS: I'm a tourist.

HARLAN: Yeah.

ROSS: Yeah, I'm just visiting.

HARLAN: The border maybe?

(Harlan stands and moves towards the door. Ross freaks and jumps. Harlan calms him quickly and moves past him to check the door.)

They feeding you?

ROSS: Fuck all.

HARLAN: Nothing?

ROSS: Rice and fucking beans.

HARLAN: They hit you? *(He's checking out the door.)*

ROSS: Door's solid, man. Whole place is solid.

HARLAN: They hit you?

ROSS: No. You from the embassy?

HARLAN: Have you been interrogated?

ROSS: You're the first.

HARLAN: You talk to anyone?

ROSS: I haven't seen anyone.

HARLAN: *(pointing at light bulb)* All the time?

ROSS: No. Who the fuck are you?

HARLAN: Harlan Cole.

ROSS: Were you arrested?

HARLAN: No.

ROSS: You here to help me?

HARLAN: Yes. What are you doing in Costa Rica?

ROSS: I'm a tourist.

HARLAN: Sure.

Scene 2
Ross is sitting on the floor. Prison sounds. Harlan goes to the door.

HARLAN: *(into the hall)* Hey. Quiero ver el gerente. *(paces; to Ross)* What are you doing in San José?

ROSS: I told you, man.

HARLAN: Visiting. But what are you doing? Where are you staying?

ROSS: A hotel.

HARLAN: Nice hotel?

ROSS: Yeah.

HARLAN: What's it called?

ROSS: The San José Hotel.

HARLAN: Luxury hotel.

ROSS: So?

HARLAN: Very expensive.

ROSS: I got money.

HARLAN: They've got a great bar.

ROSS: Yeah.

HARLAN: I go there myself sometimes.

ROSS: Yeah?

HARLAN: You ever talk to the bartender, what's his name, Pedro?

ROSS: No, man.

HARLAN: That aquarium they they've got, it's beautiful.

ROSS: Oh yeah.

HARLAN: Nicest angel fish I've ever seen. *(pause)* The strippers are pretty good, too.

ROSS: Yeah.

HARLAN: There's no San José Hotel.

ROSS: You don't know all the hotels, man.

HARLAN: I know the big ones.

ROSS: Yeah, well, this one's new.

HARLAN: Where is it? At the border?

(Ross gives up.)

You know Jim Kemp?

ROSS: Who?

HARLAN: Jim Kemp.

ROSS: Never heard of him.

HARLAN: How long've you been in here?

ROSS: Four days.

HARLAN: Long time.

ROSS: Yeah.

HARLAN: How are you feeling?

ROSS: Bored out of my fuckin' mind.

HARLAN: No, I mean ... let's see your eyes.

(Harlan moves to Ross, slowly and cautiously. He looks closely at Ross and checks his eyes.)

ROSS: You a doctor or something?

HARLAN: *(stands)* You're all right.

(Harlan slams Ross with the back of his hand and sends him sprawling off the bench.)

ROSS: *(smiles)* Hey, you are from the embassy.

HARLAN: I want to know what you're doing in Costa Rica.

ROSS: I'm not scared of you, man.

HARLAN: Good.

ROSS: I'll tell you cause I know you're from the embassy.

HARLAN: Start.

ROSS: I could beat the shit out of you if I wanted to.

HARLAN: I know.

ROSS: Hey, I don't know why they picked me up.

HARLAN: Who?

ROSS: Hey, I'm a friend, right?

HARLAN: Who?

ROSS: The fucking Costa Rican government. They got to come down on someone, they take me. Big show, everyone's happy, right? Am I right?

HARLAN: Who picked you up?

ROSS: The Civil Guard.

HARLAN: Where?

ROSS: Zapote.

HARLAN: What were you doing there?

(Ross doesn't answer.)

Look, if you want help getting out of here ...

ROSS: *(pause)* Jim Kemp sent me to pick something up. He says someone's gonna meet me where the boat docks, right, but there's no one there. So I start walking to Zapote, these two guys stop me, take me back up river to where their car is ...

HARLAN: You said Kemp wanted something picked up.

ROSS: Yeah, they had a package with them.

HARLAN: What was it?

ROSS: I figured it was C-4 plastic and that's why they're coming with, cause of what happened with the last plastic.

HARLAN: What happened?

ROSS: To the plastic?

HARLAN: Yes.

ROSS: Which time?

HARLAN: The first time. Before you went to Zapote.

ROSS: Jim Kemp brought in six charges, right, and he tells ...

HARLAN: When?

ROSS: Three weeks ago.

HARLAN: So ... Kemp brought in six charges ...

ROSS: Yeah, and he tells Vega to stash them. Later on he says go pick 'em up and Vega comes back and ... you know Ricardo Vega?

HARLAN: Yes.

ROSS: Well, Vega comes back, he's only got one charge, right? He says, "I can't find the other five, I buried 'em, can't remember where." Jim Kemp was real pissed off but he sends us across the border with the one charge and when ...

HARLAN: You crossed the border?

ROSS: *(pause)* Yeah.

HARLAN: Jim Kemp send you across?

ROSS: No.

HARLAN: Did he know?

ROSS: Fuck man, I came to fight, not to be a fucking gopher for Jim Kemp.

HARLAN: Did Kemp know?

ROSS: No.

HARLAN: Go on.

ROSS: We cross the border into Nicaragua to set the last charge, right, but there's fuckin' Nica soldiers everywhere so we go back to Amparo. Then Vega sells the last charge to some guys from Costa Rica Libre. And those fuckers blow up a power line to Nicaragua, only it turns out that the power isn't going to Nicaragua, it's going to fuckin' Amparo. They blacked out Amparo and Jim Kemp's farm too. That was real funny, cause, you know, you look at the wires and, fuck, how's Costa Rica Libre supposed to know which way the power's going? Jim Kemp was real pissed off.

HARLAN: Did you have much contact with Costa Rica Libre?

ROSS: Hey, man, when I got here I heard Costa Rica Libre this, Costa Rica Libre that, I thought they were fucking communists. Who'd think they'd have a name like that and be on our side, right?

HARLAN: Did you see them much?

ROSS: I saw them. They talked a lot with the contras, and Vega, he'd slip 'em guns and ammo, and even some plastic sometimes. Or they'd be at the farm, they were cool, but I couldn't always tell if I was talking to one of them or to a Cuban or a contra. Or a fuckin' Civil Guard. Fuck the Civil Guard though. I mean, we helped those fuckers. They knew fuck all about guns, I showed 'em how to clean 'em, how to strip 'em, even how to fuckin' shoot 'em. We'd go drinking together in Amparo, then they fuckin' arrest me.

HARLAN: So the two Civil Guard put you in their car ...

ROSS: Yeah, a Toyota, you know, a jeep.

HARLAN: Yeah.

ROSS: Yeah, and we drive, and when we get to the cut off to Jim Kemp's farm they go right by. I go to say something, the one guy, he puts his M16 in my nose. They put a hood over my head, tie me up and make me lie down in the back. We drove for a couple of hours, we spend a while in the car just sitting there, then we drove for another hour and they put me in this place.

HARLAN: They say anything?

ROSS: To me?

HARLAN: Yes.

ROSS: Just what I told you, man.

HARLAN: They didn't tell you you were under arrest?

ROSS: No.

HARLAN: They talk to each other?

ROSS: Yeah.

HARLAN: What about?

ROSS: I don't speak Spanish.

HARLAN: But they spoke English.

ROSS: Yeah, one of them.

HARLAN: Good English?

ROSS: Yeah.

HARLAN: Accent?

ROSS: Yeah.

HARLAN: Did he speak good English or not? Was it a strong accent or not?

ROSS: I don't know, he didn't say that much. Look, it was the fuckin' Guard, man.

HARLAN: Maybe.

ROSS: It was them.

HARLAN: How do you know?

ROSS: Million fuckin' spics runnin' around in camouflage, how you supposed to tell 'em apart?

HARLAN: What if it wasn't the Guard?

ROSS: Then who?

HARLAN: You tell me.

ROSS: No, it was them, man.

HARLAN: If it wasn't?

ROSS: Then you wouldn't be here.

HARLAN: What's your name?

ROSS: Ross.

HARLAN: How old are you?

ROSS: Twenty-two.

HARLAN: Why did you come to Costa Rica?

ROSS: To fight communism.

HARLAN: That the best work you could get? ... What job did you quit to come fight communism in Costa Rica? You come to Costa Rica and get your head blown off or maybe you don't. What do you do next?

ROSS: Vega said he'd look after me, maybe get me work in a training camp in Florida.

HARLAN: Good job.

ROSS: Hey man, I came down here to fight communism, that's what I'm doing here. If we don't stop them in Nicaragua they'll be in Salvador and Costa Rica and then all over Central America. That's the plan, don't you know that? Jim Kemp says when Mexico goes communist there's gonna be five million refugees crossing into the U.S. and that'll wreck the U.S. without the Russians even firing one single shot. It's guys like me and Vega and Jim Kemp that are the ones putting our asses on the line. You guys, you sit in your fucking air-conditioned rooms at the embassy and you move your little papers around. You think that's gonna beat the communists? Fuck that.

HARLAN: Jim Kemp say that too?

ROSS: No, man, that's what I say.

HARLAN: How did you meet Kemp?

ROSS: Vega brought me.

HARLAN: How did you meet Vega?

ROSS: In Miami.

HARLAN: What was he doing there?

ROSS: Hey, I thought you knew him, man.

HARLAN: I don't know him, I just heard of him.

ROSS: He lives in Miami.

HARLAN: So he's Cuban.

ROSS: He's a Cuban-American.

HARLAN: Who set it up for you to meet him?

ROSS: There's a difference, you know.

HARLAN: Okay.

ROSS: His old man was at the Bay of Pigs thing in Cuba.

HARLAN: Yeah.

ROSS: Yeah, he died on the beach there cause Kennedy wouldn't give them air support even though the CIA planned the whole fuckin' operation. That Kennedy was a communist.

HARLAN: How did you meet Vega?

ROSS: You think Kennedy was a communist?

HARLAN: How did you meet Vega?

ROSS: Do you?

HARLAN: Yes. How did you meet him?

ROSS: I answered an ad in The Defender magazine. Someone called me up and asked me what I could do, and they said okay.

HARLAN: What can you do?

ROSS: I can fly backwards.

HARLAN: *(pause)* Then what?

ROSS: I took the fuckin'—twenty-six hours on the fuckin' bus to Miami. Vega met me in this restaurant, Los something, really fancy, right. I even met the guy that owns it, uh, shit, I forget his name and some guys who were soldiers in Nicaragua before the communists took over.

HARLAN: Did Vega tell you he was acting officially?

ROSS: Oh yeah, he was.

HARLAN: How do you know?

ROSS: Well, he was always with Stassen and Martin Holme. You know them?

HARLAN: No.

ROSS: Oh, well, Martin Holme, he's from The Defender. And Stassen, he's real high up in the American Council for Freedom. I met all those guys, man. Stassen even had a letter from the President.

HARLAN: From Reagan.

ROSS: Yeah, I saw it, man, the fuckin' seal and everything. He said he read it out loud at an American Council for Freedom dinner.

HARLAN: Did you read it?

ROSS: He read it to us at the restaurant. It said "Dear Bob ..." It said Stassen was doing God's work and that Reagan personally thanked him for everything he did. And, oh, Stassen told me about all these guys who had lots of money in Nicaragua, and then when Vega took me to the airport this guy took our bags, right, and Vega was joking with him in Spanish and then Vega says to me you know that porter I was talking to, that man owned a fuckin' castle in

Nicaragua, he was a colonel in the National Guard and he had four sons and, get this, each son had a Mercedes fuckin' Benz. Now his wife makes tamales at home and the sons sell them on the street in Miami. That's what the Reds did to them.

HARLAN: So Stassen had a letter from Reagan.

ROSS: Yeah.

HARLAN: That's it?

ROSS: That's what?

HARLAN: Vega's official connection. Stassen's letter from the President.

ROSS: You don't think a letter from the President's good enough?

HARLAN: It doesn't prove he's acting officially.

ROSS: Come on, man, no one moves in Miami without the CIA sanctions it. They're all the time bitching about it, too. Vega doesn't trust the U.S. this much cause of what they did to his old man, shit, he didn't like taking orders from the CIA, but he fuckin' took 'em.

HARLAN: Why did Vega meet with Holme and Stassen?

ROSS: Holme and Stassen raise money for guns. Vega moves 'em.

HARLAN: Why did he take you?

ROSS: Because he wanted me to meet these people.

HARLAN: Why?

ROSS: Just to see them.

HARLAN: Twenty-two-year-old kid comes down from ...

ROSS: ... New Jersey ...

HARLAN: ... to fight communism. Now why does he take you with him?

ROSS: C'mon, man, he just took me with, alright?

HARLAN: How long were you in Miami?

ROSS: Six days.

HARLAN: Did they train you?

ROSS: Vega took me to see one of the training camps but he said I already knew enough.

HARLAN: About what? ... Look, I have to know about this. You want me to help or not?

ROSS: Explosives.

HARLAN: Where'd you learn that?

ROSS: On my own. I got a feel for it.

HARLAN: Yeah?

ROSS: They didn't believe me neither.

HARLAN: So they checked you out.

ROSS: Yeah.

HARLAN: But they didn't want you to teach in the camps.

ROSS: Vega said they needed me in Costa Rica.

HARLAN: For what?

ROSS: I don't know.

HARLAN: Ross ...

ROSS: I don't know, man.

HARLAN: Did you ask?

ROSS: He just said don't worry.

HARLAN: And when you got to Costa Rica, he didn't tell you what he needed you for?

ROSS: No.

HARLAN: Did you ask?

ROSS: Fuck, man, I told ya.

HARLAN: Vega tells you in Miami they want you for something special. But he doesn't tell you what. He doesn't get you yo teach the contras in Miami how to use explosives. And then you get to Costa Rica and he still doesn't tell you what he wants you for.

ROSS: Yeah.

HARLAN: And you're pissed off because no one'll let you fight.

ROSS: Yeah.

HARLAN: But you didn't ask him.

ROSS: He never said.

HARLAN: You want me to help you?

ROSS: Fuck, man, I told you.

HARLAN: How did you get into Costa Rica?

ROSS: Just walked off the plane.

HARLAN: Sure.

ROSS: This guy in a blue uniform meets us and we walk right in, didn't check our papers or nothing. Someone's waiting for us, he takes us to San José. Then another guy takes us to Jim Kemp's farm. And then Jim Kemp checked me out, said if there was anything I needed, to clear it out with him.

HARLAN: He was in charge.

ROSS: Yeah, he's the CIA liaison.

HARLAN: How do you know that?

ROSS: He told me.

HARLAN: Hi, I work for the CIA.

ROSS: Pretty near. He said he's the CIA liaison and he's the fuckin' contra liaison too. He said it like it's secret, right, but he was always joking about it, like this one time he said that every month the U.S. government puts ten thousand bucks into his Miami bank account, and then, then he said God help me if the revenue people find out about it.

HARLAN: What did you do there?

ROSS: At the farm?

HARLAN: Yes.

ROSS: Hung around. We'd off-load planes that'd land on his strip. Go to Amparo and get pissed. Then the contras'd come, and Jim Kemp and Vega and them'd talk, and I'd bring 'em coffee.

HARLAN: Did they let you listen?

ROSS: If I looked like I was interested they'd ask me to leave. They talked mostly in Spanish anyway. Fuck, man, I was getting really pissed off cause I expected to see some action and I talked to Vega about it. And then when he went to set that charge that time after Jim Kemp chewed him out, he said to me do you wanna come.

HARLAN: Vega crossed the border, too?

ROSS: Yeah.

HARLAN: He's pretty high up.

ROSS: Well, he knew Stassen and Martin Holme. And those guys treat him with respect.

HARLAN: But he crossed the border.

ROSS: Yeah, he wanted to fight, too, man.

HARLAN: And he sold the plastic.

ROSS: Yeah but it was to either Costa Rica Libre or the Civil Guard. Vega's always moving, making deals, making friends. And Costa Rica Libre can do things we can't, they got friends high up in San José.

HARLAN: Who?

ROSS: Some guy in the government. The guy that runs the police.

HARLAN: Minister of the Interior.

ROSS: Yeah, the interior, what the fuck's the interior, anyway?

HARLAN: The guy that runs the police.

ROSS: Yeah, right, thanks man.

HARLAN: You think Vega set you up?

ROSS: Fuck, man, I got no grief with Vega.

HARLAN: Maybe he told Kemp you crossed the border.

ROSS: He wouldn't do that.

HARLAN: So why did Kemp set you up?

ROSS: He didn't know I crossed.

HARLAN: Maybe he did.

ROSS: No way.

HARLAN: Maybe he had some other reason to set you up.

ROSS: I wouldn't know.

HARLAN: Looks like someone set you up.

ROSS: Yeah.

HARLAN: I think you're right.

ROSS: 'Bout what?

HARLAN: You're in prison because they have to come down on someone. Big show. Everyone's happy.

ROSS: Can you get me out?

HARLAN: No.

ROSS: I'm a U.S. citizen.

HARLAN: That doesn't matter.

ROSS: What's the embassy for?

HARLAN: The embassy didn't ask you to come to Costa Rica.

ROSS: Fuck, what do you do at the embassy, anyway?

HARLAN: I work with the cultural attaché.

ROSS: You came to get me out, right?

HARLAN: (pause) No.

ROSS: Then why'd they send you?

HARLAN: To pass the time, I guess.

ROSS: What're you doing here?

HARLAN: I don't know.

ROSS: Fuck, man, I been straight with you.

HARLAN: I don't know why I'm here.

ROSS: Who sent you?

HARLAN: I was getting into my car, two guys point guns at my head.

ROSS: But you're from the embassy.

HARLAN: Yeah.

ROSS: Holy fuck.

HARLAN: Yeah.

ROSS: Holy fuck. Going into the embassy, that's fuckin' serious, man. You must be in real shit. I come down here to fight communism and you're from the embassy, and they fuckin' arrest us. Why would they do that? You gotta have some idea, right? Maybe they don't trust you or something. You selling embassy secrets? It's gotta be something pretty heavy for them to go into the embassy. ... This is really, really fucked. You know, man sometimes I wonder what I'm doing down here. You ever think about that?

(Prison noises off.)

Scene 3
Harlan is seated as Ross does push-ups.

ROSS: You should be doing something to keep in shape. We could be in here a long time. ... You wanna do some with me? ... Fuck, man, I wish I had a gun. You don't shoot every day, you lose the edge. It's something you gotta do every day.

HARLAN: Like playing the violin.

ROSS: Yeah right. *(stops)* Hey, you know the Beretta 92SB dash F?

HARLAN: No.

137

ROSS: It's the new standard army pistol. *(mimes firing a pistol)* Short recoil, semi-automatic. Mean nine-calibre piece, man. I got the 92SB. Same thing as the dash F but, no way was I gonna pay fifty bucks extra for a few fuckin' fluorescent dots on the sights, then I read in The Defender that in a stress situation the dots'd just confuse you anyway. Six hundred bucks a piece. I got one at home, couldn't bring it with me, right? You shoot much?

HARLAN: No.

ROSS: Cultural attaché, huh?

HARLAN: Assistant to the. *(prison sounds)*

ROSS: I guess you don't need guns for that, huh? ... Don't you carry a gun?

(The door opens, Wade comes flying in, blindfolded. The door closes behind him. Harlan removes Wade's blindfold.)

WADE: Harlan, what are you doing here? ... What's going on?

ROSS: Who're you?

WADE: What's going on?

ROSS: We don't know.

HARLAN: They arrest you?

WADE: No one said I was under arrest. Two Civil Guard ...

ROSS: You sure?

WADE: Por favor, señor Sinclair. Lo siento, señor Sinclair, take me to their car, put this *(the blindfold)* on me.

HARLAN: The Costa Rican government does not arrest embassy people.

ROSS: Maybe they started.

HARLAN: Who're they gonna bring in next, the ambassador?

WADE: I hope so.

ROSS: Maybe they're picking up Americans all over Costa Rica.

HARLAN: This isn't Lebanon, Wade.

WADE: Shit, Harlan, we're here, ain't we?

HARLAN: So what's going on?

WADE: How the hell do I know? You got any ideas?

HARLAN: *(pause)* He's been at the farm.

WADE: With Jimbo?

ROSS: Yeah.

WADE: Welcome to the fifty-first state — Tico-land? Costa Rica? Wade Sinclair, son. *(offers his hand)*

ROSS: Ross Gibson Jr.

(Ross and Wade shake hands.)

WADE: Imagine them spics treatin' us like this. Even odds we bought them this place, and their shiny weapons too. How long have you been here Harlan?

HARLAN: A few hours.

WADE: *(to Ross)* You?

ROSS: Four days.

WADE: Have they been ... cruel?

ROSS: Fuck man, I haven't even seen anybody.

WADE: They feed you?

ROSS: Yeah.

WADE: Thank god for that. It's some mistake, Harl. *(pounds on the door)* Come on you friendly Ticos. I'm the first secretary at your favourite embassy, I demand to be interrogated. Stupid spics. *(to Ross)* You know they call Costa Rica the Switzerland of Central America? Truth is it's the Puerto Rico of Central America.

ROSS: No way they're gonna arrest people from the embassy.

WADE: Yeah, well maybe we're hostages. Let's think. Who'd want us? And what the fuck for? ... You start, Harlan. This is more or less your field. ... I'll start you off. The Ticos, I mean the government of Costa Rica, acting in an official capacity. Why? Wait. This place wired?

ROSS: It's all right, man, I checked it out.

WADE: Good. Okay Harlan, the friendly Ticos. Why?

HARLAN: For show.

WADE: If it was for show, they'd pick up some merc like —

ROSS: I'm not a mercenary.

WADE: Well what are you, then?

ROSS: I'm an adventurist.

WADE: They'd arrest an adventurist like Ross, here, and make a speech about Costa Rican neutrality. They wouldn't touch the embassy.

ROSS: Not unless it's sanctioned.

WADE: Big word. By who?

ROSS: The CIA.

WADE: Why?

ROSS: Kill us, blame it on the Sandinistas.

WADE: CIA. do a lot of that? ... Who's next?

ROSS: The contras.

WADE: Why?

ROSS: Same reason. But they wouldn't go near the embassy either, unless it was sanctioned. They'd want the okay from Jim Kemp.

WADE: Jimbo.

ROSS: Costa Rica Libre might do it.

WADE: Smart kid.

ROSS: They could even do it without Jim Kemp.

HARLAN: ARDE *(AR-day)*, FDN, MDN, UNO *(OO-noh)*, you know this shit, Wade, some of them like us, some of them hate us, doesn't matter, there'll be a new one tomorrow.

WADE: That don't stop any of them from wanting us dead.

HARLAN: Us. *(Harlan and Wade)* Then why's he *(Ross)* here?

WADE: *(to Ross)* Harlan's very important. He's assistant to the cultural attaché. That means he's in charge of Coke sales here in Costa Rica, the drink, not the drug. Maybe the mothers of kids with cavities are out to get you, Harl. *(pause)* What about the Company, Harlan? What do you think? *(pause)* C'mon, Harlan. This is too important for the usual rules of secrecy.

HARLAN: If the Company's involved, you know about it.

WADE: I know you mean that as a compliment, but I want to think it through. If the Company's involved, I know about it. That means either the Company isn't involved, or else I know what's going on. I don't know what's going on. So the Company must not be involved. But that doesn't satisfy me. If there's one thing I've learned in this business it's that no one's safe. Someone might not like the colour of my eyes.

HARLAN: So we're hostages.

WADE: Whose?

ROSS: Hostages are for trading. I'm not worth trading. And I got nothing to hide, not from our people. I've been in here four days, I haven't seen anybody, no one's asked me a thing. They slip food in under the door. It's like they don't want to be bothered.

WADE: I think there's a lot in what the boy says, Harlan. If ARDE's got us, well they might wanna trade for CIA money. But you couldn't trade the kid for a tortilla. Maybe the Ticos are trying to make a point but we're big fish, Harlan, too big for the friendly Ticos.

HARLAN: You're going in circles.

ROSS: What about the Sandinistas?

WADE: What about 'em?

ROSS: They're communists.

WADE: Yeah.

ROSS: Yeah, well, maybe they got the order from the Soviets. And they're pickin' up Americans all over and making a move into Costa Rica.

WADE: Call in the marines!

HARLAN: Something unusual is happening, Wade.

WADE: You think Nicaragua's invaded Costa Rica?

ROSS: There's a fucking war.

WADE: What are they gonna do?

ROSS: They're gonna to kill us.

WADE: Here in Tico-land?

ROSS: Anywhere.

WADE: They do that kind of thing?

ROSS: Yeah.

WADE: Really?

ROSS: Yeah. Those two Civil Guards.

WADE: On the border.

ROSS: Yeah.

WADE: That's the border.

ROSS: So?

WADE: Take it, Harl ... *(looking at Harlan)* Someone, I don't know who, fires across the border. The Sandinistas shoot back, they hit a couple of guards. How are the Sandinistas supposed to know they were friendly Ticos? *(to Harlan)* Did I get it right?

ROSS: Why are you defending them, man?

WADE: I'm just telling you what happened. Don't quote me.

HARLAN: What ...

ROSS: Jim Kemp says the Sandinistas are gonna invade Costa Rica and it's only cause we're keeping them pinned down inside Nicaragua that they don't.

WADE: Right, let's keep 'em there. Now, back to the Company.

HARLAN: What are you doing, Wade?

WADE: I'm just...

HARLAN: We get picked up in the middle of San José and you act like you're on a game show. Except that within two minutes of walking in here you announce to the world that we're ... CIA.

WADE: Ross here isn't stupid. He's figured out for himself that the cultural attaché doesn't need an assistant. I'm just trying to figure out what's going on, and I want to know what you think. That make you uncomfortable, Harl? Ross isn't uncomfortable, he isn't hiding anything, are you Ross? I got nothing to hide, from friends. But I'm glad you let me know you're upset, Harl, this is a good place to get things off our chests. What about you, son, you upset too?

ROSS: About being in here?

WADE: Well, Harlan says I'm upsetting him. Am I doing anything that upsets you?

ROSS: No.

WADE: See, Harlan. *(pause)* No air conditioning. I'm gonna have to talk to the ambassador about that.

HARLAN: Ross crossed the border.

WADE: Into Nicaragua?

ROSS: No, into fuckin' Afghanistan.

WADE: Good work, Harlan, what else you find out?

HARLAN: He's lying about something.

WADE: 'bout what?

HARLAN: I don't know.

WADE: You keeping secrets from us, Ross?

(Ross doesn't answer.)

So, you crossed the border. Jimbo send you across?

ROSS: Man, I came down here to see some action, I spent a thousand bucks of my own money to come ...

WADE: Did Kemp send you?

ROSS: No.

WADE: You just went.

ROSS: Fuck.

WADE: By yourself.

ROSS: No.

WADE: With who?

ROSS: Some people.

WADE: Name one.

ROSS: Ricardo Vega.

WADE: Richard Vega took you.

ROSS: Yeah.

WADE: You like Vega?

ROSS: Yeah.

WADE: You trust him?

ROSS: Yeah.

WADE: Did Jimbo explain why you couldn't cross the border?

ROSS: Yeah.

WADE: Jimbo's very sensible. Jimbo's the salt of the earth. You should listen to him. Did he tell you about his neighbour Bruce?

ROSS: Yeah.

WADE: Did he show you those pictures in Life magazine? Bruce with the wife and kids in the friendly Tico sunset? Bruce charging through the trees in camouflage, Bruce with twenty contra up to their pits in water, their M16's held high over their heads. That stream runs through Bruce's farm and it's this high *(half metre)* and they're on their asses to make it look deep. I love Bruce. Salt of the earth that man. Bruce was a poet too. "Just a little piece now and a little piece later, until we're all gobbled up by the Red Alligator. Remember, you can't play good guy with murderers and thugs ...

ROSS: ... or shake off their threat with handshakes and hugs."

WADE: Too bad the friendly Ticos had to kick him out of Tico-land. What did Jimbo say when you asked why you couldn't fight in Nicaragua? ... Tell us.

ROSS: Why doesn't the fuckin' army just invade!

WADE: What did Kemp say?

ROSS: He said they don't want U.S. citizens caught in Nicaragua.

WADE: Jimbo's a very sensible man.

ROSS: *(pause)* You gonna tell him I crossed?

WADE: I don't know.

ROSS: Come on, man, don't tell him, all right?

WADE: *(to Harlan)* What do you think?

HARLAN: Get him *(Ross)* out of Costa Rica.

WADE: That's kind of extreme, Harl.

HARLAN: There's no controls. It makes the Company vulnerable.

WADE: They're doing things for us, they're risking their lives.

HARLAN: There's procedures, Wade.

WADE: Sometimes you got to compromise.

HARLAN: There's rules.

WADE: That's funny, you talking about rules.

HARLAN: The border's a zoo.

WADE: Aw, they're just taking a little initiative, Harlan. Anyway, it's none of your fucking business.

HARLAN: You asked what I thought.

WADE: Did I?

Scene 4
Lights come up. Middle of the night, no one can sleep. Wade is tapping the bench with his fingertips.

HARLAN: Wade.

(Wade continues.)

Hey!

WADE: *(stops)* Fuckin' Tambs.

HARLAN: Something bothering you?

WADE: I like it here. The quiet, the home cooking. *(pause)* This wouldn't have happened with Windsor.

HARLAN: What wouldn't happen?

WADE: This.

HARLAN: What's this?

WADE: Us. Here.

ROSS: Who's Windsor?

HARLAN: Ambassador before Tambs.

ROSS: You don't like Tambs?

HARLAN: He's not very popular.

ROSS: What's wrong with him?

WADE: Nothing a brain couldn't fix.

(Ross laughs.)

They threw him out of Columbia.

ROSS: Yeah, I knew that.

WADE: He fucks up there, they send him here.

ROSS: Why would they do something like that?

WADE: Same reason they do anything. He's got friends.

ROSS: Jim Kemp says he's all right.

HARLAN: Kemp likes anyone that hates Reds.

ROSS: Yeah.

HARLAN: Tambs's got the speech down and it's the same speech Kemp makes, only Kemp put it together himself and it took him twenty years to write. He doesn't know you learn that speech the first day of ambassador school.

WADE: Ooo, I don't know if you should be talking about a U.S. ambassador like that, Harl. Besides, I thought you liked him, I thought he was your kind of man.

ROSS: Vega doesn't like him either.

WADE: Yeah.

ROSS: He said Tambs came down hard on drug traffic in Columbia, now he's doing it here. He said how do they expect the contras to raise money.

WADE: I thought you liked Tambs, Harlan.

HARLAN: Why?

WADE: You didn't like Windsor.

HARLAN: He was ineffective.

WADE: I thought Windsor put forward the U.S. position very well. Costa Rica should have an army. And shove neutrality up their ass.

HARLAN: And Costa Rica threw him out.

WADE: That's not true, Harlan.

HARLAN: They asked the U.S. government to remove him.

WADE: We should've refused. The U.S. gives the Ticos a few hundred million dollars every year. You'd think it'd buy us something.

HARLAN: He's a diplomat, Wade. He's supposed to be diplomatic.

WADE: You're so traditional.

HARLAN: *(pause)* We've been in here too long. The embassy knows we're missing now.

WADE: Relax.

HARLAN: Like you?

WADE: You want me to bite my nails?

HARLAN: You're too calm.

WADE: Look at the kid. He's been here four days.

HARLAN: You throw fits when you run out of staples.

WADE: My mother was like that. My brother was dying of cancer, you've never seen anyone as calm. But when she burned the toast, she cried for an hour. She said some things are God's will. Burning the toast isn't.

HARLAN: That's not good enough.

WADE: The truth is, Harlan, I set this up. I wanted a chance for us to talk. You know what a pain in the ass you've been, I thought we could have it out. *(pause)* Actually Ross and I set this up. *(pause)* Maybe Ross set this up.

ROSS: Fuck.

WADE: Maybe he's an undercover Sandinista. You a communist, Ross?

ROSS: Man, you fuck right off.

WADE: What do you think, Harlan?

(Wade threatens Ross.)

He's the one that said the Sandinistas set this up. You think he's trying to throw us off? *(to Ross)* Who you working for, kid? How many times you been to Nicaragua? You can't fool us.

(Ross is very confused.)

Look at him. You think he's just pretending to be confused? ... You're no fun, Harl.

Scene 5
Ross and Wade are doing push-ups.

WADE: One, two, three, seven. One, two, three, eight. One, two, three, one. One, two, three, two. One, two, three, three.

(Wade stops, exhausted. Ross continues.)

All right, you're making me feel bad. I can't even count anymore.

ROSS: *(continues, then stops)* I don't have a passport.

WADE: What?

ROSS: I don't have a passport. How'm I going to get home without a passport?

WADE: What the fuck you do with it?

ROSS: I gave it to Vega.

WADE: We'll get Tambs working on it. Where you from, Ross?

ROSS: Newbury.

WADE: Where's that?

ROSS: North end of New Jersey.

WADE: What do people do in Newbury, New Jersey?

ROSS: Nothing.

WADE: What's your dad do?

ROSS: He works for Goodyear.

WADE: Yeah.

ROSS: Yeah, he worked there thirty years.

WADE: Long time to work for one company. *(to Harlan)* Don't you think that's a long time, Harl? *(to Ross)* You want to work there, too?

ROSS: My brother tried to, right? My old man figured after working there so long they could get his son a job, specially since Brady's a vet. Goodyear said they had to go through the union, union said he was way down on the list.

WADE: What about you, what were you doing before you came here?

ROSS: I was gonna go in for electronics after high school, but ... I sold magazines for a while, then I was picked up for—I ripped off a car. So, then, well my brother was in Viet Nam and I was pissed that I didn't get to go.

WADE: That why you came to Costa Rica?

ROSS: I didn't care where much, I just wanted to see some action. I was in Junior ROTC and the Civil Air Patrol. I been reading The Defender for years, man, training myself.

WADE: Did you try to enlist?

ROSS: No.

WADE: They train you.

ROSS: I'm trained, man, I want to see action.

WADE: You sorry you came?

ROSS: You could spend your whole life in Newbury and not meet the people I've met or learn the things I've seen. Like Jim Kemp, I never met anybody like him in Newbury.

WADE: It's warm here, too.

ROSS: Beats the hell out of winter in New Jersey.

WADE: ¿Aprendes español?

ROSS: I don't think I'm much good at languages.

WADE: What's Jim Kemp like?

ROSS: You don't know him?

WADE: What do you think of him?

ROSS: He's doing what he wants to do, he's good at it. I don't know. This one time, this contra came in, right, with his whole fuckin' leg blown right off. Jim Kemp, he bandaged him up himself, and sent him off to the hospital in San José. After he left Jim Kemp said he's gonna lose his other leg too and you could see he had tears in his eyes, that's the kind of guy he was. Sometimes late at night we'd just sit and talk, just him and me. Like he'd explain about communists in Congress, he even knew their names. He's got one of them dish antennas and we'd watch TV, he used to watch those preachers, just like my old man. Fuck, he was really good at explaining things, like these people from the U.S.'d come, newspaper people, and like one time, you could tell she was a communist, you know, like from the questions she was asking, but Jim Kemp, he'd explain things real calm and real straight.

WADE: Harlan tell you he used to play pro-football?

ROSS: Who for?

HARLAN: I didn't.

WADE: I thought you did.

HARLAN: I could have played, I didn't.

WADE: But you were all-American, right? The Forty-Niners wanted to sign you.

HARLAN: The Rams.

WADE: You should have signed.

ROSS: Why didn't you, man?

HARLAN: I wanted an M.B.A.

ROSS: What's that?

HARLAN: Master of business administration.

ROSS: Fuck. You guys got any kids?

WADE: A boy and two girls.

ROSS: What do they do?

WADE: They're in school.

ROSS: *(to Harlan)* You got kids?

(Harlan isn't paying attention.)

Yo! Harl!

HARLAN: One's an architect, my daughter's in medical school.

ROSS: How did you get to work for the ... Company?

WADE: You looking for a job?

HARLAN: They asked me.

ROSS: Just like that.

HARLAN: I was doing a Ph.D. in economics and my uncle asked if I would put my education at the service of my country.

WADE: You should've said no. You ever wonder about that, Harl? You got all this education and you're still a fuckin' operative. I don't have a Ph.D. And I'm ten years younger than you. You ever wonder why my career has taken off and yours is still in first gear? I think it's a question of attitude. *(pause)* So, you want to work for the Company, son?

ROSS: Yeah.

WADE: You wanna help the contras?

ROSS: Yeah.

WADE: You know much about 'em?

ROSS: I know that they're fighting for freedom.

WADE: Sort of.

ROSS: Meaning?

WADE: Well, Harlan could tell you some stories that'd curdle your blood. Harlan doesn't pretty things up, he's got a mind that sees things the way they are. ... But today, I don't know why, he's holding back. See ... *(to Harlan)* I want you to listen to this Harl,

I want you to tell me if I got it right ... *(to Ross)* now the contras fight two ways. In the first, hit and run, they attack farms, health centres, schools. They blow up the buildings, kill whoever's handy. Sometimes they rape, sometimes they mutilate.

ROSS: I don't believe that.

WADE: Ask Harlan.

ROSS: That's communist disinformation. That's what Jim Kemp says.

WADE: I've said that too. I'm saying this just for you and Harlan. Now the second way they fight is called take and hold. Three hundred contras sweep into a town and hold it. They make speeches, execute some Sandinistas. We like it when the contras take territory. We like it because it makes them look like a real army and people in Congress like that. But when the Nica army finds out where the contras are, they wait with those new helicopters they got from the Soviets, and rat-ta-tat-ta-tat. So before Congressional votes we got to convince the contra commanders to order take and holds. Now they're sitting in hotel swimming pools in Honduras and Miami so they don't mind take and holds. But your actual man on the ground, he prefers hit and run.

ROSS: Shit.

WADE: Pardon.

ROSS: I talked to contras, man, they're just ordinary guys fighting for their country.

WADE: Guys like Krill, you know Krill?

ROSS: No.

WADE: He worked with Suicida, out of Honduras. An ordinary guy, an ordinary soldier in the guard, but when he became a contra, he changed. He turned into a natural leader of men. Strict, mind you. I understand he's killed at least forty of his own men, some, I've heard, for being late. But mostly he was a quiet, thoughtful guy. He liked to go off by himself and fire his machine gun into the hills.

ROSS: I don't know what the fuck you're doing, man, you got some really strange things going on inside your head.

WADE: As God is my witness.

ROSS: How come you're putting down the contras?

WADE: You want to fight, I'm just telling you ...

ROSS: No, you're putting them down. You're saying the same thing as the communists ...

WADE: Help me, Harl.

HARLAN: Leave him alone.

WADE: You're always goin' on about how we gotta know the truth. Ross is one of us, isn't he?

HARLAN: What do you want?

WADE: Stick up for me.

HARLAN: *(to Ross)* He's right.

ROSS: Fuck.

WADE: Give him some detail. Matiguas. Do it.

HARLAN: Why?

WADE: Trust me.

HARLAN: Matiguas. June nineteenth, 1985. A wedding party. Seven males, nine females ambushed by contra under the command of Oswaldo Lopez. Discovered by a Dutch television crew. The men and older women appeared to have thirty to fifty rounds each fired into them at close range. The girls were raped and strangled.

WADE: Or strangled and raped. What kind of weapons did the wedding party have?

HARLAN: They were unarmed.

WADE: And where is Oswaldo Lopez now?

HARLAN: He commands a contra camp in Honduras.

WADE: What was the name of the guy in Matagalpa? ... Harlan.

HARLAN: Gustavo Romualdi owned a coffee plantation. President of the Nicaraguan Association of Coffee Growers. Abducted from his home August nineteenth. Found dead in Matagalpa eight days later.

WADE: Don't hold back, Harl.

HARLAN: His arms, legs and head were missing.

WADE: His dick, too. But we didn't just sit on our behinds. Now follow me here. We found out that Romualdi voted against the Sandinistas in the election. We said the Sandinistas killed Romualdi and that we had very convincing evidence they'd started a highly secret campaign to exterminate businessmen. The Sandinistas censored the story in La Prensa, but they couldn't bury it. Papers in Costa Rica and Columbia picked it up. So did the Times in Washington. You know what happened then? Contra radio broadcast a warning from Honduras. They said, I'm translating here, "Coffee production in Nicaragua must be stopped. Anyone that cooperates with the communists will be dealt with. Gustavo Romualdi is an example of what will happen." They ran that broadcast four times, and the Times in New York picked it up before we killed it. I just want you to understand, son. I know Rambo and John Wayne don't rape and mutilate. But that's the kind of war we got. You still want to fight? ... Once you understood how important burning schools and mutilating corpses is in the fight against communism, shit you'll jump right in. Death is pretty much the same from one round in the gut or fifty. So I've heard, anyway.

HARLAN: Why are you doing this, Wade?

WADE: For you Harlan. I'm trying to show you I know the difference between the lies and the truth. I know how important that is to you.

HARLAN: Why're you doing this now?

WADE: ... Mid-life crisis.

Scene 6
Wade is standing in front of the door with a tray of food in his hands.

WADE: *(looks at the food)* Where do you think we are, Nicaragua? *(laughs)* Cigarettes! *(opens a pack of cigarettes)* You smoke, Ross?

ROSS: No.

WADE: Good for you. *(lights one)* See, you light the end with the brand name on it. That way, when they find the butt, they can't tell what brand it was so they don't know who smoked it. It's an old spy trick. You hungry?

(Wade offers the food to Ross. Ross shakes his head.)

Have some, keep your strength up. You know, when I was your age, no, I might've been a bit older, I was at university. There was the moratorium and everyone was skipping class to protest the war in Vietnam. My father came to school and sat with me. For two hours we sat all alone. No students, no teacher. One day I got a letter asking me if I was interested in an important government position. The duties included foreign travel and it would be like working for the State Department. When I was in training there was a party one night and this guy asks me what I'm doing in Washington. He was real persistent but I kept giving him the cover story, some shit about working for the Department of Agriculture. Then he went to talk to someone else. The next day there were a few of us missing from class and the same guy was there to talk to us about communism. He told us it was real important to watch who we talked to. He said the Soviets were recruiting agents all over the U.S. He said they prey on shy, lonely outcasts and recruit them into the American Communist Party. These people have no friends, no links to decent society. The Soviets brainwash and exploit these sad people to the point where they're willing to violently overthrow our government. He told us some of them have made it into high positions in the government, even into the CIA. He said to us, you people are not going to let that happen. We used to sing the national anthem before classes then, every morning, we'd stand up and I'd close my eyes and I'd just sing. Jesus I loved to sing it. Now the Company's different. People fuck around. All they care about is better postings and more money. The spirit's not the same. ... We need more people like you, Ross, people with the right spirit, the right commitment ... You got the makings, son.

HARLAN: For Christ's sake, Wade.

WADE: I'm serious. Why he's typical Company material. He's E-R-A, extrovert, regulated, adaptable. Mesomorph body type. Magnetic, charming and captivating, just like you and me, Harlan. Not everyone gets recruited out of university, we still hire a few Neanderthals. You know what a Neanderthal is, son? That's what we call the recruits that come up through the military side. Demolition, explosives, underwater techniques. The Company pays well, and they never fire you, no matter how bad you fuck up. Sometimes they even give you a family. The Company brought a whole bunch of new men into Costa Rica and they set 'em up in real nice houses in the suburbs. Two months later they decide these men'd fit in better with the neighbours if they had families. They did that for Harlan here. They moved in a Tico woman and her two Tico kids. Can you believe it? Whoever did that one up Harl, must be either really stupid or a great sense of humour. You know what I want to know, Harl? Are you poking her? Was that part of the deal? Are you? ... What's with you, Harl? You've got no sense of humour anymore. I noticed that. You know what your colleagues are saying about you, don't you? You're drinking too much, you're hostile, keeping to yourself, not part of the team, and no sense of humour. That's in your file, too.

Scene 7
Ross is gone. Footsteps off stage. Ross yells "no." A gun shot. Then Ross yells "Jesus Christ."

WADE: Something bothering you, Harl?

HARLAN: Why him?

WADE: Why not him?

HARLAN: Why not you or me?

WADE: It's random.

HARLAN: Come on.

WADE: Who knows what the fuck they're doing?

HARLAN: Two Company officers with embassy cover and they go for the twenty-two-year-old kid from New Jersey?

WADE: It's random.

HARLAN: It's absurd.

WADE: Take it easy, Harlan.

HARLAN: They took that kid out of here and ... you're not even thinking about it. Your mind a little foggy today? ... What's going on, Wade?

WADE: You wondering about me, Harlan? That's good. Sometimes I wonder about you, do you know that? Do you know what I wonder about, Harlan? C'mon, take a guess. ... Go on, Harlan. ... I wonder about your loyalty, yeah, that's right, Harlan. I know you been with the Company for fucking ever, how long, eighteen years? And a year and a half in Costa Rica. I know you got a fine evaluation for the time you were in Jamaica, same thing for the work you did in Chile with, what's that newspaper called, the El Mercurio? You won a fucking merit award. Course they're a dime a dozen, but still, for eighteen years no one's ever had a reason to question your loyalty.

HARLAN: Loyalty to what?

WADE: To the Company. To the United States of America.

HARLAN: You got something on me, let's see it.

WADE: What do you want, photographs, taped conversations with Soviet agents?

HARLAN: You're saying I'm compromised?

WADE: We'll have to do a series of lie detector tests. Just routine, but we are very concerned.

HARLAN: About what, exactly?

WADE: The questions you been asking about Company activity get out, it could blow six years of hard work.

HARLAN: Is there a leak?

WADE: There could be.

HARLAN: There could be?

WADE: Yeah.

HARLAN: Do you mean you think there is one or do you mean everything is possible?

WADE: I say a simple thing, you argue. You see what I mean?

HARLAN: You're accusing me of ...

WADE: It's not just me, Harlan. If it was just me ...

HARLAN: Who else?

WADE: The Deputy Director has expressed his concern.

HARLAN: I'm concerned too.

WADE: Good.

HARLAN: Why're you pushing this now?

WADE: What's your classification?

HARLAN: Why now, Wade?

WADE: What are you supposed to be doing in Costa Rica?

HARLAN: Data collection.

WADE: What have you found?

HARLAN: You've seen it.

WADE: It's not very much.

HARLAN: It's what I've found.

WADE: But there's no shortage of data.

HARLAN: Some of it doesn't stand up.

WADE: Analysis isn't your job.

HARLAN: What's bugging you, Wade? Your wife screwing around again?

WADE: The U.S. Citizens Committee in San José.

HARLAN: I watched her the other night at the Swiss embassy. She was all over the Argentinian Trade Commissioner.

WADE: The U.S. Citizens Committee isn't mentioned in your last report.

HARLAN: I think she's hot on me too.

WADE: She never had any taste.

HARLAN: The U.S. Citizens Committee is not communist.

WADE: They sit in downtown San José and they publish stuff about contra camps in Costa Rica. According to our government, and the government of Costa Rica, those camps don't exist.

HARLAN: But they do.

WADE: That's not the point.

HARLAN: I ran a check on the leadership.

WADE: What do you want, red flags?

HARLAN: I've got someone at the meetings.

WADE: That's analysis.

HARLAN: I don't think so.

WADE: What is it then?

HARLAN: As I understand it, I am supposed to collect evidence of communist activity in Costa Rica. ... If I'm collecting rocks for a geological survey, before I send off a sample I make sure it's a rock. I do this to avoid wasting time on tennis balls and potatoes. Is that simple enough for you? What do you want, Wade? Every time a Russian or Cuban sets foot in the country, I report it. There's statistics on land expropriation, state ownership, rationing, tax increases, export controls. What the fuck do you want?

WADE: You attached news clippings of Nicaraguan border violations to a memo saying you want information about their origin and you sent the memo to our offices in Managua, Guatemala, Honduras ...

HARLAN: Salvador, Bolivia and Chile.

WADE: And Langley, Harlan, don't forget Langley, Virginia. What were you doing exactly?

HARLAN: Verifying the authenticity of the reports.

WADE: Why?

HARLAN: To verify the authenticity of the reports.

WADE: Why is that any business of yours?

HARLAN: I'm trying to separate rocks from potatoes.

WADE: And I'm trying to separate good old boys from communists.

HARLAN: Look, Wade. Listen to me. When I was in Jamaica, when I was in Chile, it was my job to fabricate reports. I made things up. A bomb'd go off somewhere, we call the local paper and claim responsibility in the name of some left wing group. I'd fake a story that there were 3000 Cuban military advisers and plans for a Soviet air base. We'd surface the stories through agents in Venezuela or Columbia. If we worked it right they'd show up in the NBC news. But that's not my job here. Here in Costa Rica I'm supposed to gather information about Communist strength, activity, that kind of thing. Not disinformation, but information. You with me so far?

WADE: One hundred percent.

HARLAN: Now here, in Costa Rica, I'm taking this slow, step by step so you'll understand, somebody else does for Nicaragua what I used to do in Chile and Jamaica, right? They fake that information if necessary but they get it circulated. I've got no trouble with that but it's not my job. My job is to do research. So. One day I'm sitting in my office, cutting out clippings to send to Langley, and I say to myself, I know this style, I recognize this. This is just like what I used to write. I thought it was funny. Here I am sending off evidence of communist activity and it's probably the operative in the office next to mine that made it up. I thought this is not good research. So I started to make sure that I only sent in actual intelligence.

WADE: You missed the whole point.

HARLAN: I'm talking about good intelligence.

WADE: What about direct orders? Does it matter to you that you've been told more than once, by more people than me, to stop separating rocks from potatoes?

HARLAN: Yeah, it matters to me.

WADE: That you went over my head.

HARLAN: It matters a lot to me.

WADE: Yeah?

HARLAN: I was sure I'd find support up the line.

WADE: How high?

HARLAN: Anywhere. Christ, Wade, I would have been happy with you, I wanted you to understand. I am saying that I don't mind us making up shit. I used to do it and I did it well. But isn't it important that we know the difference between intelligence and disinformation? We said that the Sandinistas were responsible for the attack on Pastora. Good. But we believed it. We listed the Corinto bombings as a contra operation. There it was, the one biggest operation of the war. We're telling each other, three months, six at the most, we'll be celebrating in Managua. Then we find out, the whole fucking world finds out, it was a Company operation, planned and executed by us. If we want to win this we should know what they are really doing. If I send in phony data, it gets analyzed, the conclusions are wrong because the data is wrong, and Langley, never mind Langley, the State Department starts making policy based on completely wrong assumptions about communist strength and strategy.

WADE: So what's the truth?

HARLAN: What do you mean?

WADE: What's lies, what isn't?

HARLAN: Go on.

WADE: Where's it end, Harlan? Nicaragua some nice little country? We making a mistake here?

HARLAN: You've been through my files.

WADE: Yeah.

HARLAN: It's all there.

WADE: Yeah. When I was a kid, my father used to make me hunt cougar with him. One time, I was fourteen, it was almost summer but in the mountains there was still snow. It was cold and wet, and I noticed the sound my boots made coming out the mud. I started running, just to hear the sound, and feel the pull of the mud on my boots. I ran past my father and the dogs took off ahead of me. Christ I ran. Over fallen trees, through creeks, jumping over boulders, I just ran. I wasn't tired or feeling that pain under my ribs. I just felt the cold air sting my skin. I was running through this gully and there was a ridge on my right. It got bigger and steeper until it was like a wall. Then I saw the dogs. They were barking at a patch of trees by the ridge. I moved closer and I saw a big cougar, trying to get a foothold in the rock, but it was too steep. She moved towards us, the dogs barked, and she'd try the ridge again. My father caught up to us. He said, "She's a big one." He said, "She's yours. Go ahead." He shoved me with his rifle butt. "Shoot. Shoot." I lifted the rifle and aimed. The cougar just stood there, looking right at me. I squeezed the trigger. She fell. *(Wade goes to the door and knocks.)* See I liked the mountains. I liked running. But before that, I didn't like the kill. I know you find part of your work distasteful. But you can't say "I like this, I don't like that." It's all part of the hunt.

> *(Prison sounds. The door opens and Ross is thrown in. His wrists are tied and he's been beaten.)*

ROSS: *(to Wade)* What the fuck's going on, man? I thought you were running this thing. You never fuckin' told me, what the fuck they beat me up for? I thought I was coming in here to get him to talk, then you give me this communist bullshit and I get the piss taken out of me. Why don't they beat him up, he's the fuckin' traitor.

WADE: You should sit down.

ROSS: I'll fuckin' stand.

(Wade throws Ross down. Wade's violence is precise and controlled.)

WADE: You got a big secret, Ross. I want to know what it is.

ROSS: I don't know what you're talking about.

WADE: Yes you do.

ROSS: You never told me about this. This wasn't part of the plan.

(Wade hits Ross.)

I don't know anything.

WADE: I'll start you off. You were in on a plan to hit the embassy.

ROSS: I don't ...

WADE: I want to know about it.

ROSS: *(to Harlan)* He set this whole thing up, man, to trap you.

(Wade hits him.)

WADE: Tell me.

ROSS: You're crazy.

WADE: I don't have time.

(Wade hits him again, then Harlan gets in Wade's way. Wade pushes Harlan away, Ross jumps Wade, Wade kicks Ross, Ross goes down.)

(to Harlan) I want you to listen to this.

(He makes Ross sit up.)

You want to go back to the States, you start talking now. The plan to hit the embassy. Who was in on it? The Civil Guard?

ROSS: No.

WADE: Costa Rica Libre?

ROSS: I don't know.

WADE: Who? ... I'll smash your fucking head in.

ROSS: Fuck, man.

WADE: Who? *(hits him)*

ROSS: I'll tell you. I'll tell you.

WADE: Who?

WADE: Vega.

WADE: Who else?

ROSS: Stassen. Holme.

WADE: In Miami.

ROSS: I wouldn't do it.

WADE: Whose idea was it?

ROSS: I wouldn't go along with it.

WADE: Whose idea was it?

ROSS: Stassen said it came from upstairs.

WADE: From who? *(another threat)*

ROSS: Maybe Bush.

WADE: Vice-President Bush?

ROSS: Yeah.

WADE: Did Stassen say the order came from Bush?

ROSS: He said Bush knew about it. And Vernon something.

WADE: Vernon Walters?

ROSS: Yeah. Stassen talked to him on the phone.

WADE: You heard him.

ROSS: I was in the room, man.

WADE: Did Reagan know?

ROSS: No one said.

WADE: Did they mention Tambs?

ROSS: Yeah.

WADE: What about him?

ROSS: He was the fuckin' target, man.

WADE: *(pause)* You're sure?

ROSS: That was the whole plan. We blow up Tambs, the Sandinistas take the rap, we send in the Marines. *(pause)*

HARLAN: They talked about this, in front of you.

ROSS: Fuck, they had maps of the embassy and everything, I swear it. I didn't believe it neither, you ask them what's this about, what's this mean, they say you don't need to know. You sit quiet, you hear it all.

WADE: Did they say when they wanted to do it?

ROSS: No.

WADE: What else?

ROSS: That's it. That's the last I heard about it.

WADE: No one ever mentioned it to you on Kemp's farm?

ROSS: No.

WADE: Jim Kemp never talked about it?

ROSS: I swear.

WADE: You're sure?

ROSS: I swear.

WADE: *(hits Ross)* Look, son. I don't want to hit you again. I'll just tell you what I'm asking is for the good of your country. I know you want to protect him. I know he's your friend. But it's very important that we know if he knew about the plan.

ROSS: *(pause)* We were at this sawmill ...

WADE: When?

ROSS: A month ago, maybe more.

WADE: Where?

ROSS: Near the border. There was stuff stashed there. We went to pick up some shit for the contras. I grabbed some M79 grenades and some Claymore mines. Jim Kemp said to leave 'em. He said, "We may need 'em to do an embassy later on."

WADE: That's it?

ROSS: I swear, I'll never fucking forget it.

WADE: That wasn't very hard, was it? What do you think, Harl?

HARLAN: Other sources?

WADE: One.

HARLAN: Vega.

WADE: Yeah.

HARLAN: Very reliable.

WADE: He's okay.

HARLAN: And Bush is in on it?

WADE: Vega said the same thing.

HARLAN: Bomb the embassy, kill the ambassador.

WADE: There were fucking phone calls ...

HARLAN: To Vernon Walters. Maybe.

WADE: Why wouldn't Bush be in on it? We're losing. We fucked Nicaragua, people make more money selling oranges in the street than they do working in factories and there's fucking food shortages but you can count contra supporters on one hand. Nicaragua isn't gonna attack anyone. If we want to invade, we're gonna have to make our own reason. So okay, Bush isn't in on it, let's say. But Kemp's in on it and Kemp don't jack off without word from higher up. I didn't believe Vega either. He told me about the kid, *(Ross)* said ask the kid. You think he's lying?

HARLAN: No.

WADE: No.

HARLAN: *(pause)* So you want to hit Tambs.

WADE: Yeah.

ROSS: Fuck!

HARLAN: You're serious.

WADE: One hundred percent.

ROSS: No fuckin' way am I gonna kill Americans.

WADE: You think the U.S. should invade?

ROSS: Yeah.

WADE: So who's gonna die if we invade? Americans. Kids like you. Maybe ambassadors should get to die, too.

ROSS: And CIA assholes like you.

WADE: I don't mind. *(to Harlan)* What do you think, Harlan?

HARLAN: It got stopped.

WADE: We hit the embassy, we set the whole thing in motion.

HARLAN: Maybe they had a reason to stop it.

WADE: Some of them are soft, some of them are scared. They're afraid it'll come out. You worried about that? It came out in Chile, a few people got transferred. But Chile's ours now, that's what counts.

HARLAN: What if you hit Tambs, and the U.S. doesn't invade?

WADE: Americans might be getting soft but things aren't so bad that we'll sit back and watch the communists kill U.S. ambassadors.

HARLAN: What do you want me to do?

WADE: We'll need information ready to go, Harlan, and you know how to do it. The best agents you've found in eighteen years, AP, Reuters, UPI, all gotta be primed. We can't let 'em know what's up, but they gotta be primed.

HARLAN: You hit Tambs, it'll get headlines without me.

WADE: No, I've thought this through. If it hadn't been stopped, Nicaragua'd be surrounded by U.S. troops on manoeuvres, everything'd be ready. But when we hit Tambs it'll be a surprise, they won't be ready. It'd take, I figure, minimum 36 hours, maximum 72 to invade. For 72 hours we've got to flood it. Headlines won't be enough. We'll need hard evidence that the Sandinistas did it, not the Libyans, not the Ayatollah, not the—we'll need editorials, backgrounders, analysis, all that in depth stuff you're so good at. What do you say, Harlan? You're the only one that can do it right, you got years of contacts. *(pause)* I need you Harlan. There's no one else in Costa Rica.

HARLAN: What if I say no?

WADE: It's easy. It's all set up. We get to do for them what they already wanted to do. We lost Cuba, Harlan. We don't want any more communists on our turf.

HARLAN: Christ, you talk about following orders, about the team. Where are the orders for this? Where's the team when ...

WADE: Don't you remember how a team works, Harlan? If you got the right attitude, if you know what direction you're moving in, you don't need orders, you know what's right for the team. We're not talking details here, forget the details, look at the whole picture. What's the team trying to do? That's all you gotta know. ... It's a war, Harlan, all over the world. It's freedom against communism, we gotta take action, and all I'm asking you is to make it possible for that to happen.

HARLAN: I can't.

WADE: I knew it wouldn't be easy for you.

HARLAN: No one knows what's going on anymore ...

WADE: Fuck, you and I know. Ross knows.

HARLAN: No one knows what's lies, what isn't ...

WADE: Everyone's got doubts, but that's small shit. You look at anything hard enough, it starts to look funny.

HARLAN: There's too many lies.

WADE: We're here to lie. That's what our job is, to clear the way for what has to be done. And we know what we want to do, we don't need your research to tell us what we want to do. Forget this lie shit. The bottom line is Nicaragua's communist. We'll bomb the fucking embassy and we will prove to the people of America and to our government that the Sandinistas did it. They will want to hear lies and we will give them lies. It'll be for the good of the U.S.A., and I have no trouble living with that.

HARLAN: I can't.

WADE: Fuck, Harlan, in Washington, they got to worry about politics. What do you expect, a letter from the President "Dear Harlan. Bomb the fucking embassy. Sincerely Ron." It don't happen like that. And that's what makes us different. We can take action. And there's people in Washington that understand that. There's people there that want it.

HARLAN: What are you saying?

WADE: Harlan.

HARLAN: What are you saying?

WADE: Just what I said.

HARLAN: Are you saying there's authorization for this?

WADE: I didn't say that.

HARLAN: But I'm supposed to believe it.

WADE: Believe whatever the fuck you want.

HARLAN: I need time to think, I don't know who to talk to, I don't know what to do.

WADE: Harlan.

HARLAN: I can't do it. ... I can't do it.

WADE: Alright, Harlan. You cut your own throat a long time ago. I gave you another chance. You're gonna be all alone. You're gonna find out what a lonely place the Company can be. ... You're real good at explaining things, Harl. You can explain this to yourself any fucking way you want. But this is war. And you let down your country.

(Wade exits, leaves door open. Harlan looks at the door but stays. Lights fade.)

(The End.)

LEARNING TO LIVE WITH PERSONAL GROWTH

Learning to Live with Personal Growth was first produced by the Great Canadian Theatre Company in Ottawa, Canada, on November 18, 1987, with the following cast:

Ginny	Rebecca Campbell
Marla	Heather Esdon
Jeff	Terrence Scammell
Link	Alan Templeton

Director	Patrick McDonald
Set	Arthur Penson
Lighting	Martin Conboy
Costumes	Sheila Singhal
Sound	Ian Tamblyn
Stage Manager	Season Osborne

Characters
Jeff: a social worker, Marla's husband, warm and friendly, late 30s

Marla: lawyer, Jeff's wife, smart, caring, ambitious, 33

Link: real estate investor, energetic, gregarious, 30s

Ginny: single mother on welfare, Jeff's client, forthright, tired, 23

Setting
Ottawa, Canada, circa 1987.

Learning to Live with Personal Growth consists of 66 scenes, ranging in length from one line to several pages. Scenes take place in a restaurant, a café, a living room, a country road, a hotel room in France, a bar, a health club's locker room, etc. The set must be minimal, scene changes very quick, accomplished mostly with lights and, occasionally, props. It's not always necessary to establish location. I've offered suggestions, but it's up to you.

Jeff is present in every scene, even if he does not speak. He often addresses the audience directly.

Scene 1
Jeff addresses the audience.

JEFF: It's good to see you. I'm glad that you could make it. Yeah, I know, I've been busy, too. It's funny how things add up and you have to schedule time to take a shower. I'm doing pretty good. Yeah, all in all, no complaints. No big complaints. I wouldn't have said that a year ago. A year ago, well, five years ago too, I had complaints. What was it, a mid-life crisis? I'm a little young for that, maybe they happen earlier these days. A lot of things happened at once. A lot of things started to bother me at the same time. It was nothing serious, just that, well, I noticed that the only place I liked to go to anymore was restaurants. I used to go to bars and listen to bands. I stopped. I stopped going to movies—not completely, but I only went to movies because Marla wanted to go, if it were up to me I wouldn't have gone. I just really liked sitting in those restaurants, usually Italian but not always, where there's six-course meals, and you get to take a little rest between courses, and the waiters never get in the way of a conversation, but they're always there when you need them. And you just sit, drink wine, and talk. I still love those places. Then there was Marla. We weren't getting along. No, maybe that's too strong. There was something wrong. I didn't know what. But something was bothering me. Where were we going?

Scene 2
Jeff and Marla at home.

MARLA: What do you feel like?

JEFF: I don't know.

MARLA: Italian?

177

JEFF: No.

MARLA: Szechwan?

JEFF: No.

MARLA: Mandarin?

JEFF: No.

MARLA: Cantonese?

JEFF: No.

MARLA: Thai? Vietnamese? Lebanese? Hungarian? Kentucky Fried?

JEFF: No.

MARLA: What then?

JEFF: You decide.

MARLA: I don't care.

JEFF: I don't care either.

MARLA: Why don't I just poach us some eggs?

JEFF: No.

MARLA: An omelette?

Scene 3
Jeff addresses the audience.

JEFF: Whatever the problem was, I couldn't talk to Marla about it. Marla and I can talk. We have really good talks sometimes, we can talk for hours about a movie we've seen, or people we know. But Marla always wants to talk about our relationship, and I don't mind, it's not that, it's just—I don't feel like there's very much to say. Marla thought that was a problem. I didn't. I've talked to guys I know, and I've asked women about it and it just seems to be one of those constants about couples. Women want to talk about their relationship, men don't. Women think it's a problem that men don't want to talk. Every night, I'm sure there's a lot of guys out there saying, "I think it's alright. I don't see any serious problems." For me, the problem was something different, it was bigger than that. I remember hearing on the radio one time about a couple who were celebrating their sixtieth wedding anniversary. I started to sweat. I thought, Marla and I have been married for eight years. That leaves fifty-two more years. Is Marla going to want to talk about our relationship for another fifty-two years? I couldn't very well say to her, "I have this problem. I can't imagine us living together for another fifty-two years. Nothing personal." But the thing was, it wasn't personal. It wasn't Marla that depressed me. It was the image that depressed me. I felt stuck. I could see myself in fifty-two years, sitting in an Italian restaurant, spilling over the sides of the chair, and Marla asking me, did I really love her, or why I wasn't as excited about her birthday as I used to be.

Scene 4
At home.

MARLA: You know that apartment building across from the church?

JEFF: Which church?

MARLA: The one across from the park with the geese.

JEFF: Swans.

MARLA: You know that apartment building?

JEFF: The one you keep pointing at, with stained-glass in the front door.

MARLA: And the courtyard.

JEFF: And the courtyard.

MARLA: Cathy moved in there.

JEFF: Oh, good.

MARLA: I was there today.

JEFF: How is Cathy?

MARLA: It's a beautiful apartment.

JEFF: That's nice.

MARLA: The rooms are enormous.

JEFF: Where'd she get the money?

MARLA: It still has the original fixtures.

JEFF: Is she going to sell them to raise money for the rent?

MARLA: Jeff?

JEFF: You want to move.

MARLA: Yes.

JEFF: I like it here.

MARLA: It's starting to feel small.

JEFF: It is small.

MARLA: If we had an extra room, I could have an office at home.

JEFF: I don't want to move.

MARLA: I swear, you'd think we were broke from the way we live.

JEFF: It has nothing—

MARLA: Grow up.

Scene 5
Jeff addresses the audience.

JEFF: I felt paralyzed. I felt like I had to do something because I was getting a bit scared. Wait a second. I don't want to give the impression that I was falling apart or having a breakdown because it wasn't that at all. I'm sure to the rest of the world I looked quite normal. I don't even think Marla knew what I was going through.

Scene 6
At home.

MARLA: Jeff? Listen, I guess I've been kind of a grump lately. I, I don't know. Sometimes I get impatient with you. But the thing is, I worry about you. You're not, I don't know how to say this, you're in a rut. Don't you think so? You don't like your job, you don't like—anything. That's what it seems like sometimes. I know, we go out to eat, we—what else do we do? What do you like doing on your own? I go to meetings, I do things with people, there are things that I'm involved in that mean something to me and let me express myself. I don't think what you're doing is healthy.

Scene 7
Jeff addresses the audience.

JEFF: And at one point I thought, maybe I'm afraid of getting old, which makes sense and isn't unusual. I'm getting older. I should get more exercise, I should take care of myself. So I joined a health spa. Three times a week, I worked out on these machines and I ran around in circles. It was expensive, but I'm not the kind of guy who can jump out of bed and do push-ups and sit-ups for half an hour first thing in the morning. And this place is incredible. It's beautiful. It comes as close as anything I've ever known to making exercise fun. When I told Marla I was going to join she couldn't believe it. She made it sound like I was changing my whole life.

Scene 8
Link and Jeff in the change room at the health club.

LINK: Hi, what's your name?
JEFF: Jeff.

LINK: Link.

JEFF: What?

LINK: Link. That's my name.

JEFF: Oh. Hi.

LINK: Listen, a bunch of us are going to play basketball. You want to play?

JEFF: Well—I haven't played for a while.

LINK: It's no problem, we'll get someone—

JEFF: No, I used to be good in high school. I'd like to play.

LINK: Alright.

Scene 9
Jeff addresses the audience.

JEFF: My parents grew up in a world where a woman on her own was destitute. No decent man would even think of leaving his wife. And a woman would never leave her husband unless he was an absolute failure and couldn't support a family. But the world's different now, women can survive on their own. They work more, and there's things like welfare so women and their children don't starve to death. There isn't as much pressure now to stay together. Not getting along is now reasonable grounds for divorce. So getting along, or love, becomes the only reason to stay together. You have to spend all this time working it out. I thought, maybe my problem is that I'm a traditionalist caught in a modern world. I never really felt like I needed an excuse to stay with Marla.

Scene 10
In the change room.

LINK: You're a social worker? Fuck. Hey, you know what get's me? Acid rain, what it's doing to the lakes and trees? Fish dying? Maple trees dying? I don't know how those guys get away with it. I'd put them all in jail.

Scene 11
At home.

MARLA: Richard called.

JEFF: Oh, shit. I've got a meeting tonight. I don't have time to go out to eat. Oh, shit.

MARLA: Now what?

JEFF: I was supposed to have something ready and I completely forgot. I just won't go. I'll tell Richard something came up.

MARLA: You sure?

JEFF: No, yes, no, yes, yes.

MARLA: What's the meeting?

JEFF: S.S.C. executive committee.

MARLA: And you're going to miss it, just like that?

JEFF: I don't know.

MARLA: That's a change.

JEFF: I know.

MARLA: You sure you should?

JEFF: No, I know I shouldn't but I'm going to anyway.

MARLA: Jeff, I don't care about the Social Service Council.

JEFF: Good.

MARLA: But it used to be important to you—

JEFF: Are you ready?

MARLA: Yes.

JEFF: Let's go.

MARLA: Jeff?

JEFF: What?

MARLA: Do you have to wear those pants?

Scene 12
Link and Jeff outdoors.

LINK: See that building? There's what, twelve, sixteen units? This old lady owns it, she can't afford to fix it up, the place is falling apart, but she won't sell. Centrex's bought up everything around it, they want to develop the whole block and they're paying incredible taxes. She could make a pile but she won't sell.

Scene 13
At home.

MARLA: Who is he?

JEFF: A guy I met at the health club.

MARLA: A new friend?

JEFF: I guess.

MARLA: I can't go. That's the night of the cookie exchange.

JEFF: The what?

MARLA: The cookie exchange.

JEFF: Oh, the cookie exchange. What's a cookie exchange?

MARLA: I told you about it.

JEFF: No, I wouldn't forget about a cookie exchange. What do you do at a cookie exchange, exchange cookies?

MARLA: Everybody bakes cookies, and we get together and buy them from each other.

JEFF: And you won't miss this cookie bake-off to have dinner with Link and his wife?

MARLA: They happen once a month and at the beginning everyone decides on where the money goes. It's my first one, I don't want to miss it. We'll go out with Link some other time.

JEFF: I can't believe that a bunch of lawyers get together to—What is it, moonlighting? Lawyers not making enough these days?

MARLA: It's not lawyers. It's women. It's a chance for us to get together.

Scene 14
In the change room.

LINK: Your wife's a lawyer? Your wife is a lawyer? Lots of bucks, eh? What are you doing when you're through here? A bunch of us are gonna grab a pint.

Scene 15
At home.

MARLA: I would really appreciate it if you came with me. Jeff? I would really appreciate it. I don't think it's too much to ask. Sometimes I go with you out of duty, just because you ask me to. Occasionally you come with me out of duty. I think that this is one of those times. I don't like it when other board members say to me, "Is your husband here? I was so looking forward to meeting him," and I have to make excuses for you. I know you think I should just say you don't like painting, but they won't leave it at that. I will soon have to say, "My husband thinks art is boring." You don't have to look at the paintings. You drink wine, and eat cheese, you ignore me and find someone to talk to just like you do at parties. Some board members think it's important that my husband has never set foot into the art gallery on the board of which I have been a member for four years. If you were there I wouldn't have to talk about you, I'd be able to talk about shows and acquisitions for a change. Promise you'll come to—four openings in the next six months? To set a trend?

Scene 16
Jeff addresses the audience.

JEFF: Tell me what you think about this. I go to Marla and I say, listen, Link had this great idea. A bunch of us go down and catch a Blue Jays double header, make a whole day of it, Link and his wife and me and Marla and maybe two or three other couples, we go to Toronto, watch the game, stay in a hotel for the night, I thought it sounded like a good time. Marla says, "I hate baseball." I said, "Never mind the baseball, it's just a chance to have some fun, to spend some time with some new people." Marla says, "I hate baseball, I don't want to go."

Scene 17
Jeff at work.

GINNY: Excuse me.

JEFF: Mrs Sheridan?

GINNY: Yes.

JEFF: What can I do for you?

GINNY: I was told to come here.

JEFF: Right. You've got two children.

GINNY: Yes.

JEFF: Both in school.

GINNY: No.

JEFF: No?

GINNY: One's in school, one isn't.

JEFF: Oh. How old?—is the one that isn't in school?

GINNY: Three.

JEFF: See, there's a mistake in the file. A boy?

GINNY: No.

JEFF: Uh, then it's a girl. What's the matter, don't you like my jokes? What can I do for you, Mrs Sheridan?

GINNY: I was told to come here.

JEFF: Do you know why?

GINNY: No.

JEFF: Do you have any idea?

GINNY: What do you want?

Scene 18
In the change room.

LINK: You missed a great time in Toronto, buddy. Have a nice weekend with the wife?

Scene 19
Jeff addresses the audience.

JEFF: You know how when you're a kid you feel like one day you're going to be an adult? Well, does it ever happen? Does there ever come a time when your parents decide that it's up to you whether you eat desert, dress warmly enough or have kids? That's not what I mean. When I was younger I assumed that one day I would be a married man, a husband. But I started noticing, it just started bothering me that I had trouble saying the word "wife." Marla just says, "You might as well call me your wife because that's what I am," straightforward, right to the point. But when I introduce her to someone—"I'd like you to meet ..., well, this is ...," my mate, my spouse, my partner, my companion, my co-vivant, the woman with whom I live. It was the image that was bothering me. The image of being stuck.

Scene 20
At home.

MARLA: Do you remember last year when we went out to buy wine glasses?

JEFF: Yeah.

MARLA: And because of you we bought Czechoslovakian crystal?

JEFF: Yes.

MARLA: Do you know that we have an automatic dishwasher?

JEFF: Yes.

MARLA: And it was your idea to buy it.

JEFF: Yes.

MARLA: Do you know that we have a very fancy sound system and a colour television with remote control, which you bought?

JEFF: Yes.

MARLA: And a VCR?

JEFF: Marla.

MARLA: Do you remember all that?

JEFF: Yes.

MARLA: Good.

Scene 21
Jeff and Link in a bar.

LINK: That's the trouble with this country, there's too many people telling you what you "should" do. You should do this. You should do that. Nobody tells me what I "should" do. Some people can tell me what "to" do, that's different. If I've got a boss, he can tell me what "to" do, that's what bosses are for, and if I don't like it, I know where the door is.

Scene 22
At home.

MARLA: What's the matter with people? Why do they want to go to court over who keeps the can opener? I'm thirty-three years old. Am I going to be dealing with fighting couples for the rest of my life? I talked to Graham, he says they don't need anyone in the property section. I said, "Look, I need a change." He said I'm doing a fine job where I am. What am I supposed to do? I swear, I'd start out on my own but you know what you have to do when you start out on your own? Divorce. If we ever split up, Jeff—let's just not, it's not worth it. I'm going to take a shower and then maybe I'll feel better, and then I'm going to lie down for a while. Maybe you'd like to come lie down with me?

Scene 23
Jeff addresses the audience.

JEFF: For a long time I was going to university and I lived like a student. You get a loan, a grant, there's not much money. Then you get a job and suddenly there's more money coming in, but that doesn't mean you have to change your whole life. I was perfectly comfortable where I was. Why would I want to spend thousands of dollars on a new place to live? But Marla just went on and on about it.

Scene 24
At home.

MARLA: I think you should see someone. You know, like a counsellor or something.

JEFF: Thanks.

MARLA: I'm being serious. Judy suggested it.

JEFF: Tell Judy that it's none of her business. Who's Judy?

MARLA: You know who Judy is.

JEFF: Give me a hint. Is she tall?

MARLA: I can't believe your ability to block whole areas of my life.

JEFF: I know four different Judy's.

MARLA: My therapist.

JEFF: I didn't know her name was Judy. So you and Judy decided that I should see a therapist. She looking for work?

MARLA: She says that it would help you face some things about yourself.

JEFF: Like what?

MARLA: Like why you don't want to move.

JEFF: I can't believe it.

MARLA: She says—

JEFF: I'm sorry. I took psychology in university. I got As, and, as far as I remember, liking where you lived was not one of the ten warning signs of insanity.

MARLA: It has nothing to do with insanity. Seeing a therapist could help you ...

JEFF: Help me what?

MARLA: Deal with what you're going through.

JEFF: What am I going through?

MARLA: It just might help you to talk to someone.

JEFF: Does Judy think that everyone should see their own therapist?

MARLA: We're not talking about everyone.

JEFF: You've been seeing her for three years—

MARLA: Three months.

JEFF: What are you talking about? You've been—

MARLA: I have been seeing Judy for three months now. It was someone else before that.

JEFF: Oh.

MARLA: Mrs Fleming?

JEFF: Oh, it used to be Mrs Fleming. Now it's Judy. Is this something new? First name therapy? How long will you be seeing Judy?

MARLA: I don't know.

JEFF: Is she good?

MARLA: Yes.

JEFF: Then that means that you should be cured soon.

MARLA: I am not sick. It's not a question of being cured.

JEFF: So you'll be seeing her for the rest of your life?

MARLA: Never mind.

JEFF: I want to know. Does everybody need a therapist, for their whole life? I'm a kind of—I work with people with real problems, I'm sort of a therapist actually, I do a lot of counselling, but I've never counselled people with your particular problem. Maybe I should get into it. "Can't decide between that snappy condo by the river or that tastefully renovated townhouse? Come see Jeff, specialist in living environment crisis intervention."

MARLA: I won't let you turn this back against me. It is possible that at some point I'll feel like I don't need a therapist anymore, but we're talking about you. I think when someone who's been married for eight years introduces his wife as—Don't ever call me your "room-mate" again.

JEFF: Okay, I'll call you "the wife" from now on.

MARLA: It's an improvement.

JEFF: I'm cured.

MARLA: And someone who turns a simple decision about moving—

JEFF: Here we go.

MARLA: You see, you can't deal with it rationally.

JEFF: Forget it.

MARLA: You can't.

JEFF: I don't want to move, so of course that means I'm crazy.

MARLA: Proof.

JEFF: Of what?

MARLA: That you can't deal with it rationally.

JEFF: Okay. I'll be rational.

MARLA: We'll talk about it later.

JEFF: I'll be rational.

MARLA: You're too upset now.

Scene 25
Change room.

LINK: So?

JEFF: I like where we're living, that's all.

LINK: You might get to like a house.

JEFF: I don't want to mow the lawn, I don't want to shovel snow, I don't want to paint windows.

LINK: You hire people to do that. How long have you lived where you're living?

JEFF: Five or six years.

LINK: There's got to be some forward motion. Take a look behind you, what do you see? ... Take a look.

   (Jeff looks.)

   What do you see?

JEFF: Lockers.

LINK: No.

JEFF: Naked men.

LINK: You see yesterday. And if yesterday looks the same as last week, or the same as today, you're spinning in the mud. There's got to be some forward motion.

Scene 26
At home.

MARLA: I don't want to have any children.

JEFF: You're thirty-three years old.

MARLA: And my biological time clock is running down.

JEFF: You're sure.

MARLA: I don't want to be pregnant, I don't want to go through labour, and I don't want to look after babies.

JEFF: But what happens in five years when—

MARLA: My maternal instincts awaken?

JEFF: Yes.

MARLA: I'll stifle them. Anyway Jeff, how would I get pregnant? Not in the usual way, not through sexual intercourse, or would you make an exception just this once?

Scene 27
Jeff in his office.

GINNY: Jeff?

JEFF: Ginny. Do we have an appointment?

GINNY: I was near here, I ...

JEFF: What's up?

GINNY: I just wanted to say thanks.

JEFF: You're welcome. For what?

GINNY: For coming by. Hey, they liked you.

JEFF: I liked them.

GINNY: And I've been working on budgeting. I might be able to make the money last, a little longer, anyway.

JEFF: Somebody once said that asking poor people to budget more carefully is like asking starving people to eat less.

GINNY: So why did we spend all that time going over my budgets?

JEFF: It's what they pay me to do. So, your kids liked me.

GINNY: Yeah.

JEFF: Ginny, why don't I take you all out to eat?

GINNY: You don't have to.

JEFF: No, no. I want to.

Scene 28
Jeff addresses the audience.

JEFF: I was watching Link work out on a rowing machine. When he worked out that was all he was doing. I mean I was working out and getting into shape but no matter what I was doing, my mind was always somewhere else, thinking about work or Marla's wanting to move or how our sex life was or anything, but Link was doing what he was doing. Same thing in the bar after basketball, he was really funny, really quick, didn't matter what he was talking about, he said what he felt, he didn't hold back at all. He knew how to have a good time. And his friends, too, they knew how to have fun. One guy taught psychology, another guy was a designer or something, I don't know exactly. Another guy was an accountant and one guy was a partner in a car dealership. I mean a car salesman and an accountant were having fun. I thought, I don't know, what kind of stereotypes do we have about car salesmen and accountants? Aren't they supposed to be, sort of out of it? But I felt like I was out of it. I was. But I had a good time.

Scene 29
Change room.

LINK: What I do doesn't matter, Jeff. The thing is, I have a good time. That's what we're here for, isn't it? Are you having a good time?

JEFF: Yeah.

LINK: Yeah, yeah. Yeah ain't good enough. It's gotta be yes. Are you having a good time? Yes. We're not here very long, tomorrow you could be crossing the street, pow, run over by an elephant, curtains.

JEFF: Yeah, well ...

LINK: Fuck "Yeah, well" Jeff. Yes or no. Are you having a good time or not? I've been watching you, you know what your problem is? You don't want to have a good time. You're a good-looking guy, look at the way you dress. Don't argue, listen to me, you don't know the first thing about having a good time. It's like one of those beer commercials. Everyone's having a good time, telling jokes, making deals and there's this guy with his arm around a girl and they're both laughing and he takes a drink out of his Molson Golden, he's got his arm up, and as I look at him, I catch, through the crook of his elbow, a little bit out of focus, you, drinking soda water, your brow wrinkled with worry, thinking about—life.

> *(Jeff laughs.)*

You want to have a good time, Jeff, you gotta enter into a contract with yourself, you gotta to make a deal. If you're doing something and you can't say, "I am having a good time," then go and do something else. You're too important to put up with the shit, life is too short.

Scene 30
At home.

MARLA: Does he smoke?

JEFF: Yes.

MARLA: Well you better tell him.

JEFF: Mm.

MARLA: Are you going to tell him?

JEFF: Sure.

MARLA: Look, we both agreed our home would be smoke-free. If he's going to come, just warn him, okay?

Scene 31
Change room.

LINK: I live by the contract, buddy. If we have a contract, I'm there. No contract, then count me out. Family, okay, that's different. Kids, if you got any, kids are a contract even if there's nothing written down, I figure kids are a contract for life and you don't break that, and the wife's the same, but that's it. I care about me, I care about my family, but that's where I draw the line. Unless we got a contract. I've got a contract with my banker and with my insurance company and with the people that work for me. But I don't have a contract with my neighbour and I don't have a contract with the guy down the street and I don't have a contract with you, right, so I don't owe you anything, you know what I mean? I mean if I say I'll meet you for lunch tomorrow, I'll meet you for lunch tomorrow and I'll be on time but that's not what I'm talking about here. I'm talking about the bigger things. I'll be straight with you, cause that's the way I am, we're getting to be friends, I'm starting to think of you as my friend, I am, but if you show up tomorrow and you say, "Oh, I just lost my job and the wife ran off with the mailman, and I broke my leg, too," well, I might give you a place to sleep and bacon and eggs in the morning but then again I might not, too, you know what I mean? What it is is, I won't put up with bullshit, I got to have things clear and straight so there's no questions when the spit hits the fan. See, I'm not one of these people that says, "I don't owe nobody nothing." If we got a contract, you can count on me.

Scene 32
At home.

MARLA: What does he do?

JEFF: Who?

MARLA: Link.

JEFF: I don't know exactly.

MARLA: He's your friend and you don't know what he does?

JEFF: He doesn't talk about it.

MARLA: He called. He can't make it.

JEFF: Oh.

MARLA: Did you tell him he couldn't smoke here?

JEFF: Yeah.

MARLA: Liar.

Scene 33
Coffee shop.

GINNY: What would you do if you quit?

JEFF: I don't know. Is there such a thing as a job that's fun?

GINNY: I'd be happy if I found a job that paid enough to get off welfare. If it's such a drag, how come—why did you become a social worker in the first place?

JEFF: *(excited)* Oh, well— *(thinks)* To help. When I started doing social work, I thought all people needed was a good talk with someone who was sympathetic and intelligent, like me. I thought I'd be able to fix things between husbands and wives just by talking to them. And between parents and children. And children and teachers, and kids and cops. I'd make sure kids got another chance. And after talking to me, those kids'd make it. Are you uncomfortable?

GINNY: I guess, a bit.

JEFF: Why? There's nothing wrong with going out for a cup of coffee. Is there?

GINNY: No.

JEFF: Anyway, I found out talking doesn't help much. Maybe it helps people get through the weeks but not through the years. And there's no time to talk, there's too many people to see, there's too much work. So what happens? I get to be a cop. Did you make any extra money this month? Next. Mary's teacher says she hasn't been to school all week. Next. When was the last time you saw your husband? Next. You're going to have to budget more carefully. Next. Why'd you quit school?

GINNY: You're not supposed to do this, are you?

JEFF: Do what?

GINNY: See your clients, out of the office...

JEFF: Well, there's no rule against it.

GINNY: What would your boss say?

JEFF: She would trust me to remain objective and maintain professional distance. So, why'd you quit school?

GINNY: I hated it.

JEFF: To get married?

GINNY: That's not why.

JEFF: Were you pregnant?

GINNY: I wanted to get pregnant.

JEFF: Why?

GINNY: It's the best way to have a baby.

JEFF: Why did you want to have a baby when you were seventeen, when it would mean quitting school, when it would change your life?

GINNY: It was something to do.

JEFF: Did it change your life?

GINNY: I don't remember. Look, I've got to split.

JEFF: Wait. Do you think you and the kids would like to go for a drive in the country?

Scene 34
At home.

MARLA: Do you love me?

JEFF: Yes.

MARLA: No, you don't.

JEFF: Marla ...

MARLA: Define love.

JEFF: I can't.

MARLA: Then how can you say you love me?

JEFF: Marla ...

MARLA: Do you love me?

JEFF: It's a trick question. If I say, yes, you won't believe me. If I say, No—

MARLA: Do you love me?

JEFF: Yes.

MARLA: Then say it.

JEFF: I love you. But I think my idea of love is different than yours.

MARLA: What's your idea of love?

JEFF: Love develops over a long time. It comes from spending time together, it's the product of a shared past.

MARLA: Oh, good.

JEFF: What's wrong with that?

MARLA: You make love sound like a bad habit. What's the difference between love and boredom? Don't you ever get excited? By anyone?

JEFF: I don't know. Do you have to be excited about someone to love them? Do you love me?

MARLA: I love some things about you.

JEFF: How do you define love?

MARLA: I don't think love can exist without passion.

JEFF: And do you feel passionate towards me?

MARLA: Well ...

JEFF: No.

MARLA: Not very.

JEFF: So you don't love me.

MARLA: Not by that definition of love.

JEFF: Which is your definition.

MARLA: But I feel comfortable with you.

JEFF: But that's not love.

MARLA: No.

JEFF: I'm glad we've had this chance to talk.

MARLA: That's the difference. I want there to be passion in our relationship. You seem quite happy to let it just go on.

JEFF: We could try drugs.

MARLA: You could try to be more passionate.

JEFF: But ... you said you didn't feel passionate towards me.

MARLA: If you were more passionate towards me, I'd feel more passionate towards you.

JEFF: That makes no sense.

MARLA: I don't care, it's true.

Scene 35
An afternoon in the country.

GINNY: This feels great.

JEFF: Yeah.

GINNY: Thanks for taking us out here. *(to off-stage)* Bobby! Watch Amy!

JEFF: Take it easy.

GINNY: *(to off-stage)* Bobby!

JEFF: They'll be alright. You're supposed to relax in the country.

GINNY: Amy!

JEFF: They're having fun. I used to come here a lot. I used to bring Marla here. The last time we came here she got out of the car and put on her walkman. I thought we'd have a nice quiet walk in the country and she's wearing her walkman.

GINNY: Look.

JEFF: Where?

GINNY: On that branch. See it?

JEFF: Yeah.

GINNY: It's pretty.

JEFF: Yeah.

GINNY: What do you think it is?

JEFF: A bird.

GINNY: You sure?

JEFF: You can tell by the feathers. They fly, too.

GINNY: It's not flying.

JEFF: Maybe it's not a bird. See that? A flower.

GINNY: And that?

JEFF: Tree.

GINNY: And what's that big grey thing?

JEFF: Rock. Might be a stone. I didn't bring my guide book.

GINNY: Where'd you learn all this stuff?

JEFF: Oh, you know, here, there. You spend a lot of time in the country, you pick it up.

GINNY: Jeff, are you feeling better about your job?

JEFF: Yeah.

GINNY: I asked Bobby what he wanted to be when he grew up.

JEFF: He wants to be a policeman.

GINNY: A fireman.

JEFF: Kids that age always want to be something with a uniform. Then, when they're ...

GINNY: What?

JEFF: Nothing.

GINNY: What were you going to say?

JEFF: I remember something from university, a study, it showed that most kids, after they were six or seven, wanted to be something else, usually something that one of their parents or a relative did, but kids from poor families kind of gave up. They weren't excited about being anything anymore. I get really depressed by that.

GINNY: Yeah, me too.

JEFF: You ever feel that way, like it's not worth it, like you should just take off?

GINNY: Yes.

JEFF: I think it's amazing, the way you hang in. I don't know how you do it.

GINNY: There's nothing else to do.

JEFF: If I had to put up with what you do ...

GINNY: Look at those things. *(She points up.)*

JEFF: Tell me about your husband.

GINNY: Why?

JEFF: What was he like when you married him?

GINNY: See those fluffy white things? Clouds. ... Aren't you going to ask me how I know that?

JEFF: How did you know that?

GINNY: I've seen them on TV. You want to race? I'll race you to that tree. Come on.

Scene 36
A bar.

LINK: So this is Marla. Jeff's told me all about you.

MARLA: What did you tell him?

JEFF: What did I tell you?

LINK: Just that Marla was the best thing that ever happened to you.

JEFF: Oh, that.

MARLA: What kind of work do you do, Link? Jeff's never mentioned it.

LINK: Let's decide what we want first. The specials are good, and the lamb is excellent.

MARLA: I'll just have a salad.

LINK: Now, I don't want any arguments. It's on me, so let's have a proper meal, to celebrate our first time together. Let's have some wine? Red, white?

JEFF: White.

MARLA: *(at the same time)* Red.

LINK: There's a Gioberti Burgundy that's just right. You know, I was sitting here, waiting for you guys, and—see that woman behind me, brown hair—

MARLA: Pulled back?

LINK: Yeah.

MARLA: No make-up?

LINK: I thought that was you.

MARLA: Thanks.

LINK: I was going to go up to her, but Jeff came just in time. If you'd come first, I wouldn't have thought you were Marla. I'd have thought you were ... an artist.

   (Marla laughs.)

A successful artist.

MARLA: I used to paint.

LINK: But ...

MARLA: Not anymore.

LINK: Why'd you stop?

MARLA: No time. No room.

JEFF: She's still involved though.

LINK: Yeah?

MARLA: I'm on the board of an art gallery.

LINK: Oh, great. They're always short of money, right?

MARLA: Yes.

LINK: I'll send you a cheque.

MARLA: Link—

LINK: Who do I make it out to?

MARLA: The Electric Gallery for Visual and Media Arts Development Fund.

LINK: Snappy name. It's the way you dress.

MARLA: What is?

LINK: Why I wouldn't think you were a lawyer. Too ...

MARLA: Too what?

LINK: Too creative to be a lawyer.

MARLA: Link?

LINK: Marla?

MARLA: What do you do?

LINK: I play basketball, I ski, I read detective fiction, listen to early blues, I ...

MARLA: Do you have a job?

LINK: That's the same question as "What do you do?" I don't like that question. It makes me feel like people are trying to pin me down.

MARLA: That's probably what they're trying to do.

LINK: Maybe I'm a drug dealer. Maybe I'm a banker.

MARLA: You won't tell me?

LINK: First I want to know more about you.

MARLA: What would you like to know?

LINK: How a woman like you ends up becoming a lawyer.

MARLA: Rather than ...

LINK: A wife ...

MARLA: Jeff and I are married.

LINK: You guys are more like pals. Wives have children.

MARLA: You're married.

LINK: Eleven years in November. Three children.

MARLA: I don't want to have any children.

LINK: I know that. That's why I asked you. How a woman like you ends up becoming a lawyer?

MARLA: What are you saying?

LINK: I'm not saying anything, I'm just asking, cause I'm curious. Why would an intelligent woman like you give up having children to be lawyer?

MARLA: Because I want to be a lawyer. Because I don't want to have children.

LINK: To me that's what life's all about. Having children. Having a family. Being part of something bigger than yourself. Listen, I didn't invite you here to lecture you about the way you live.

Scene 37
At home.

MARLA: What is it that you like about Link?

JEFF: I don't know.

MARLA: He's the last person I thought you'd be friends with.

JEFF: Why?

MARLA: I wouldn't have thought he was your type.

JEFF: What is my type?

MARLA: Tormented. Link is not tormented.

JEFF: He's smart, he's got this kind of "I don't care" attitude, but he thinks about things. We talk.

MARLA: About what?

JEFF: Lots of things. He's excited about life, he's got good energy.

MARLA: He's not tormented.

JEFF: You're right. Everyone I know, including me, and even you, is always asking themselves, "What's wrong? Who am I? What am I doing?" Link knows what he's doing. It's refreshing.

MARLA: Have you ever talked to him about buying a house?

JEFF: Let's not start ...

MARLA: I'm not starting anything. I just wonder what he would think about your obsession.

JEFF: It's not my obsession.

MARLA: Did you talk to him about it?

JEFF: Yes.

MARLA: And?

JEFF: And what?

MARLA: What did he say?

JEFF: Nothing.

MARLA: Did he think we should buy a house?

JEFF: No.

MARLA: Did he think we shouldn't?

JEFF: We didn't talk about it much. He didn't understand why I didn't want to buy a house but he didn't think I needed to see a therapist either. Look, can we go now?

MARLA: Look at me.

JEFF: I'm looking at you.

MARLA: Look at me.

JEFF: Why?

MARLA: Do I look like I'm ready to go anywhere?

Scene 38
Change room.

LINK: Why does that bother you?

JEFF: I don't know. Every Monday she's afraid to leave the house in case over the weekend her clothes have gone out of style.

LINK: What's wrong with her wanting to look nice?

JEFF: No, it's more than that, it's a basic lack of confidence.

LINK: Not everybody's as casual as you are about how they dress.

JEFF: Link, here's this woman, she works for a big legal firm, she's got to be tough all day, she stands up and talks in front of judges, and I don't understand it.

LINK: Clothes make the man, Jeff.

JEFF: I hate that expression.

LINK: It's true, take a look around. I don't much care what people wear either, but you can tell if people have pride in themselves by the way they dress. If you don't take yourself seriously, nobody else will.

Scene 39
Coffee shop.

GINNY: I think I know what you mean.

JEFF: Do you think I dress alright?

GINNY: It suits you, but ...

JEFF: But what?

GINNY: If I had more money I'd spend more on clothes.

JEFF: I like the way you dress.

GINNY: I couldn't dress like this if I had a job. I mean, clothes are important, you know.

JEFF: No, they're not.

GINNY: Yeah, they are. Like when I was eleven or twelve, and I started noticing boys and—I wanted to dress like a girl, and I wanted nice clothes. I needed nice clothes, but there was no way, we didn't have the money. I got crazy about it and we had big fights and for the first time I knew that my mother was a loser. And no wonder she was a loser, you just had to look at her. She could've been pretty, if she took care of herself, but no wonder she didn't have a man, and, and that's why she was a loser. And I wasn't going to let her make me a loser like her, and that's what she was trying to do, I was going to be pretty, I wasn't going to be like her—I told her that and I screamed at her. I hated her, but there was nothing she could have done. I remember that that now, I'm surprised she'll even talk to me, it was ten years before we could talk to each other. I think that, you know, Amy's three now and, and she doesn't know I'm a loser.

Scene 40
Bar.

LINK: Maybe Marla feels financially insecure, did you ever think about that?

JEFF: Come on.

LINK: Oh, you got money now. But what happens if she has a kid and wants to quit working, could you live on what you make?

JEFF: Yeah.

LINK: I mean live. She makes more than you, right?

JEFF: Yeah.

LINK: And what would happen if you lost your job? I know, you probably got bonds and shit. How long could you live on that? And what happens if you blow a major gasket? And she's left with two kids? I got things set up so's if I die tomorrow, or if I take off and leave, which I won't do, my wife's looking at two hundred thou a year. Women want that kind of security. So do I.

Scene 41
Jeff addresses the audience.

JEFF: Two things were bothering me. I kept telling myself that Marla didn't really like sex, she believed that it had to be part of a successful relationship, so she wanted there to be sex. But when I thought about where things were going, I got scared. I mean we were heading into separate bedroom territory. How did I feel about that? Is it a fact of life that after couples have been together for a while things cool off? Did I really believe that sex was kind of childish, and that Marla would grow out of it? That seemed to be where I was headed. But what really bothered me, or started to bother me, was Ginny. Why was I spending so much time with her? Was I really concerned about her? Yes. Was that all? Why did I keep thinking about that day in the country? Why did I go see her right away when she called and told me she was depressed about moving? And how come, even though there was nothing I could say that would make her feel better, how come it made me feel good that just my being there seemed to comfort her?

Scene 42
Jeff at work.

GINNY: I got this in the mail.

JEFF: What is it?

GINNY: Read it.

JEFF: Oh great.

GINNY: Yeah.

JEFF: "Major renovations ... 120 days ... first day of May."

GINNY: What does that mean about option to the tenants that live there?

JEFF: You won't be able to afford it.

GINNY: They can raise the rent?

JEFF: As much as they want. Listen, we'll find you another place to live.

Scene 43
Bar.

LINK: So what?

JEFF: What do you mean so what?

LINK: She's on welfare. She's been evicted. What do you want me to do?

JEFF: I don't know. I'm worried about her. It's my job to worry about her.

LINK: So why don't you tell whoever's renovating your friend's apartment they can't do that. And watch what happens. You want people to build new houses? You want people to fix windows? Things grow or they decay.

JEFF: Tell her that.

LINK: What happened to the guy?

JEFF: Her husband?

LINK: The father of her children.

JEFF: He left, I don't know.

LINK: Why did he dump her?

JEFF: I don't know.

LINK: Don't you think it's important to know that?

JEFF: Look, she's on her own, she's got two kids, she's being thrown out of her apartment.

LINK: You're always saying you want to understand things. Try to understand this. What happens when you give people welfare?

JEFF: They live in shitty houses, the kids grow up without hope, and at the end of every month they're eating spaghetti and peanut butter.

LINK: In the long term.

JEFF: What happens?

LINK: One. They get used to welfare and they stop trying to be independent. Two. The men take off. Why? Cause they know that the government's going to look after their women so they don't have to be responsible. Three. The women throw their husbands out. Maybe the guy drinks, maybe he fucks around so she throws him out. Cause she knows she is going to be taken care of. That's just off the top of my head. You want some more?

JEFF: What about the kids?

LINK: If they really gave a shit they'd finish school, they'd try harder. Like kids who play hockey twenty hours a day cause they're looking for some way out. Look man, I didn't start with much. I didn't go to college cause I wanted money quick. I got a job at Eaton's and I worked hard and I got to be floor manager. It was alright but it went better with coke. I was doing a lot of coke and I started getting it for friends, at cost. Then I started getting it for people who weren't my friends. So I started taking a cut. I took some stupid risks in those days, but I made money.

JEFF: These kids are supposed to deal coke to—

LINK: Why the fuck not? It was good enough for those guys that sold liquor in the thirties.

JEFF: So a few poor kids make it. What about the rest?

LINK: Why are you so wrapped up in this?

JEFF: Cause I care.

LINK: You're sure?

JEFF: Yeah.

LINK: You're sure that's all?

JEFF: What are you talking about?

LINK: I'm talking about you and Ginny. I'm just wondering if there's a little more happening here than you're letting on.

JEFF: Forget it, Link.

LINK: Maybe you want something to happen.

JEFF: Forget it.

LINK: You keep bringing her name up. Is she pretty?

Scene 44
Jeff at work.

GINNY: They put me on hold for forty-five minutes.

JEFF: And?

GINNY: I went into the office and filled out a million forms.

JEFF: And?

GINNY: They told me I'd have to wait a long time.

JEFF: Yeah.

GINNY: At least a year.

JEFF: At least you're on the list.

GINNY: Where am I going to live?

JEFF: We'll keep looking.

GINNY: Where?

JEFF: Ginny, maybe you're going to have to live in ...

GINNY: A park.

JEFF: Some place smaller. That place you went to last week, you sure you couldn't live there?

GINNY: Shit.

JEFF: Why not?

GINNY: It was in a basement, there were two rooms, the pipes were dripping, there was a broken window, it smelled like shit and it was too expensive.

JEFF: Alright.

GINNY: You want to see it?

JEFF: No.

GINNY: Go look at it if you don't believe me.

JEFF: I believe you.

GINNY: I'll live in a park first.

JEFF: Alright.

GINNY: It's not alright.

Scene 45
At home.

MARLA: Jeff? How are things at work?

JEFF: Shitty.

MARLA: Why?

JEFF: The usual.

MARLA: You seem more depressed than usual.

JEFF: It builds up.

MARLA: You want to tell me about it?

JEFF: Nothing's changed, there's nothing to tell.

MARLA: Link said he thought maybe you were getting in over your head.

JEFF: Link said that.

MARLA: He said he was worried about you. And a woman from work. He said you might be getting too involved with her.

JEFF: What's that supposed to mean?

MARLA: I think it just means that you're getting too close to someone that you're supposed to have a professional relationship with, in the way that social workers, and lawyers, sometimes get over-involved.

JEFF: Where did you see him?

MARLA: Link?

JEFF: Yeah.

MARLA: Lunch.

JEFF: Oh.

MARLA: Oh?

JEFF: It means, how did you come to have lunch with Link?

MARLA: Link called me up at work and asked me to lunch. He said there was something he wanted to discuss.

JEFF: Thank you.

MARLA: Do you want to know what we discussed?

JEFF: You want to tell me, tell me. You brought it up.

MARLA: I brought it up cause I was worried about you.

JEFF: Oh, good. I've got two people worried about me now.

MARLA: I thought you liked him.

JEFF: I do.

MARLA: He asked about Barker, Bartlett and Graham. I said they were good. He said he called them about some real estate work and he asked if I was available. Graham told him it would have to be someone from the property division. So Link asked me if I had enough time to do some legal work on the side.

Scene 46
On the phone.

LINK: Jeff, listen, can we meet for lunch tomorrow?

Scene 47
On the phone

GINNY: Bobby asked if he'd have to change schools. And I started thinking about my friends here and what moving's going to mean. It's kind of a group. We help each other out. My mother lives a block away. I couldn't sleep all night.

Scene 48
At home.

MARLA: Guess what? The cookie exchange has split. We had a big fight about who the money we raised should go to. One group, led by Alison, I don't think you know her, thought the money should go to Nicaragua. The other group, led by Cathy, thought we should avoid controversial issues. I said I thought the whole idea was for us to have a chance to get together, and we were only talking about fifty dollars a month and why didn't we just proceed by majority vote. Cathy wanted a two-thirds vote. Alison called her "a fucking liberal," and then Cathy called Alison "a political fanatic." So next month, the political fanatics are going to meet at Alison's place and the fucking liberals are going to meet at Cathy's.

Scene 49
Bar.

LINK: Okay, Jeff. This is it. I've talked it over with the boys and we want you in. One-point-two hectare lot, forty-eight, luxury, no, but nice units. Total cost, three-point two million. Cash up front, fifteen percent. Your cost for one share, fifty thou. Talk it over with the wife but no bullshit, eh, I know you got the money. Two good salaries, no kids, and I've seen where you live. Marla can do the legal work if you want. And don't do it if you don't want to do it.

Scene 50
At home.

MARLA: Ginny?

JEFF: From where I work. She's got two kids, she's been evicted.

MARLA: The one Link was talking about.

JEFF: Yes.

MARLA: You're still worried about her?

JEFF: I spent four hours on the fucking phone, and I still can't find her a place to live.

MARLA: And?

JEFF: I don't know. I don't know.

MARLA: You shouldn't let it get to you.

JEFF: It's my job, I just want to do my job.

MARLA: You're doing it.

JEFF: I know.

MARLA: You can't do any more than that.

JEFF: I know.

MARLA: Did you see Link?

JEFF: Mm.

MARLA: What did he want?

JEFF: He wants us to invest in an apartment building. He wants you to do the legal work.

MARLA: What did you say?

JEFF: I'd told him I'd talk to you.

MARLA: What do you think?

JEFF: I don't know. What about you?

MARLA: I don't know the details.

JEFF: Yeah, well, you'll talk to Link. But in principle, what do you think?

MARLA: Why are you asking me?

JEFF: What do you mean?

MARLA: You've never wanted to invest in anything before.

JEFF: Oh, well. Can we do it?

MARLA: Yes.

JEFF: We've got the money?

MARLA: It's just sitting there.

JEFF: I thought it was in—

MARLA: Bonds, pensions—

JEFF: And we can get it?

MARLA: A phone call.

Scene 51
Change room.

LINK: You run a business, you gotta worry about employees and customers and products. I don't need the headache. The stock market's for old ladies, it's like putting money in the bank. Now real estate, it's the only way I know to make money quick, you don't have to work too hard, and it's legal too. But. If I had a whole lot of money, you know what I'd do? I'd check out currency speculation. I like the concept. You never buy or sell anything but money.

Scene 52
On the phone.

GINNY: I talked to this woman today. She's got three kids. They've been living in a motel room for three months.

Scene 53
Link drops in.

JEFF: Link. Hi.

LINK: How you guys doing?

JEFF: Pretty good. Pretty good.

LINK: And the beautiful, charming and intelligent Marla?

MARLA: I'm fine, thank you.

LINK: Listen, I've got some news for you guys, I hope you don't take it too bad. It's about our apartment building.

JEFF: What?

LINK: I, uh, I, we sold it.

JEFF: It's not built yet.

LINK: No, we never even started.

JEFF: Why?

LINK: Well, I thought that because of certain financial considerations we better unload.

JEFF: So you just did it on your own, you didn't even bother—

LINK: There wasn't time, Jeff.

JEFF: Come on, Link, you can't tell me—

LINK: Let me explain—

JEFF: Damn right, and you can start by—

MARLA: Jeff.

JEFF: What?

MARLA: Let him explain.

LINK: Um, it's a bit complicated, it has to do with there being a tight market and—

JEFF: What did you sell it for? What do we get?

LINK: Your share? Eighteen thousand.

JEFF: You sold that place and you never talked to us and, and we're—

LINK: Profit.

JEFF: Profit?

LINK: Yeah.

JEFF: Eighteen thousand dollars profit?

LINK: And change.

JEFF: In two weeks, we made twenty thousand dollars on a building that doesn't exist?

LINK: Eighteen.

JEFF: Holy shit!

LINK: Hey. Schmuck.

JEFF: Twenty thousand dollars!

LINK: Listen to me. It's not always this easy.

JEFF: *(to Marla)* Twenty thousand dollars.

LINK: Hey! Put a lid on it.

JEFF: We've got to celebrate. We've got to have a drink.

LINK: Well I just happen to have a little bottle of champagne with me. *(He reaches for his cigarettes.)*

JEFF: This is fantastic.

LINK: It's a good champagne. I wouldn't call it fantastic.

JEFF: This is amazing. Listen, Link, you can't smoke in here.

LINK: Marla, get us some glasses.

Scene 54
At home.

JEFF: Why did he do that?

MARLA: He was just having fun.

JEFF: Why did he even offer us a share?

MARLA: Why shouldn't he?

JEFF: I'm sure he could have borrowed the money and then he could have—

MARLA: It's better to have investors. You should believe what he said.

JEFF: About what?

MARLA: That we were lucky. You do lose money sometimes.

JEFF: It sure looks easy.

MARLA: Does it bother you that we weren't consulted?

JEFF: You know what I think? I think that Link knows we don't know a whole lot about investing in real estate. And I think when we learn more, and our opinion is worth something, then he'll consult us. Twenty thousand dollars. Just like that.

MARLA: Let's go to Europe.

JEFF: Tonight?

MARLA: Saturday.

JEFF: Can you?

MARLA: For a week. You?

JEFF: I think so.

MARLA: Then let's do it.

JEFF: We'll go to Europe. And then, we'll get rid of this dump. But first ...

MARLA: Let's go to bed.

Scene 55
On the phone.

GINNY: I called eight places. And I went to see three of them.

Scene 56
Jeff and Marla in bed.

MARLA: You know what I'd like to do? I decided. I want to be a diplomat.

JEFF: You?

MARLA: I'd be good at it. I'm good at negotiating.

JEFF: You'd be good at the parties.

MARLA: Yeah, I would. I'd be good at that too.

JEFF: I suppose I'd serve drinks.

MARLA: No, no, we'd have servants for that. You have to have servants when you're a diplomat, they come with the house. We'd get a big house with a ballroom—

JEFF: And big pillars holding up the roof.

MARLA: A formal garden.

JEFF: I don't know.

MARLA: Silver tea service and fine crystal.

JEFF: I don't think I could live with servants.

MARLA: Okay, Jeff. We'll be in some poor but strategic third world country where people are desperate for any kind of work, but if you want to fire the servants—

JEFF: Okay, servants.

MARLA: Now you ...

JEFF: Maybe I could just travel around.

MARLA: No, you'd have to stay and help me entertain. It's part of being a diplomat, you have to have a spouse to help entertain.

JEFF: I'd get bored.

MARLA: I know, I'm thinking.

JEFF: I'd write my memoirs.

MARLA: I know! I know!

JEFF: What?

MARLA: It's perfect.

JEFF: What?

MARLA: Guess.

JEFF: I don't know what it is, tell me.

MARLA: Guess.

JEFF: I'd be a social worker. I'd be a painter. I'd be a servant. I don't know. What?

MARLA: A spy.

JEFF: A spy.

MARLA: What do you think?

JEFF: I'd love to be a spy.

MARLA: You'd make friends with Russian physicists and—Can you be trusted?

JEFF: I don't know. Maybe I'd be a double agent.

MARLA: It's so exciting, Jeff. Can't we do it?

JEFF: I don't see why not.

MARLA: Would you scratch my neck over here? A little lower, a little lower, yeah, right there. Yeah. That feels really good.

Scene 57
On the phone.

GINNY: I found this place that was alright. But they don't take people on welfare.

Scene 58
At home.

MARLA: Link called.

JEFF: How is he?

MARLA: He has another investment property.

JEFF: Tell him we're in.

MARLA: It's a thirty-two unit apartment building. Clear.

JEFF: Clear?

MARLA: Clear.

JEFF: What does clear mean?

MARLA: It means that there won't be any outstanding leases when we take possession.

JEFF: Is that important?

MARLA: It's downtown, it needs renovating. It's the same as last time, fifty thousand dollars a share.

JEFF: We're in, right?

MARLA: I told him we might want two.

JEFF: A hundred thousand? We don't have that much.

MARLA: We can borrow it.

JEFF: Does he want to renovate it, or are we just going to sell it like last time?

MARLA: I don't know. He said it's going to be very spiffy, he thought we might want to move in.

Scene 59
Bar.

JEFF: Alright. Tell me what I have to know to be good at investing in real estate?

LINK: Nothing.

JEFF: C'mon.

LINK: It's a talent, Jeff. Something you're born with. I don't know if it can be taught.

JEFF: I've got the talent. Now I want to know a few details.

LINK: I get lawyers to look after those.

JEFF: Link.

LINK: You buy something before the price goes up. And you sell it before the price falls.

JEFF: How do you know when the price is going to fall?

LINK: You guess.

JEFF: Come on.

LINK: That a new sweater?

JEFF: Link.

LINK: The price goes up when investors are investing. The price falls when they stop.

JEFF: Why do they stop?

LINK: They get cold feet. First one gets cold feet, then another one, then a third one, then it's an avalanche. If you've borrowed money to buy the property in the first place, it's curtains.

JEFF: How do you know when there's going to be an avalanche?

LINK: You guess.

JEFF: Come on.

LINK: Are the pants new, too?

JEFF: Yup.

LINK: And the shoes?

JEFF: What do you think?

LINK: It's good you're trying.

Scene 60
At home.

MARLA: Sorry, Jeff. Can't go out for dinner tonight. Too much work.

JEFF: You got to eat something.

MARLA: Fix me a sandwich?

JEFF: Sure.

MARLA: Mind if I take over the dining room table?

JEFF: What are you doing?

MARLA: There's some problems with the new property. Link asked to me to look it over.

JEFF: Anything serious?

MARLA: Link wants to put some stores on the ground floor.

JEFF: Oh yeah.

MARLA: That means converting apartments into stores. There's by-laws that make it a bit tricky. Link says it's all a plot to make work for lawyers.

JEFF: What's this?

MARLA: It's the title to the property.

JEFF: Our names aren't on it.

MARLA: You'll notice Link's name isn't on it either.

JEFF: So?

MARLA: Jeff, dear, don't worry about it. It's all taken care of on a separate contract.

JEFF: Can I see the contract?

MARLA: Why?

JEFF: I'm trying to learn about real estate.

MARLA: I don't have it with me.

JEFF: Oh.

MARLA: Jeff.

JEFF: Mm?

MARLA: That sandwich? Jeff?

JEFF: What is this?

MARLA: I told you.

JEFF: I didn't know where the building was.

MARLA: Uh-huh. *(pause)* Something wrong?

JEFF: It's where Ginny lives.

Scene 61
Change room.

LINK: You're serious?

JEFF: Yeah.

LINK: That's a drag.

JEFF: Link, I ...

LINK: You want out, you can get out. I shouldn't do this, but I'll do it if you want. ... What do you want me to do?

JEFF: I don't know.

LINK: You didn't throw her out, I didn't throw her out. In fact, she was evicted before we even bought the place.

JEFF: She still lives there.

LINK: Level with me. Are you two sleeping together?

JEFF: No.

LINK: Look, you did what you could. Is it part of the job description where you work, that you can't live your own life?

JEFF: I'm not sleeping with her. It has nothing to do with my job description. I just care.

LINK: Oh. Jeff cares. Jeff's a concerned individual. I get a little tired of this. We're talking about one person, here. You care? Well why don't you give a hundred bucks to the United Appeal and get it off your chest.

Scene 62
At home.

MARLA: What did you decide?

JEFF: Doesn't it bother you?

MARLA: The deal will go through and Ginny will be evicted whether we're in on it or not.

Scene 63
On the phone.

LINK: It's all cause she happens to live in the same building. You know what I mean? If she lived somewhere else you wouldn't even know about it. It's just bad luck. Anyway, I got some people who are willing to pick up the slack, and I'm holding them off, so can you let me know by noon tomorrow?

Scene 64
Voices in Jeff's nightmare.

GINNY: I got this in the mail.

MARLA: She'd be evicted anyway. There's nothing you can do.

LINK: You want out, you can get out.

MARLA: You've done your job. What more can you do?

GINNY: On that branch. See it?

LINK: It's all because she happens to live in the same building. It's just bad luck.

Scene 65
Jeff at work.

JEFF: Ginny, do you know Lisa MacKenzie? I'm not going to be your caseworker anymore and Lisa's going to take over. Do you know Lisa? I'm sure you'll get along. ... I talked it over with my supervisor and we both agreed that I shouldn't be working with you anymore. ... Lisa'll help you find a place to live. Actually, she wants to put you in touch with a tenants' group that, that'll fight the eviction. ... I'm sure it'll work out.

GINNY: Jeff?

JEFF: What?

GINNY: What are you doing?

JEFF: Just what I have to do.

GINNY: What happened?

JEFF: Ginny—

GINNY: You can't do this. Not without telling me. I have a right to know why you're doing this.

JEFF: Look, it's just—It's just a conflict of interest for me to keep working with you. That's all. Nothing to do with you.

GINNY: Jeff, tell me what happened. Can't you tell me?

JEFF: Yeah, but, we'll talk about it later, okay.

Scene 66
Jeff addresses the audience.

JEFF: So that's what happened. It's been quite a year. But I came out of it alright. We finally bought a house. I didn't think I could live in that apartment building after everything that happened, and it's worked out. We've got a sunroom with a skylight, and I never thought I would but I've really gotten into working in the garden. Link came by to see the house, asked us how much we wanted for it. Marla and I are getting along, better than ever. I went to one of her gallery openings. And I quit my job. I finally realized it was pointless, I really wasn't doing anybody any good. I've done a lot of thinking about that. You have to be able to see the difference between the intention of something and what it's actually doing, and I'm not sure how much good welfare really does. Wouldn't it be better if instead of spending money on welfare, we reduced taxes? Then people would have more to spend, more to invest, we'd get the economy going. Anyway, I feel good about some of the things I've done, some of the things I've faced up to and admitted to myself. For example. I've always known that you have to take responsibility for things, but I've finally figured out you can't care about everything or you'll go crazy. You have to say, "This is my area of responsibility," and that's it. I think that's a kind of personal growth. I really am more comfortable with myself now and I think that's what's most important. Anyway, I should be going. I'm glad we had this chance to talk.

(The End.)

SISTERS IN THE GREAT DAY CARE WAR

Sisters in the Great Day Care War opened at the Great Canadian Theatre Company, in Ottawa, Canada, on June 14, 1990, with the following cast:

Evelyn	Mary Burns
Diane	Mary Ellis
Carla	Heather Esdon
Alice	Catherine MacKenzie
Bonnie	Beverley Wolfe
Director	Linda Balduzzi
Set and costumes	Roy Robitschek
Lighting	Cedric Broten
Stage Manager	Nancy Oakley
Production Manager	Alexandra Lunney

Sisters in the Great Day Care War was commissioned and produced by Local 2204 of the Canadian Union of Public Employees (Day Care Workers) with funding provided by the Ontario Arts Council's Artist in the Workplace program. Special thanks to Dave Hagerman.

Author's Note
Sisters in the Great Day Care War is based on interviews with seven women involved in a 1981 strike at a number of privately-owned day care centres. Any resemblance to the truth is intentional—but resemblance to the truth should not be confused with fact. *Sisters* is concerned more with how people remember the strike than with the strike itself. Each of the characters is a composite. Details of events have been altered and some relevant events have been entirely omitted. Names, except for those of public figures, have been changed.

To have shared in both the public excitement and the private intensity of the strike was a great privilege. I am grateful to CUPE 2204 for making *Sisters* possible, and to the "sisters" for their courage and honesty.

—A.M., 11 June 1990

Characters
Alice: sarcastic, early 30s
Bonnie: sentimental, early 30s
Carla: conservative, early 30s
Diane: pregnant, a leader, early 30s
Evelyn: bossy, early 30s

Setting
A large room in the basement of a church or day care centre. Downstage, a video camera lying on its side in an open case. Chairs, stools, paint, paint brushes, etc., as required. A large rectangle of drawing paper covers most of the central stage area. The actors paint on the paper as the play proceeds. At the end of the play, the paper is raised, through a system of pulleys, to form a backdrop.

Diane and Alice enter.

DIANE: *(calls)* Evelyn. Evelyn.

ALICE: Maybe she's not here yet.

DIANE: She's supposed to be here. *(calls)* Evelyn. *(to Alice)* And the door wasn't locked.

ALICE: Right.

DIANE: There's paper all over the floor.

ALICE: Right.

DIANE: Video camera.

ALICE: Okay, she's here.

DIANE: *(walks across the paper and calls)* Ev—

> *(Evelyn enters from the other side, wearing overalls, carrying paint brushes, paints, overalls.)*

EVELYN: *(to Diane)* Don't walk on the paper.

> *(Diane gets off the paper.)*

ALICE: How are we going to paint?

DIANE: Did you get the keys alright?

EVELYN: Yeah. Thanks. Put these on.

> *(Evelyn throws each a pair of overalls, and exits. Alice and Diane put them on.)*

DIANE: They have different paint.

ALICE: So?

DIANE: I've been on leave four months and they get a different brand of paint.

ALICE: They should have checked with you first.

DIANE: It's just weird.

ALICE: That they didn't check with you.

DIANE: When I come back to work it'll be a different place.

ALICE: Cause they switched paint.

DIANE: There'll be new kids, maybe new staff.

ALICE: The last day care I worked in doesn't exist. You're falling apart cause they switched paint.

(Bonnie and Carla enter. Bonnie is carrying a case of beer.)

BONNIE: Hi, guys.

(much joyful screaming and shrieking)

DIANE: Bonnie.

BONNIE: Diane.

ALICE: Carla.

CARLA: Alice.

BONNIE: Where's the big movie director?

ALICE: Getting paint.

BONNIE: Why?

ALICE: To paint. On the floor. Remember?

BONNIE: Oh, yeah. Another one of Evelyn's bright ideas. How are you guys? *(to Diane)* How's Matthew?

DIANE: He has a cold.

BONNIE: How's the mother?

DIANE: I miss work.

ALICE: They got new paint.

BONNIE: You were the last one to have a baby.

DIANE: Yeah.

CARLA: *(to Diane)* Getting any sleep?

(Bonnie walks across the paper to the video camera and plays with it.)

DIANE: He sleeps right through.

ALICE: *(to Carla)* When are you moving?

BONNIE: *(to Diane)* Come on.

CARLA: *(to Alice)* On Monday.

DIANE: *(to Bonnie)* For three or four weeks now.

ALICE: *(to Carla)* Excited?

BONNIE: *(to Diane)* Want to trade?

CARLA: *(to Alice)* Yes, and sad—about leaving.

ALICE: *(to Carla)* Yeah.

CARLA: Even though, well, we hardly see each other.

ALICE: Moose Jaw.

CARLA: Bill says it's nice.

ALICE: It's like the end of the world.

DIANE: She's never been there.

ALICE: I've heard.

(Evelyn enters with more paint.)

EVELYN: *(to Bonnie)* Don't touch that.

BONNIE: Hi, Evelyn.

CARLA: Evelyn.

EVELYN: You can't touch it.

BONNIE: Hi, Evelyn.

ALICE: It's not a toy.

EVELYN: I borrowed it.

BONNIE: How are you?

EVELYN: You know how much that thing cost?

BONNIE: Twenty-nine, ninety-five.

EVELYN: If it gets broken, it's me that—

BONNIE: Okay.

EVELYN: I promised no one would use it but me.

ALICE: That's no fun.

DIANE: Alice.

ALICE: I thought we'd all get a turn.

BONNIE: It's not a toy. Hi, Evelyn.

CARLA: Hi.

EVELYN: Hi, guys.

(*Bonnie walks across the paper.*)

Don't walk on the paper.

ALICE: "How are we going to paint?" I ask again.

EVELYN: We're going to take off our shoes.

ALICE: I think you should go back to working in day care. If you could order kids around, you might be a normal person.

BONNIE: She was always like this.

EVELYN: What else do we need? Water.

DIANE: I'll get it.

CARLA: (*stands*) I'll get it. (*to Evelyn*) What are we going to paint?

EVELYN: Why are you asking me?

(*Carla exits.*)

BONNIE: You're in charge.

EVELYN: No, I'm not.

BONNIE: We thought you were.

EVELYN: I just thought it was important to do this before Carla moves away. I thought it was important to you guys, too.

DIANE: Some day care friends in Toronto—they're trying to organize a union—they said as soon as we do the video, to send it to them.

EVELYN: We always said we should write something down. I'm sorry if I ...

(Bonnie goes to take a beer.)

BONNIE: It's just like you to come up with a great idea, do all the work and then apologize.

EVELYN: It's up to all of us what we do. Okay?

ALICE: I like it better when you order us around.

BONNIE: Do we have a bottle opener?

ALICE: Aren't they twist-top?

BONNIE: No.

ALICE: Lucky I have my trusty penknife.

(Carla enters with water and empty yogurt containers. Alice takes out her penknife and passes it to Bonnie.)

BONNIE: Diane.

(Bonnie offers beer to the others.)

DIANE: No, thanks.

(Evelyn takes one. Alice doesn't. Bonnie takes one for herself. Carla steps onto the paper to mix paint.)

What do we paint?

BONNIE: Take off your shoes.

ALICE: *(at the same time)* Take off your shoes.

(They all take off their shoes. Alice and Carla take off their socks.)

EVELYN: *(to Bonnie and Carla)* Don't forget your overalls.

(Bonnie starts to put on her overalls. Carla takes hers and sits down. Alice, Evelyn and Bonnie start mixing paint.)

DIANE: What should we paint?

BONNIE: Some kind of day care scene.

DIANE: What kind?

BONNIE: Use your imagination.

DIANE: It's at home.

BONNIE: What do you tell your kids?

ALICE: "It doesn't matter ..."

DIANE: "Paint whatever you like."

ALICE: *(at the same time)* "Paint whatever you want."

EVELYN: How about a picket sign?

ALICE: I'm going to paint me with the kids in the park on a beautiful day with a blue sky.

DIANE: Can I help?

ALICE: You have to do your own.

DIANE: Who says?

ALICE: It's in the rules.

DIANE: Which rules?

ALICE: The new ones they made since you've been on maternity leave.

EVELYN: How about we just paint quietly and we talk about—

ALICE: We can't be quiet and talk at the same time.

EVELYN: Alice, why don't you tell everyone how you started working in day care?

ALICE: Is that a suggestion?

DIANE: She doesn't take suggestions.

BONNIE: Don't you hate it when people say "everyone" when they mean "me" or "us"?

ALICE: It's a disease.

EVELYN: Carla, why don't you start?

ALICE: No. I'll start. My great grandparents on my mother's side first came to this country—

EVELYN: Alice.

ALICE: Should I talk into the camera?

(Alice lies down to face the camera.)

It all started—

BONNIE: You're cut off. No more beer.

ALICE: *(stands)* I haven't had any yet. *(to Carla)* Why are you just sitting there?

CARLA: I'm thinking.

ALICE: Ms Picasso is thinking about what to paint. Okay. The first day care I worked in—

(Carla puts on her overalls and joins them.)

DIANE: Talk about being in the Navy.

ALICE: Why?

BONNIE: You were in the Navy?

ALICE: In the Navy Reserve. After high school.

BONNIE: I didn't know that.

ALICE: Yes you did.

BONNIE: I did not.

ALICE: I told you about—

BONNIE: You never told me.

ALICE: Well, I was. I had a wonderful time. A friend of mine talked me into going and we learned how to—

DIANE: Tie knots.

ALICE: ... tie knots. Shoot guns. Climb ropes.

BONNIE: Did you really?

DIANE: That's where she got her training for day care.

243

BONNIE: Did you have to do push-ups and stuff?

ALICE: Every day.

BONNIE: Oh God.

ALICE: I wore Navy boots. Fatigues. It's down at Dow's Lake at the barracks. I worked there all summer and then part time. Then I went to Algonquin College. I didn't have a clue what I wanted. Someone said, "Take this course." I took this course and I thought, "Let me out of this course."

CARLA: Yeah, me too.

ALICE: You too, what?

CARLA: I didn't like ECE either.

EVELYN: What's ECE?

CARLA: What?

EVELYN: What's ECE?

CARLA: Poor Evelyn's mind is going.

BONNIE: Gone.

EVELYN: You can't say "ECE." Some people when they watch the video aren't going to know what "ECE" is.

CARLA: The camera isn't on.

EVELYN: We should get in the habit.

ALICE: I kept working in the Navy Reserve part time and then I did some supply work for the Region. And then I got called in for an interview at Valley. I got the job and I just loved it.

BONNIE: When I was young I wanted to live in the country. I wanted to have a horse. I grew up in the West End—

CARLA: We had cousins on my dad's side, they're all farmers and they had horses, we'd go out to the farm and—

BONNIE: I had an imaginary horse.

DIANE: I always wanted a horse.

BONNIE: Me, too.

DIANE: All girls want horses.

ALICE: Not me.

CARLA: I did.

ALICE: I never wanted one.

CARLA: You probably did. You just forgot.

DIANE: *(to Evelyn)* Did you want a horse?

EVELYN: Yes.

DIANE: *(to Alice)* See?

ALICE: See what?

DIANE: Evelyn wanted a horse.

ALICE: If I wanted a horse, I would remember.

BONNIE: You probably wanted a boat.

CARLA: Yeah. You wanted a boat.

ALICE: I wanted a baby.

BONNIE: When I was ten, I wanted to be a housewife. Lots of kids. Rich husband.

CARLA: I could go for the rich husband.

ALICE: I wanted a baby, but the husbands—at that point, I didn't know there was a connection.

BONNIE: Is there?

ALICE: I always thought when I was a kid that I'd be like my mother. That I'd have kids and I'd stay at home and look after them.

DIANE: And you do.

CARLA: Well—

ALICE: And now that's what I do.

BONNIE: You're different than your mother.

CARLA: There's nothing wrong with what your mother did.

ALICE: I'm not saying there is. It's just something I feel I have to defend because a lot of people don't think I should be doing it.

BONNIE: I feel guilty going out to work, like I should be staying home with my kids. You get it for staying home. I get it for going out to work.

ALICE: Like they say, "What do you do?" "Oh. Are you brain dead?" But, I guess deep down I always thought that's what I'd end up doing and I think that's why I didn't worry about finding a job where I would make a lot of money.

BONNIE: I had a B.A. in history from Carleton and I had no idea what I wanted to do. My sister was a supervisor at a day care, I started doing substitute teaching and then I was offered a job. I never had any other job. I worked at the day care until after the strike and then I went to Teachers' College because I thought I needed to make more money and then I went back to day care again. I quit after the strike because I—

ALICE: You wanted another going-away present.

BONNIE: I didn't get one.

(pause)

ALICE: Ev?

EVELYN: What?

ALICE: How did you start?

EVELYN: Oh. I had no idea what I wanted to do. For some reason I studied psychology. I did "peer counselling" at the Women's Centre. When I think about it now, I can't believe I had the nerve to give anyone advice, abortion counselling, all that—I was such a mess. I graduated and—a B.A. in psychology was useless. Nobody ever told me in university I wouldn't be able to get a job.

CARLA: At least you took child psychology.

EVELYN: I got a job in Ogilvy's cafeteria, as assistant manager to this barracuda woman. They were Portuguese working there and they'd be teaching me Portuguese words. Well, the barracuda says, "You can't be friends with people you are supposed to supervise." I almost had a nervous breakdown getting out of there. I have memories of watching soaps and watching soaps every day. My U.I.C. ran out, I was lost. I was on tranquillizers. I didn't think I could do anything. I looked in the paper and I saw, well, day care looked okay, working with kids looked okay.

DIANE: I didn't know what I wanted to do after high school either. Most of my friends automatically went to university and I didn't have the money. I thought, "What's the point of getting into debt if I don't know what I want to do?" So I worked for a year. As a store clerk.

ALICE: I did that.

DIANE: Zeller's?

ALICE: No.

DIANE: I worked in the toy department.

CARLA: I was a telephone operator.

DIANE: I worked for the Unemployment Insurance. And in a nursing home.

CARLA: I worked at Fairweather's. I got fired cause I didn't dress well enough.

ALL: You?

ALICE: I got fired from the Bayshore Hotel and then I kind of fell into day care.

DIANE: We all did.

BONNIE: I did.

DIANE: When I started out, I didn't have any idea of the way day care worked or how it was funded or anything. When we worked at Valley, Irene told us, "You have to lobby for funding." We wrote letters, I got my friends and my parents to write letters, and by the time the strike happened, I felt like I knew what day care was.

CARLA: Originally, I applied for the Child Care Worker Program— working with kids with severe behavior problems—but I was too young. I was only 17. I got accepted into ECE—

ALICE: Early Childhood Education.

BONNIE: *(at the same time)* Early Childhood Education.

CARLA: My guidance counsellor in high school said: "Your marks aren't good enough, you'll never get accepted." I did my first practice teaching at Valley and that was '78-'79.

DIANE: I always thought you were older than me.

ALICE: She was more mature.

CARLA: I remember feeling there were way too many people in the class and I felt—

DIANE: What year did we start at Valley?

BONNIE: '77?

CARLA: I started in '78.

ALICE: I finished high school in '74, so I started at Valley in '78.

DIANE: I started in '77, you had to be there in '76.

ALICE: So I finished high school in '73?

DIANE: I don't know.

ALICE: In grade eight I was fourteen and that was the year we moved from—so I started high school in—

EVELYN: Who cares?

ALICE: '74. I finished high school in '74.

DIANE: I grew up in a public housing project and I knew my mom was a single parent so I was a bit more keyed into what was going on I think than other kids my age. I wanted to work in something that was kind of humanitarian. I wanted to work with children or old people.

ALICE: I wanted to help people.

EVELYN: That's what I wanted.

BONNIE: And children was a nice way to do it. But when I got into college there was this "children are flowers" kind of thing.

ALICE: Some are weeds.

BONNIE: "They're flowers reaching for the sun." I remember this woman made purple paint and they went, "We only use blue and red and yellow."

ALICE: "Never, never use black."

BONNIE: "We don't introduce purple, it's too traumatic for the children," and I went, "This is very weird."

CARLA: Remember the teachers always saying, "Oh, Valley, that's a profit centre," and I thought, "This place is great." It was purpose-built, it was actually built to be a day care, not a church basement or something.

ALICE: I remember saying to myself, "Well, the owners aren't making any money, Irene isn't making a profit."

DIANE: We believed that for years.

ALICE: I think the teachers were warning us.

CARLA: But they never explained why profit day care was so bad. It was like, "Don't go out in the dark. Men are waiting in the bushes. Wink-wink, nod-nod." But they never'd say what these men were waiting for. There was no, "What does that mean, profit day care?"

ALICE: I didn't know what they were talking about.

CARLA: Then I started saying it, too. "It's a profit day care."

ALICE: Our salaries at that time were average and our benefits were probably better than most places.

BONNIE: In the Regional centre where I work now, we still don't have the equipment we had then at Valley.

DIANE: I remember doing a placement in a co-op day care, they had nothing. It was like a-hundred-and-one ways to use egg cartons. And parents who worked in the government brought office supplies that they "borrowed."

ALICE: Remember you told us about Dorothy Anne, where she would take—

DIANE: She was the administrator in a co-operative day care and she told stories about going down to the baby room and she'd pick whichever kid looked most pathetic that day. She'd hold this kid on her lap while she talked to the bank manager and she'd say, "We really need a loan."

BONNIE: Then the kid threw up.

ALICE: I remember thinking, "Valley's pretty good. Irene knows what she's doing."

EVELYN: Irene was the owner of Valley Day Care.

ALICE: Right.

DIANE: Irene was good. If she'd been on our side—

CARLA: I felt proud to work there.

ALICE: Me, too.

CARLA: It was sort of more—I hate this word—professional. There were things we were doing that weren't happening yet in the co-ops, like we did themes and programming.

DIANE: We spent a lot of time working out programs.

ALICE: A lot of overtime.

BONNIE: Free overtime.

ALICE: And we got politically involved. Laura was involved in the O-D-C—

BONNIE: O-C-D.

ALICE: O-D-C-D-A.

BONNIE: O-C-D-C-A.

ALICE: Ottawa-Carleton Day Care Organization.

BONNIE: "A."

ALICE: Association.

EVELYN: Who's Laura?

CARLA: Where's Laura?

DIANE: In Vancouver, I think.

ALICE: Victoria.

EVELYN: Who's Laura?

CARLA: Where's Laura?

ALICE: Victoria.

DIANE: She left.

BONNIE: Right in the middle of everything.

DIANE: She split.

EVELYN: Who was Laura?

ALICE: She was our supervisor.

EVELYN: Thank you.

BONNIE: And we were her proteges.

ALICE: And she just took off, right in the middle—

EVELYN: That was later.

ALICE: I remember going into her office and—

EVELYN: Let's go in order. What happened next?

CARLA: Look at this. *(her drawing)*

BONNIE: What is it?

ALICE: It doesn't have to be anything.

BONNIE: What does it mean?

EVELYN: Where were we?

ALICE: We were—well, Laura got us to go to Day Care Association meetings. We learned about funding and she encouraged us to unionize.

DIANE: And we all went, "Unions. Ugh."

CARLA: Oh, God. "Unions make you do things."

ALICE: The ten labour myths. "Unions force you to go on strike. Unions force you—"

CARLA: "Unions make you change your workplace."

BONNIE: Unions make you wear clean underwear.

ALICE: That was your mother.

DIANE: And "Should we even have higher salaries?" Because if we did parents wouldn't be able to pay the fees.

CARLA: God.

DIANE: Someone said to me, "You are subsidizing day care by accepting low wages." A light went on. "Right. We're responsible for looking after the kids, but if the parents can't afford it, that's the government's job."

ALICE: I used to think we were stealing money from the parents if we asked for higher salaries.

CARLA: I think when people—women—were making career choices, the last thing we looked at was money. Because in the back of our minds was—we were looking for something to do that's going to be fun until we get married.

ALICE: I felt that way.

BONNIE: Oh yeah.

EVELYN: I did.

BONNIE: You did?

EVELYN: Yes.

ALICE: I'm not ever letting my daughter feel that way. Most women are going to work, and my daughter's going to be prepared.

CARLA: People look at things like Early Childhood Education and they say, "I don't want to make less than a zoo keeper."

ALICE: What does a zoo keeper make?

BONNIE: But I loved it. I thought when I got married, I'd open this cute little day care in my house.

CARLA: When I went for the first day of ECE—

ALICE: Early Childhood Education.

BONNIE: *(at the same time)* Early Childhood Education.

CARLA: The teacher went to the blackboard and put the salaries up. She said, "This is what you are going to be making. If you're in this for the money, you might as well leave now." Some people got up and left.

DIANE: We made 6K when we started.

CARLA: It was possible to live a meagre existence.

ALICE: Especially if you planned to get married.

BONNIE: I said I wasn't going to get married until I was 25. I got married when I was 21.

ALICE: I was 25.

BONNIE: *(to Alice)* You don't meet many eligible men in day care.

ALICE: In day care you meet fathers.

EVELYN: In Early Childhood Education, too, you don't meet many men.

ALICE: Diane was telling me about student teachers she's had recently. They don't say to the children "poo" and "pee."

DIANE: You have to say "urinate" and "bowel movement."

ALICE: So they go up to this little two-year-old and say, "Do you need to urinate?" The kid goes, "I don't think so." Then they pee their pants.

BONNIE: And they can't say "don't."

ALICE: You can't use the word "don't" and you can't use the word "no" so if the kid's running inside you say: "We use our walking legs here."

BONNIE: And the kid goes and looks for them.

DIANE: I tell student teachers: "That's what you learn in school, this is real life. If two kids are beating each other up you can't take the time to figure out how to stop them without saying 'don't.' You stop it."

BONNIE: Student teachers have to write down how many times they hear us say "don't" and "stop" and then they discuss it in class.

CARLA: It's confusing for them.

DIANE: Sometimes I see this look of excitement on their faces like, "I'm in a day care and it's real and that teacher's getting paid," and it's the same feeling I had when I was practice teaching.

BONNIE: I remember that feeling.

DIANE: I think teaching has improved because now they see day care as a political thing.

EVELYN: Not in the course though. It's not part of the course.

DIANE: Well, I've been invited to speak about the union.

EVELYN: It's still negative. They'll go, "So this is a unionized centre."

BONNIE: Or "a co-op."

ALICE: "A co-op." Oh yeah. "A co-op." It's like doodoo.

EVELYN: "A co-op."

ALICE: When I was working for the Region, we were doing a job description of what we did and I said, "Help children learn to resolve conflict," and everyone looked at me, like, "What are you talking about?" I said, "Kids fight and you help them resolve conflict." They didn't write that down. It was not going to go on paper that kids fight in day care.

DIANE: Kids fight.

BONNIE: And they throw up on your shoes and they poop their pants and they miss the toilet. The first day of the course or the first week or something the question was put on the board, "What are children to you?" One woman stood up and went, "A child is a flower growing and bending in the wind," and I went, "Excuse me, is this the horticulture class?"

CARLA: I remember this film they showed about how education can take place without coercion and everyone was saying how wonderful this was and I said, "It's garbage," and they said, "Well, why," and I said, "Okay, six kids are sitting in a circle, and one boy's showing pictures from a book. Those other kids won't just sit there. They want to show the book. There's going to be a problem." So they said, "What would you do?" "Well, I would say, 'If you can sit nicely while he's having a turn, you'll be able to have one, too, but if you can't then you won't have a turn,'" and they said, "What's wrong with that?" I said, "It's coercion. We're not going to beat them black and blue, but it's still coercion."

ALICE: It's been called "knowing the consequences," which is a nicer way of putting it, but it's still—

BONNIE: Yeah. Coercion.

CARLA: You can have all the right answers from the book but some people just don't have the knack.

ALICE: It's something you have.

CARLA: If you don't have this thing inside you, all the courses in the world won't do any good.

BONNIE: It's like that, "What's wrong with this child because they use black paint?"

CARLA: Kids love to use black paint and purple paint.

BONNIE: It shows up.

DIANE: Every student I've ever talked to said, "There needs to be more practical work."

BONNIE: Students are told they have to wear skirts.

ALICE: Still?

BONNIE: They come in for their practice teaching in skirts.

CARLA: You wear skirts, you start saying to the kids, "Don't touch me, don't come near me with the purple paint."

ALICE: I once wore a pair of brand-new, baby blue cords. I got puke all over them.

DIANE: In the co-op day care where I work, I call parents by their first names. At Valley—

ALICE: It was always Mrs so and so or Mr so—

EVELYN: I didn't call them anything. It was like after I got married, my in-laws wanted me to call them "mom" and "dad" and I couldn't. So I never called them anything.

ALICE: "Hey, you."

BONNIE: My first practice teaching was at a Catholic school—she made the children call me "Miss Bonnie." I thought I was on Romper Room.

ALICE: We should have studied that in ECE. The philosophy of name calling.

DIANE: We studied philosophy of education.

CARLA: Piaget. Montessori.

ALICE: But not name calling.

DIANE: There was drama and children's art and music and—

CARLA: Art and art and art and—

ALICE: Not mutual biting.

BONNIE: Mutual biting. I'd pull the kids down off the ceiling and I'd go through there like the wrath of God. "You, on a chair. You, on a chair. You, into the bathroom." Lynn—remember Lynn?—she'd just sit there. The supervisor goes, "Lynn has such a wonderful way with children. She never raises her voice."

ALICE: "So good with the little ones. She never—"

BONNIE: There was a bench this long in our room and we had sixteen two-year-olds. Every day Lynn would say to them, "As soon as your shoes are on you can sit on the bench," and every day they were fighting and pushing and I'd go, "Lynn, that bench doesn't hold sixteen kids." And every day she'd say, "You're right."

EVELYN: There were the Lynn types who knew she didn't have it but wasn't sure what she didn't have. Then there was the Jody type—

ALICE: Jody. God.

EVELYN: She didn't have a clue what was doing but she thought she was great.

DIANE: There was a substitute teacher and I said, "The minute I leave six heads are going to pop up and say, 'Can I go to the bathroom?' Tell them, 'No,' cause they've all gone." I come back ten minutes later and half the kids are in the bathroom.

CARLA: We were like that at the beginning.

ALICE: But we learned. Some people never learn.

BONNIE: We were good teachers.

EVELYN: We were.

BONNIE: We were strict teachers, we set limits and expectations. Some people thought they were good teachers because they let the kids have their way but if the kid had a choice to run to Lynn for a hug or me, they'd come to me.

EVELYN: We respected the kids.

ALICE: We did.

EVELYN: Kids are smart.

DIANE: Like they know how to use Velcro.

ALICE: Oh, God. Velcro.

BONNIE: Chitch, chitch, chitch, that's all you hear all day. Reading a story and the kids are sitting there, chitch, chitch—

DIANE: We thought our lives'd be easier when Velcro came in.

EVELYN: Technological change.

ALICE: Carla put up a poster telling parents to "Please buy shoes—"

CARLA: "Shoes with laces."

ALICE: "No Velcro."

DIANE: We sewed Velcro onto sheets so they wouldn't fall off the cots. We thought we finally had the perfect sheet and—

BONNIE: The kids are supposed to be asleep and all you hear is chitch, chitch, chitch—

CARLA: But that was part of it. We had fun but—

ALICE: Lots of fun.

CARLA: ... we took it seriously. We learned things and we cared—I mean, we were all good with children and we worked hard.

DIANE: And we knew that day care was important. Not just working with kids, but—

EVELYN: I started taking day care seriously when Laura—

ALICE: Our supervisor.

EVELYN: Laura decided that we should have a counsellor come talk to the parents about parenting—one of the staff had to be there. We sat around, eight women, talking about our lives and these women trashed men from beginning to end. "Well, I got married and as soon as I had the kid, the bum took off." Or, "I worked in his store fifteen hours a day, I didn't get a dime, and then he just hit me one too many times and I walked out." These women were ordinary parents, they were really struggling and they had to make ends meet with a kid or three kids, mostly on their own. Day care was the best thing in their lives. It got them through the day. It was there for them. Then, if they got a slightly better job, they'd lose their subsidy, so they'd lose their space. I began to understand what the waiting lists meant—these parents that would come in the office and cry, desperate to get a space. People told horror stories about babysitting, like they came to pick up their child early to find the diaper soaked, with the babysitter drinking beer, watching

TV. And these people had no choice. They could quit their job and they'd lose their apartment.

DIANE: It was that kind of stuff that started me thinking there should be more day care.

EVELYN: Which is why we got involved in the union.

ALICE: Not in the union at first. The—

DIANE: The OCDCA.

EVELYN: Right.

ALICE: Ottawa-Carleton Day Care Association.

BONNIE: We didn't get involved to get more money. We got—

CARLA: It was to get more day care.

EVELYN: In those days we didn't think about the money.

BONNIE: I didn't.

CARLA: Later we came to think of day care as a place to work in a more serious—

ALICE: Diane made us think that way.

CARLA: She twisted our arm.

DIANE: I went through that too you guys.

ALICE: You went through it first.

DIANE: Well, Laura—

ALICE: Laura, too.

BONNIE: Because, well Laura—

EVELYN: Our supervisor.

BONNIE: We had meetings and she asked us, "What do you think?" and, "What are we going to do?" She made us take our jobs seriously.

CARLA: We really got into if it was relevant to the kids. It kept you changing program materials.

DIANE: And fine-tuning.

CARLA: Like for Halloween, finding the right shade of orange milk shake.

BONNIE: I had only been working a week, I remember walking in and going, "Jesus Christ, they're yelling at one another, 'You use ketchup.'"

CARLA: Oh, God.

DIANE: Alice and I went to Europe, we were away for three weeks, and when we came back the ketchup war was on.

ALICE: Should the kids be allowed to have ketchup on macaroni, on fish, on peas, or on eggs, or—?

CARLA: Some kids put it over their whole lunch.

BONNIE: Some people felt it was okay on meat but not potatoes. Some people thought it could go on anything. Evelyn thought it shouldn't be allowed, ever.

DIANE: We came back from Europe, we're in culture shock, and people are going, "Where do you stand on the ketchup question?"

ALICE: And we're going, "What?"

BONNIE: We decided they could squirt a bit on their plate and that's what my kids still do.

ALICE: A little pool.

BONNIE: A little pool.

EVELYN: A reasonable size pool.

BONNIE: And this is the general practice and the law from one end of the country to the other. They teach it to you now in Early Childhood Education.

ALICE: Ketchup 101. Some have lost their lives over it.

CARLA: Then there's the mustard and relish question.

BONNIE: No.

DIANE: Let's not get into that.

EVELYN: Let's keep going. The union.

ALICE: Well, I was against the union at first—

CARLA: We all were.

ALICE: And then it was, "Okay, I'll unionize, but don't ever ask me to go on strike." It took a lot to get me angry and to make me aware of what it was really like. But I liked my job and I admired Laura.

DIANE: Oh, I did, too.

CARLA: We all did.

EVELYN: She had a company car.

ALICE: But she let us drive it. We got to do field trips.

CARLA: And Laura was fair.

BONNIE: Laura said to me one time, "I'm going to get you a raise because you have a B.A.," and I went, "I shouldn't get a raise because I don't have ECE." And she went, "You should be making more."

EVELYN: She was reasonable.

ALICE: She was really reasonable and money didn't mean much then.

DIANE: I was satisfied.

CARLA: I was already married and we could have lived on my husband's salary so I didn't depend on it to survive.

ALICE: I did. But I survived.

EVELYN: The only thing I really regretted was that I remember thinking, "I will never own a car."

BONNIE: Some things were just out of your realm.

ALICE: So you didn't think about it.

BONNIE: I didn't worry about being sixty-three years old and making seven thousand—

EVELYN: I went to a benefit dance at Glebe Day Care and they had that woman working there. She was going to retire.

BONNIE: Oh right.

EVELYN: I thought, "Someone's going to retire from day care."

BONNIE: It was mind boggling that someone over thirty was actually working in day care.

ALICE: Diane and I took a three-week vacation to Europe just after the first year we worked there.

DIANE: It was part of that "alligator syndrome." You grow according to the size your bathtub is.

BONNIE: I went to Florida but I didn't have a stick of new furniture in my house.

ALICE: I didn't buy anything. I went on trips.

BONNIE: Early given. That's how I decorated my house. Early given.

EVELYN: My roommate was working for Bell Canada. She got overtime. And if she had to work late, she'd get taxi fare, when she worked on a holiday she got double-time or time-and-a-half—standard employment things that we weren't getting.

BONNIE: I remember talking to a—

ALICE: *(at the same time)* I remember thinking—

BONNIE: ... friend that worked in a bank—he made a lot more money than me. He said what he did was really important because he could make a mistake and lose thousands of dollars and I said to him, "Big deal. I could make a mistake and someone's child would be dead."

DIANE: The year after we got married, Stephen was a student at Ottawa U. So I was supporting two people.

ALICE: And you ate eggs. She'd come into work and say, "We had eggs for supper again."

DIANE: But it never occurred to me that it was my job's fault. It was just, "This is what day care pays."

EVELYN: You're a professional and you accept this because you're doing important work.

BONNIE: Like important work shouldn't be paid well.

ALICE: Like martyrs.

DIANE: Like you can't have job satisfaction and good salaries.

ALICE: How much did Joan of Arc make?

DIANE: The things is, we were really committed to day care so instead of going somewhere else to make more money, we said, "No, we want to stay here and we want to make more money here."

BONNIE: And we thought if the pay was so bad then good people wouldn't stay in day care and the quality would suffer.

DIANE: People say to me, "But you must love working with children." Well yeah, I do, but on the other hand, I should be able to afford a car. I mean I'm making a decent salary now.

ALICE: It's not decent.

DIANE: I guess it's not.

ALICE: Not when you look at what other people make. It's only decent compared to what we used to make.

DIANE: Yeah. That's true. That's true.

EVELYN: Well, what's a decent salary?

DIANE: I guess I'd be happy with what I make if I didn't know there were all these assholes making sixty, a hundred, a hundred and fifty thousand.

ALICE: I don't see why day care teachers should make less than school teachers.

EVELYN: Well, maybe school teachers are making too much.

BONNIE: You never hear that.

EVELYN: A lot of people make too much money.

ALICE: Oh, yeah.

DIANE: This is for sure.

ALICE: But I don't think school teachers necessarily do.

CARLA: You'd never say, "They make too much." I go, "They're working hard and I'm working hard so we should make the same."

EVELYN: But I don't think—we can't all in this country make sixty thousand a year.

DIANE: Well, that's the other thing.

EVELYN: For you to make more, someone else is going to have to make less.

CARLA: But then who decides what job gets what?

ALICE: Men.

DIANE: Remember that council meeting where that alderman said, "If these women want to make more they should go out and get real jobs."

ALICE: There was that task force where we were writing a description of what a teacher in day care does, and one guy just kept going, "I can't believe you do all this."

EVELYN: Wasn't he that guy that said, "Do you walk—?"

ALICE: Yeah, "Do you walk on water, too?"

BONNIE: I was practice teaching in a school and this seven-year-old kid had an accident in his pants and the teacher said, "Well, you're going home." I remember thinking, "Teachers in schools only teach," but in day care we taught, we cared, and we mothered.

CARLA: When I think about that time now, I don't know how we did it. There was so much work, and meetings every—

ALICE: Day care meetings, the Day Care Association meetings, strike meetings ...

CARLA: I saw you guys more than I saw my husband.

DIANE: How many times did we all go to work on three hours sleep?

ALICE: Oh, yeah.

BONNIE: Hangovers and—

ALICE: We had a good time.

DIANE: The co-op where I work now is really good. But I'll never have those same relationships that we did.

CARLA: Even though, well we don't see each other that much these days.

DIANE: Just at baby showers.

BONNIE: Boring things like baby showers were fun. Wedding showers were fun.

ALICE: Not mine.

BONNIE: Except for yours.

EVELYN: But we used to laugh. It's been six years since I worked in day care and coming in here today and looking around, seeing the toys and supplies, and the little chairs and tables—and painting like this—

ALICE: And no kids. That's the only problem with day care is the kids—

BONNIE: We can't put that in the video.

EVELYN: It was so much fun to go to work and lunch hour would come and I'd be exhausted and we'd just kill ourselves laughing. I think we laughed all the time.

CARLA: Not all the time. We weren't a lot of big fools or anything.

BONNIE: We laughed all the time. We'd hit one word and we'd—

ALICE: Like you *(Diane)* saying people shouldn't come to Canada and change their children's names.

DIANE: Those Vietnamese kids in the day care with names like Christopher and Melissa.

ALICE: Diane said they shouldn't change their names because it's their cultural identity. I had this boyfriend and he said when he came he changed his name and Diane said—

DIANE: "What was your name before?" And he says—

ALICE: He says, "Horst."

DIANE: I started—

ALICE: Diane bursts out laughing. She says, "Good idea that—"

DIANE: "Good idea, Howard."

ALICE: "Good thing you changed your name."

EVELYN: I used to get asked, "Don't you have any other friends?"

BONNIE: "Isn't there anything else to your life?

EVELYN: And trying to respect what we did. People would say, "Oh, you babysit," and I'd go, "No."

BONNIE: You had to explain yourself a lot.

CARLA: Diane called us "day care workers." I thought I had to call myself a "day care teacher" to make what I was doing sound important.

ALICE: People thought that we had a preoccupation with what we did. Like at parties when we'd all congregate together.

CARLA: I went to a party where I was the only woman who wasn't a nurse. Nobody talked to me.

BONNIE: We went to a lot of day care functions.

EVELYN: Benefits at the Glebe.

ALICE: Wedding showers. Baby showers.

CARLA: Leaving day care parties.

ALICE: Coming back parties.

BONNIE: I really liked everything I was doing.

ALICE: Irene used to tick us off.

EVELYN: Who's Irene?

ALICE: The owner. Every once in a while she'd come in to say something stupid.

CARLA: Or be condescending.

ALICE: We'd sort of go, "Pfff."

CARLA: She came in one day and said, "Come here, little girl. I'll help you with your coat." The kid goes, "No. I don't want you," and Irene went, "Fine. Do it yourself," and stomped out of the room. That was Irene's contact with the kids.

ALICE: We could handle her.

DIANE: There were some weird things, like—

EVELYN: We were told never to discuss with anyone what we were making.

ALICE: But we did.

DIANE: And there were some really arbitrary things, like—

CARLA: The girl who was—she didn't have ECE or anything, and she was making more than any of us.

BONNIE: And they wouldn't say if a job was coming up. If you heard there was going to be an opening for like a supervisor, you'd have to go and say you were interested.

ALICE: And they'd say, "We have another relative." I remember thinking that having a union would at least mean there'd have to be a system.

DIANE: Sick leave.

ALICE: Oh boy, if you were sick, you were—

DIANE: One time I was in the hospital for a week and I got told in evaluation that I had bad attendance.

ALICE: You couldn't be sick.

BONNIE: They wanted you to say, "I'm planning to be sick in a week, is that okay?"

ALICE: Irene thought it was unreasonable to be sick.

DIANE: And that if you said you were sick, you were lying.

CARLA: We got Christmas bonuses.

BONNIE: We got angora mittens one year.

ALICE: Little pins with Valley Day Care.

CARLA: We had four weeks holiday.

BONNIE: Two weeks and then three weeks.

CARLA: Four weeks.

BONNIE: It was the union that got us four weeks.

CARLA: I had four weeks.

BONNIE: Oh, wait one minute ...

CARLA: I had four weeks the first day I walked through the door.

BONNIE: It was three weeks your first year—you're right. It was four weeks in your second year.

EVELYN: Our benefits were as good as anywhere else.

BONNIE: We got half OHIP, right?

EVELYN: And long-term drug benefits.

CARLA: We used to go in for Sunday clean-up and she'd order pizza.

ALICE: And Saturday meetings for program evaluation.

BONNIE: Once a year. Clean-up twice a year, staff meetings—

ALICE: Once a month at least.

BONNIE: You'd work until six and then have a four-hour staff meeting.

ALICE: And program planning on our lunch hours.

BONNIE: All of which was unpaid.

CARLA: I remember thinking it was unprofessional to expect to be paid for meetings.

DIANE: You gave all this time, then you'd phone in sick, they'd think you were lying.

BONNIE: So we started going to the OCDCA.

ALICE: Ottawa-Carleton—

DIANE: Well, first, Laura—our supervisor—was going. She asked if we were interested and I started going with her and then you (Alice) started. There were people from the co-ops, and—

ALICE: You could tell where they worked by how they dressed. From the co-ops, they had long hair and granny glasses. From the community-run centers, in their cashmere sweaters and pearls. And from the private day cares, in their ...

BONNIE: Tacky clothes.

CARLA: You mean us?

BONNIE: Irene.

ALICE: And remember the staff?

BONNIE: Which staff?

ALICE: Of the Day Care Association—those intellectual outside agitators from the School of Social Work. They'd get in yelling matches.

DIANE: Irene was actually very smart. The Region would say to day cares, "You're getting a four percent increase," and Irene'd say, "I need ten percent, cover my ass or I'm out of business."

BONNIE: That's when we found out Valley got more money than anyone else.

ALICE: We started asking questions and Laura was really keen to have us involved.

CARLA: Irene was too. They froze the day care budget—and Irene said, "We all have to fight this together," and we went, "Yes, we all do."

BONNIE: Irene was involved and not just for the money.

EVELYN: Well ...

BONNIE: I think so.

EVELYN: She didn't care about kids and she didn't care about day care.

BONNIE: I don't know. I think—

EVELYN: She liked money and she liked power.

BONNIE: I'm not saying she didn't. I'm just saying she also got her teeth into—

EVELYN: She was paying a housekeeper on day care salaries.

BONNIE: I'm just saying that—

ALICE: She was buying her groceries through the—

BONNIE: She was also interested in day care.

EVELYN: Any effort she made was self-serving.

BONNIE: Oh, yeah. I'm not saying that it wasn't.

EVELYN: But at that point the interest of day care and her own interests were the same.

BONNIE: Oh, yeah.

DIANE: I knew Irene for a long time. Her own family shit on her. They thought she was pushy and overbearing and she wanted to show the world. Irene was paying her sister a salary that no one else was making in day care and her sister'd come in and say, "Don't tell anyone I'm Irene's sister."

ALICE: Irene came back one time from haggling budgets. She said, "You know what they called me? An 'entrepreneur.'" I had to look it up in the dictionary.

DIANE: It pleased her to be called that.

ALICE: She thought it was great.

CARLA: There was that big meeting at City Hall and Irene drove up in her Buick Riviera and everyone thought that—

ALICE: We were all trying to look poor.

CARLA: Poor, but neat.

BONNIE: She was so tacky.

ALICE: She was really tacky.

EVELYN: She always looked like such a mess at the parents meetings. Her hair all over the place, her slip hanging way down and she'd yell at the parents.

CARLA: She had a bad dye job.

BONNIE: She always had roots.

DIANE: It shocks me to think that she was only thirty or thirty-one then.

CARLA: She could wash her hair and an hour later it was greasy.

BONNIE: The same age as us now.

ALICE: That is shocking.

BONNIE: But at the beginning she didn't get in the way. We didn't join the union because of her.

ALICE: It was Laura—

DIANE: The supervisor.

BONNIE: *(at the same time)* Our supervisor.

ALICE: ... that convinced us.

BONNIE: Laura said, "Workers in unions get decent wages and workers who don't have unions don't."

EVELYN: Regional day care workers were already unionized.

ALICE: And we knew they had better pay.

CARLA: Thirty percent more.

ALICE: At least thirty percent more.

EVELYN: And someone on City Council said we'd be more effective if day cares could say to the Region, "Our employees are unionized and they're demanding higher salaries ..."

ALICE: But we all thought unions made you do things.

DIANE: Like the Postal Workers. We all said to each other, "The union forces the Postal Workers to strike."

ALICE: And, "We have a job that's too important and—"

DIANE: "We could never walk out on the kids and the parents."

ALICE: When I started going to the meetings, it was like, "I'm going to be there so that they can't make me do something I don't want to do."

EVELYN: I said I'd never ever strike.

CARLA: We all said that.

DIANE: We even talked about, "Should we have the right to strike?" because nobody ever thought there could be one.

ALICE: And then we had to decide, "Which union?"

DIANE: There was SORWUC—

BONNIE: It was that sort of feminist union from—

EVELYN: They said we were welcome to join.

DIANE: They couldn't really help because they had very little money.

BONNIE: They were based in the west.

DIANE: And we went to CUPE and—

ALICE: Canadian Union of Public Employees.

DIANE: They sent that old guy to talk to us, that great big guy. We were sitting in tiny, little day care chairs and he's telling us, "I was in the coal mines in Cape Breton and we went on strike and we fought the bosses and the army was sent in," and we're—half of us are like, "Wow," and the other half are going, "Oh, my God." He's going on about, "We'll be in the OFL and the CLC and the CLC's linked to the NDP."

ALICE: And the A-B-C, R-N-A and X-Y-P-L-N-F—

DIANE: And we're going, "What does CLC stand for?" and "Do we have to be in the NDP?" and, "What's a collective agreement?"

ALICE: Remember Phil?

DIANE: He was a parent in a co-op centre—

EVELYN: And he knew his way around unions.

ALICE: He worked for CUPE.

EVELYN: He's the one who said we should join CUPE but we should have our own Local—

ALICE: Twenty-two-o-four.

EVELYN: Just for day care workers.

DIANE: Phil understood that we weren't just interested in the money, that we wanted to help day care and actually help our employer.

CARLA: It wasn't against Irene. It didn't have a damn thing to do with Irene.

DIANE: Then.

CARLA: We thought unionizing would help her.

BONNIE: Were we surprised when she got mad at us. "You mean, you don't like this?"

ALICE: None of us were radical about it.

CARLA: We didn't have any reason to be.

ALICE: Then we got that letter.

EVELYN: God, it was offensive.

ALICE: "You met with a representative of the union on Valley Day Care premises."

BONNIE: That was a lie.

ALICE: (at the same time) Which was a lie. It talked down to us like we were in kindergarten—"Mommy and daddy are going to take better care of you, you've been bad and silly and ..."

DIANE: It was a classic union-busting letter actually.

ALICE: Every time I think about it I get mad.

CARLA: It convinced me about the union.

DIANE: At that point we'd already signed cards.

CARLA: When?

DIANE: It was during the waiting period.

BONNIE: We had to go out in the hallway to sign the card and come back into work.

CARLA: Then there was that meeting that I missed.

ALICE: In February.

CARLA: She said we weren't going to get paid.

EVELYN: That was when?

DIANE: Well which maternity leave were you *(Carla)* on?

CARLA: Nathan. February '81.

DIANE: That's when we didn't get paid.

BONNIE: Then Laura decided she wouldn't be in the union.

EVELYN: Well—

BONNIE: She didn't join.

EVELYN: She couldn't join. She was the supervisor.

DIANE: She was making decisions about hiring and firing—

EVELYN: She couldn't be in the union even if she wanted to.

ALICE: She was still supportive.

DIANE: Oh, yeah.

CARLA: Oh, definitely.

BONNIE: On the other hand, she had her kids in the day care.

ALICE: When you think about that—like I can't afford to work because I can't pay to keep my kids in care and she got free day care for two kids. Plus the car.

BONNIE: It was sort of, "The union is good for you, not for me."

EVELYN: She couldn't join.

ALICE: But all the teachers signed.

DIANE: I'm still proud of that.

BONNIE: You had to pay a dollar to join. It had to be your own dollar.

ALICE: We went to see Phil at CUPE and he said, "Remember, you've got to sign fifty-five percent of the people working at Valley, fifty percent isn't enough, you need fifty-five—just to be safe." Diane says, "Okay." Phil says, "How many have signed cards so far?" And Diane goes, "Oh. A hundred percent."

DIANE: He was shocked.

ALICE: We just smiled.

CARLA: Well, no one thought there'd be a problem, it wasn't—

BONNIE: It wasn't until we got the letter that we realized—

DIANE: We knew before that. That's why we had to keep signing the cards a secret.

BONNIE: I didn't know it was a secret.

DIANE: Cindy told us, "Don't do it on the premises. Do it on your own time."

ALICE: And Laura made us be careful.

CARLA: I never understood why.

BONNIE: No one ever told me it was a secret.

ALICE: Well, did you sign cards in the lunchroom?

BONNIE: No.

ALICE: It was always off the premises. *(to Diane)* I remember you and me walking home that night, by the Catholic school.

CARLA: You got her in the back yard.

DIANE: I made her pay me a dollar.

ALICE: And I remember saying, "Okay, but I'll never go on strike."

DIANE: And I said, "Yeah, well don't worry about it."

EVELYN: I said it up until she held back the cheque.

ALICE: We went to that meeting with Cindy and Anne and—

BONNIE: Who were Anne and Cindy?

ALICE: They were—they worked at a co-op day care and they helped us and they were really involved in the union and they—anyway, we went for a drink downtown to a sidewalk cafe.

DIANE: We were excited at being downtown.

ALICE: It was—

DIANE: Romantic.

ALICE: We were only nineteen and we were—

DIANE: I was twenty.

CARLA: I was—

ALICE: We were really—

BONNIE: I was twenty-one.

CARLA: I was—

ALICE: We were really—

BONNIE: No. I was twenty, too.

DIANE: You were twenty-two?

EVELYN: Who cares?

BONNIE: I was also twenty.

CARLA: I was twenty—

EVELYN: Who cares?

ALICE: We were really young. And we were excited. Not about, "We're going to get that bitch," or, "We're going to get paid more." We were excited about, "We'll get more funding for day care."

EVELYN: And then when we went to that labour conference in Toronto.

DIANE: One woman said, "You do work women have traditionally done for nothing and that's where you're starting from." I thought, "That's why we all think it's worthless."

ALICE: It started out by us saying, "It's good for day care and maybe Irene can lobby and get us more money," and by the end it was, "We're worth a lot more, we're not five-year-olds, we don't need her to talk down to us. We don't need a slap in the face like that. We don't need to be two years behind everyone else. We—"

DIANE: And, "We need a union cause it's our only way to talk to her."

CARLA: What started me off was when we read the standard CUPE agreement—that part about not discriminating.

DIANE: We give it to Irene—We thought, "Who could object to that?"

EVELYN: "Article 1, denied. Article 1A, denied."

CARLA: I looked at that and I thought, "They're not even willing to say that they won't discriminate against us."

ALICE: Mel said—

EVELYN: Who's Mel?

ALICE: Mel was Irene's husband. He said in negotiations, "We don't want guys coming in here dressed in drag, you know."

BONNIE: He said that?

ALICE: Right at the negotiating table.

EVELYN: I couldn't believe it.

ALICE: I started to realize what little scuzzes they thought we were.

DIANE: Irene set that strike up. She set herself up to put herself out of business. She did it. We didn't do it.

EVELYN: First she fought recognition ...

CARLA: We had recognition then. Cause I was married in '78.

DIANE: They'd already approved the catch-up. We better go over that.

EVELYN: The Region agreed that in three years we'd be paid the same as Regional workers.

DIANE: One-third every year.

EVELYN: Until we caught up.

ALICE: That's why it was called a "catch-up."

DIANE: What happened was the co-ops went ahead and—

BONNIE: They got it.

DIANE: They got the first 33 percent.

BONNIE: Everybody got it.

ALICE: Except us.

BONNIE: It wouldn't have cost her one cent.

ALICE: The co-ops just asked for it and if Irene asked for it we would have got it too.

BONNIE: It wouldn't have cost her one cent.

EVELYN: And the next year she asked for it and she just kept it.

ALICE: She kept it.

BONNIE: I couldn't believe it.

EVELYN: She just kept the money.

BONNIE: I couldn't believe it.

EVELYN: I still can't.

DIANE: That was it.

ALICE: That's when I first said I'd go on strike.

EVELYN: "Let's walk."

DIANE: I wanted to walk out right then.

CARLA: She was saying she can't pay us more because the money is just not there and meanwhile she had a car, maid, groceries—

BONNIE: Cars? Fleets.

CARLA: All bought through the business.

ALICE: We found out other day care centres didn't have photocopying machines, or full-time secretaries, or executive secretaries, they didn't have a rented apartment, or a suite of executive offices.

CARLA: And she's still saying, "Oh, I'm not making a profit."

ALICE: It was pure spite on her part.

BONNIE: Yeah.

EVELYN: "These are my slaves," and—

BONNIE: "No one will tell me—"

EVELYN: *(at the same time)* "No one's going to tell me what to do."

BONNIE: She could have gotten the money from the Region.

ALICE: All she had to do was ask.

BONNIE: She wouldn't have had to cut her own income.

ALICE: It was pure spite.

EVELYN: And then she got the money from the Region she didn't give it to us.

ALICE: She just kept it.

BONNIE: I couldn't believe it.

EVELYN: I still can't.

BONNIE: That was it.

ALICE: We had to fight like dogs. We had to go in one by one and launch a grievance.

BONNIE: We all had to go in and say, "I grieve."

CARLA: The whole time this is going on we've got sixty-four children to look after.

BONNIE: And we're all crying.

CARLA: Going in that office to launch my grievance.

BONNIE: We're all crying.

DIANE: I try to remember that now, when I'm trying to get women to sign grievances, how painful it can be.

BONNIE: Laura sitting at her desk and crying while we read the grievance.

CARLA: Then Irene said she didn't get money.

ALICE: That was just shit.

CARLA: She said there was a problem at the bank.

BONNIE: *(to Diane)* Then she came right out and told you on the phone that we weren't going to get paid.

ALICE: And we're going: "She can't do this. It's against the law."

DIANE: I was sitting in her office going, "Irene, I need that bloody pay cheque. Irene, you can't keep my pay cheque, I have rent to pay, I've got medicine to buy. Irene, do you understand, that money is what makes us live. We live on that money, don't you understand what you're doing you stupid bitch, this isn't funny anymore ..."

CARLA: Remember Bonnie was crying and the kids—

ALICE: And the kids saw.

CARLA: We're all having lunch and one of the kids says *(kid's voice)* "Why is Bonnie crying?" *(adult's voice)* "She doesn't like rice."

EVELYN: We finally got the money.

BONNIE: I had mine framed. A framed photocopy.

DIANE: I still think we did a damn good job with the kids. We'd run into the cupboards and we'd go—where else did we go?

BONNIE: To the bathroom.

CARLA: We turned the water on so they wouldn't hear.

BONNIE: And that day we sat in the staff room and ate four-and-a-half dozen chocolate chip cookies.

EVELYN: We were in a legal strike position and we're being told, "Don't go yet, don't go yet."

ALICE: And we'd be sitting there and the slightest thing would happen—a light bulb would blow, the toilet'd plug—and we'd go, "That's it. We're out."

EVELYN: We had that petition.

BONNIE: We started talking to parents.

EVELYN: We would stand outside after our shifts—that was our first official contact with parents.

DIANE: There was still a bit of that attitude—we always called the parents, "Mrs this," and "Mr that."

EVELYN: Parents started asking me, "What do you make?"

DIANE: I remember them saying, "You're kidding, aren't you?"

EVELYN: Irene put that letter out where she actually said to the parents, "We have a mortgage to pay on our house. And a maid"—things that didn't make any sense.

ALICE: Any parent who actually met her was immediately on our side.

DIANE: It was the same with the press.

ALICE: She set herself up.

BONNIE: She was a basket case.

CARLA: We did our best at keeping things away from the parents.

ALICE: Until then.

CARLA: "We're professionals."

ALICE: "It's not their problem."

CARLA: "We don't want to bother anybody about it."

ALICE: "We don't want to look greedy."

EVELYN: I remember going to one of the parents' houses for that meeting and seeing how they lived.

ALICE: Oh yeah.

EVELYN: I thought, "Why do I feel sorry for these people?"

CARLA: Not the ones who were subsidized, they were as broke as we were.

EVELYN: The fee payers.

DIANE: And we had mostly fee payers.

EVELYN: Which meant they were making a lot of money—and we're sitting there going, "Oh no, we can't ask you to pay another penny just because we want decent salaries."

BONNIE: That was a bizarre meeting.

CARLA: It was a horrible meeting.

BONNIE: We went outside and we were crying our eyes out.

ALICE: For a change.

BONNIE: And then we had that big meeting at City Hall. We had a great turnout—how many parents were at the meeting?

CARLA: Over a hundred. We were trying to set up the Alternate Care.

DIANE: We had to find space, we had to get a licence, we had to get equipment. I was getting angrier and angrier, and there was a point where I thought, "To hell with the Alternate Care." Cindy or Anne went, "Look, the parents aren't the enemy. If you go on strike without Alternate Care, parents are just going to cross your picket line. You're not going to have the kind of picket line that parents are going to be afraid to cross."

EVELYN: Remember that parent at the meeting, he was dying to be P.T.A. president.

ALICE: With his flip chart and his magic markers.

BONNIE: All of a sudden, they got scared. That this was bad for their kids, that they had to choose between us and their kids.

EVELYN: We were talking about setting up a co-op and that woman stood up and said, "This is communism."

DIANE: We tried to explain—

EVELYN: Parents on the board, and staff on the board—

DIANE: And all the staff paid the same.

BONNIE: All this incredible hostility coming at us.

DIANE: We walked out the door and burst into tears.

ALICE: For a change.

EVELYN: And then the same woman who called us communists came out and went, "That was awful in there. It was like a witch hunt," and we're going, "It was you lady. It was you that started it."

ALICE: The rest of us were in a bar and you guys came in and you looked—

DIANE: They just turned on us.

EVELYN: Everybody was getting uptight and—

DIANE: We thought we deserved a voice in the centre and—

EVELYN: We were trying to reassure parents—there was still going to be qualified teachers and a place for them to take their children. The service would continue—

DIANE: But we would run it as a co-op.

EVELYN: And we'd equalize salaries.

DIANE: "It's communism."

ALICE: The day the strike started—

EVELYN: Not yet.

ALICE: Well, it was still—

EVELYN: We were in a legal position to strike. The Region had withdrawn Irene's purchase of service and in the same motion they said they would give us money for the Alternate Care.

CARLA: We were so excited we screamed.

BONNIE: We were having beans for the fourth day in a row.

CARLA: Days and days and days of beans.

BONNIE: Irene's executive secretary was cooking lunch.

ALICE: She wouldn't talk to us, she just slopped the beans on the table.

CARLA: But the thing that was really sad was that Laura left.

ALICE: Right.

DIANE: She called me into the office and she said she was leaving and I said, "Just a minute," and I went and got Alice.

ALICE: She couldn't handle it.

CARLA: She just left everybody and everything.

ALICE: She just took off.

DIANE: She was trying to justify her position on both sides of the fence and all of a sudden we looked at each other and we went, "She's gone. She's not with us anymore."

ALICE: She was saying, "This is getting too big, it's getting scary." Cindy gave me that book "One Hundred Songs of Protest" and this song was going through my head, "Which Side Are You On?"

CARLA: We were all scared.

ALICE: Terrified.

CARLA: That whole summer they'd been jackhammering the garage next door—

BONNIE: You couldn't see the back of the room.

CARLA: There was cement dust all over the place. We kept saying to Laura, "We're going to lodge a safety grievance if you don't do something." And I thought, "She's letting us down, and she's letting the kids down."

ALICE: The health inspector took one look ...

CARLA: I always admired Laura, she was so strong and confident, but then she got scared.

BONNIE: We were all scared.

CARLA: But we handled it.

DIANE: We were ready.

EVELYN: We trained by picketing the Perley Hospital.

CARLA: My first picket line.

DIANE: It was an illegal strike.

ALICE: And it was pouring rain.

BONNIE: In February.

ALICE: It was freezing cold.

CARLA: My husband came and took pictures.

DIANE: Then Steve and Howard came to that party and totally humiliated us.

ALICE: People were going to jail and—we were standing around the kitchen and—

DIANE: The hospital strike was folding, it was really serious, and we were—

ALICE: They'd been out drinking.

DIANE: And they're going, "It's illegal," and, "Unions are stupid" and "They just want this, they just want that," and I told them in front of everybody to fuck right off. "Fuck off Stephen. Just fuck off." People were in tears, their lives are falling apart, and these assholes are debating whether or not unions should exist.

ALICE: "Do you really think everybody should make the same?"

DIANE: Right. Yeah. That night we started seeing some of the things that were happening in the labour movement, not just in day care.

EVELYN: We realized we were part of a movement.

CARLA: *(to Diane)* I remember you telling me about that woman that was fired four times and me thinking, "Gees, to believe in something that much and she just kept fighting and—"

ALICE: *(to Carla)* You were fired.

BONNIE: What was it? You were on the phone to the—

CARLA: I was with the caterer.

BONNIE: Oh, right. In the kitchen.

CARLA: The staff room.

BONNIE: You were setting up the food for the Alternate Care.

DIANE: On her premises.

CARLA: Irene came in and she was beet-red. The poor guy didn't have a clue what was going on—he was a caterer. She's screaming, "Fired. Fired. Fired."

EVELYN: Then she came flying into—we're all sitting at the lunch tables and she goes, "You're fired. You're fired. You're fired."

CARLA: I said to the caterer, "Um, we'll have to continue this some other time."

ALICE: And in the middle of all this was that extravagant party at Irene's wonderful house.

BONNIE: I put my finger in her carpet and it disappeared.

DIANE: *(to Alice)* Remember on the way to negotiations, Anne and Cindy'd stop at this health food store and buy little bits of food in bags and we'd sit at this huge mahogany table in this ritzy office and we'd go, "Pass the sesame seeds."

ALICE: Sunflower seeds.

DIANE: And Irene didn't come to that one meeting and her husband fell apart. He's going, "Maybe we should just sign this agreement," and "Maybe we should do something to make day care self-sufficient, maybe we could sell light bulbs."

ALICE: He was serious.

DIANE: He's going, "I don't know where it all went wrong," and his lawyer sort of elbowing him and René—the CUPE staff rep, a real character—

ALICE: "Fuck" is in every sentence.

DIANE: We had René with us cause we figured, even Cindy and Anne figured, we needed—

ALICE: We needed René.

DIANE: We needed a strong-arm, someone with experience. Irene's husband's blathering, "I don't know what happened. I don't know where it all went wrong."

ALICE: "You want the day care? Take the day care."

DIANE: "I want this to be over. I want it to end. I don't know what happened. I don't know what went wrong."

CARLA: "Irene never tells me anything."

ALICE: And the lawyer's going—

DIANE: The lawyer says, "Well, uh, it looks like, uh, my client wants to give up. We'd, uh, like to come back tomorrow with some sort of agreement." And I was, like, "Fuck this. It's fucking bullshit.

It's bullshit again." René's going, "Listen to him." I'm going, "This is shit. This is just a tactic. They don't want us to strike. They're stalling. Let's go for it. Let's go for the touchdown." The lawyer comes back and says, "My client wants you to have the day care. He wants to do it amiably." René and I are screaming at each other, he's telling me to fuck off, I'm telling him to fuck off. René says, "We've got to listen to what they're saying. We've got to give this twenty-four hours." And I'm yelling, "No fucking way." Anne and Cindy are trying to calm me down, and we go, "Okay, tomorrow morning." And—

ALICE: The next morning—

DIANE: The next morning—

ALICE: ... we're out at the CUPE office and—

DIANE: We're waiting for the phone call and René picks it up and he listens ... he hangs up ... he says to us ... "They want another twenty-four hours."

ALICE: We look at him. He looks at us. And he goes, "We're pulling the fucking pin." "We're pulling the fucking pin. Boom."

DIANE: We tear back to the day care. Everybody's coming out, everybody's going, "Tomorrow, it's tomorrow."

BONNIE: We're telling the parents—

DIANE: "Tomorrow morning, take your kids to this address. This is it, we're in motion."

ALICE: I was in the centre and I thought, "I'm never going to make it out that door."

BONNIE: I will never forgive you for that. Never. As long as I live.

ALICE: I couldn't, I—

BONNIE: It was the last day before the strike, you guys are all waiting outside, the kids are almost gone and I had to stay until six and you *(Alice)* promised you'd stay.

ALICE: I couldn't.

BONNIE: I begged you.

ALICE: I couldn't.

BONNIE: I hung onto this parent, I begged him—

ALICE: I was walking around, taking down the schedules, routines, everything we'd put up—Irene comes up behind me—"What the hell are you doing?" "Nothing. I'm leaving."

BONNIE: I'm going, "Don't go, Alice. Only ten more minutes."

ALICE: Everyone was gathering outside the door.

BONNIE: I was the only teacher left in the centre. One of the parents came in and I begged him to wait and walk out with me. I couldn't stand it. I couldn't stay by myself.

CARLA: It was so intense.

DIANE: We knew at that point we had her by the balls. We had every parent on our side.

BONNIE: I just wanted to be out of there.

DIANE: We'd been like that for a month.

CARLA: I didn't even get to be on the picket line. I could ring Laura's neck. If she hadn't quit—

ALICE: We're sorry.

CARLA: I'll never forgive myself for agreeing to be supervisor.

ALICE: We're sorry.

CARLA: I didn't want to be at the Alternate Care. I wanted to be on the picket line.

BONNIE: Which you let us know about.

CARLA: I did mention it.

BONNIE: Once or twice.

CARLA: I was seven months pregnant and all I could think about is, "I want to walk that picket line."

BONNIE: Oh, it wasn't that great.

CARLA: Sure.

BONNIE: It was really boring.

EVELYN: We fell asleep all the time.

DIANE: It rained a lot.

EVELYN: It was just, you know, like waiting for the bus.

ALICE: I got blisters on my feet.

BONNIE: Yeah, it was—

DIANE: It was great.

BONNIE: Yeah.

EVELYN: It was exciting—

ALICE: The only thing that rivals the first day of that strike was the birth of both my children.

CARLA: *(to Diane)* And you guys led it.

DIANE: Well—

CARLA: You and Cindy and Anne.

BONNIE: We were all interested, but—

ALICE: A lot of us were interested but people weren't that educated.

CARLA: Like Maggie—what was it?—"Now I understand why it's so important not to cross a picket line, and the next time I go to the Post Office, I'll use the back door."

BONNIE: A lot of us were getting a hard time from our families.

ALICE: Parents, husbands, sisters, cousins—

DIANE: My sister the day care worker who thinks unions are awful and that day care's bad for kids.

BONNIE: My father was a union member and he was on strike once. Except it wasn't their strike, it was another section of the same union. He felt he had no choice—he crossed the picket line and went back to work. Our strike brought up a lot of bad memories for him.

ALICE: My parents thought it was kind of cute. "Oh, she's always been like that."

BONNIE: Ron thought it was cute, at first.

ALICE: Remember he picked us up from some meeting and he's talking about productivity and we're going, "You can't measure productivity with kids, it's not a factory."

DIANE: That's another stage we went through. The whole thing of, "We're different. We're a union, but we're a different kind of union."

EVELYN: "We have a real cause. We're not ordinary union people."

DIANE: "We're like the Teachers' Federation."

CARLA: Remember the pamphlet came out that CUPE did, the one on building better day care?

BONNIE: With the song.

DIANE: The song.

> *(Bonnie sings but mocks the song. Alice joins in forcefully. Bonnie stops singing.)*

BONNIE: "Play fair with day care ..."

ALICE & BONNIE: "Play fair with day care

Someone in the crowd is shouting ..."

ALICE: "Play fair with day care

'One, two, three, four"

BONNIE: Alice.

ALICE: "Who are we for?"

BONNIE: Alice.

ALICE: "Day care, that's us."

CARLA: In that pamphlet—

ALICE: With the song.

CARLA: ... they talked about six centres organized, four were co-ps and two "profit" centres.

BONNIE: I hate that song.

EVELYN: We were cheesed off because they called us "profit centres."

ALICE: I remember, right up until the strike, being cheesed off at the co-ops—we're going through hell and they're just sitting there.

DIANE: Well—

ALICE: We were the black sheep of Local twenty-two-o-four.

DIANE: Well—

BONNIE: They thought we were slowing things down.

ALICE: They didn't have to fight to get what they wanted.

BONNIE: They thought we were holding things back because we couldn't get our contracts signed.

EVELYN: We used to think the people in the co-ops were a lot more political.

BONNIE: It was easy for them.

DIANE: It was easier.

BONNIE: They thought they were more progressive but they never had to fight.

DIANE: I don't know if they thought that.

ALICE: We thought they were.

EVELYN: We thought they were all like Anne and Cindy.

ALICE: And then we found out they watched "Another World" and "General Hospital."

DIANE: There was a sense that the union was only co-ops.

BONNIE: We'd go to their meetings and they'd vote two hundred dollars for such and such a strike in Sudbury.

DIANE: The Local wasn't really organized then. Now we'd get support from the Labour Council, too.

EVELYN: We did get support.

BONNIE: It was more from individuals.

DIANE: We got a lot of support, really.

ALICE: Die-hard trade unionists on the picket line.

DIANE: The Perley Hospital workers.

BONNIE: People used to bring us breakfast and—

ALICE: It just never felt like enough.

DIANE: The day care community gave us equipment for the Alternate Care.

BONNIE: Yeah.

DIANE: We got a lot of help, really.

EVELYN: We did, but—it was our whole lives and we couldn't understand how it might not be somebody else's.

ALICE: I remember people'd come to the picket line for an hour and they'd say, "We're going to a movie tonight and I'd think, "How can they go to a movie?" One time, I was on the picket line with Vivian, and these guys from the—International Socialists—

DIANE: I.S.

ALICE: ... tried to sell us their newspaper and Viv says, "You mean you're here to take money from us and we're on strike?" Poor Viv. I got her run over by a truck.

BONNIE: That was terrible.

ALICE: Irene had that scab working for her, he was seventeen, he was driving around trying to scare us. He was coming fast out of the parking lot and Viv wanted to run. I grabbed her arm and said, "We're going to walk. We have a right to be here." And he hit her. He hit her right in the shoulder. I felt really awful. It should have been me that got hit.

ALL: Yeah.

EVELYN: We used to do great stuff on the picket line.

BONNIE: Alice and I dressed up as clowns.

ALICE: Not me.

BONNIE: I thought it was you.

EVELYN: She didn't have to dress up.

DIANE: Marion Dewar was mayor—she really supported us.

ALICE: And that big wig from CUPE—

EVELYN: Grace Hartman.

ALICE: She came out.

DIANE: CUPE was really proud of us. We were living proof that unions weren't always just out for more money.

EVELYN: We weren't.

DIANE: We might have had things like benefits done for us except we were pretty rich for people on strike. We had all the salaries from the Alternate Care.

EVELYN: We better go over that.

DIANE: Well, we were getting money from the Region and we hired a bunch of people to work in the Alternate Care. We split the money with them and—

CARLA: Those of you who were on the picket line.

BONNIE: It wasn't much.

DIANE: No. Actually Stephen and I were really broke. He was still a student.

ALICE: He made you that lunch pail.

DIANE: For my birthday. It said, "On Strike, D.M." He cut the letters out. This little worker's lunch box.

ALICE: Stephen was honestly trying to understand why you felt the way you did. He'd say, "Well, I've gone to school for 'x' number of years and I should make more than people who cook in day care," and we'd go, "No, they work hard, too."

DIANE: He really struggled with it.

ALICE: He was going for his Ph.D. in engineering. Electronics.

DIANE: Electromagnetism. I remember cause I typed the fucking thesis. Stephen used to say to me, "You used to be such a nice day care worker. You loved the children and now you're angry," and he couldn't understand it. He was insecure. He was a student and I was working.

ALICE: He needed your money.

DIANE: It's true.

ALICE: She'd stay up all night and type his papers for him.

DIANE: I worked like a dog. I don't know how I did it.

ALICE: Well, you didn't make it to work in the morning.

DIANE: There was that big rally at City Hall and Anne picked me up in the car and said to me, "You're going to make a speech." It was like—"What? Are you crazy?" I was the kid in school who passed out when she had to read a poem out loud. Stephen came and heard my speech—he says, "I'm so proud of you." But when the phone rang for the thirty-fifth time that night, it would be like, "You love the union more than you love me." He was afraid of the change in me.

ALICE: I got a call in the middle of the night. "I've left Stephen."

DIANE: I'd just come back from Grenada—I got sent on that solidarity trip—I was wearing my "Long Live the Revolution" T-shirt. I was like—"Oh, my God. I've been to Grenada."

ALICE: He got really scared. "Holy shit, she's a communist."

DIANE: We'd been out in this bar—it was about one-thirty—and Alice and I were talking about meeting the next morning at a demo about Nicaragua or El Salvador and Stephen jumps up—"I can't take it. I can't take it. I can't take it." Stephen and I alone were great but out in the world there was no place for us. I felt like it was my fault, cause it was me that changed. I moved out—I moved downtown. I got very sick—I was really poor—it took me a long time to get back on my feet. Then I stayed with him for a week before his defence—to type up his notes and iron his pants and hem his suit and do the slides—I felt like it was my responsibility. Then, when I broached the idea of money, he said, "You want support." I said, "No, I want my turn to go to school." Because that was our plan, that I would go to university after he did. He hated me. He still hates me. He loves me, he hates me. Years later, he called to tell me how he met this women and how great she was—she did the dishes and all those things.

CARLA: I got the guilt trip. "I need you, the kids need you, the dog needs you to come home and feed her." My kids had allergies, they'd be up all night and Bill got really fed up—I'd have to bring the kids to meetings—I remember thinking, "How can I do this to these little babies?" None of you had any kids—you'd all look at me as if to say, "Well, come on." I felt pressure from you guys, I felt pressure from Bill. I'd go to work at seven in the morning. I'd be home at five. I'd get supper ready. Get the kids into bed. I'd get back in the car by eight, we'd work till about three or four in the morning, then I'd drive home, get the kids ready, be back at work for seven, home at five, prepare supper ...

DIANE: The time it took was incredible. Working all day—

EVELYN: And after work, standing outside talking to parents. Organizing the Alternate Care—

BONNIE: Ron and I were planning our wedding—talk about being torn—I felt I had to be with you guys. But I was excited about getting married. I'd be making arrangements for the catering and the invitations—and you guys would laugh at me—

ALICE: We didn't.

BONNIE: You did, and I used to feel really cheated. "Why can't I just get married like a normal woman? Why do I have to be going through all this? I just want to walk into the supermarket like everybody else. I don't want this conflict in my life all the time." But I didn't want it to stop.

EVELYN: I didn't have a relationship then and the strike was my life. And I didn't care about anything else. Except I remember saying to myself, "I have no future. I'm going to work in day care forever and I'm going to be alone forever."

CARLA: It was like a roller coaster ride. Your emotions went up and down—

DIANE: All over the place.

ALICE: My boyfriend—

DIANE: Horst.

ALICE: He tried to be supportive, but he just didn't understand what I was doing. You *(Bonnie)* came into the bar that night crying, and he kept saying, "Why are you doing this to yourself. Is it worth it?"

BONNIE: I'm crying and going, "It's worth it. It's worth it."

ALICE: Through her tears—"It's worth it. It's worth it."

BONNIE: At first Ron thought the strike was so neat and I was so neat and he'd take me to parties and say, "Tell people what you did." Then as soon as we're married, he says, "Don't go to meetings." If I went to a meeting, he was always in bed when I came home, the lights would be out and—

ALICE: Subtle hint.

BONNIE: He's never given himself to anything except me and the kids. There was no way he could understand what it was about.

ALICE: *(to Bonnie)* Your reception couldn't have happened at a better time.

EVELYN: It was sure one hell of a party.

BONNIE: Well, it was right at the end of the strike. It was like a victory party that I happened to get married at.

CARLA: Through that whole time, it was hard on Bill and me but we would never talk about it. There was a strain but I just wanted to be with you guys.

ALICE: We wanted to be together a lot.

CARLA: We needed to be together.

DIANE: It was like we all crossed this bridge and there was no looking back. The night we were at your *(Bonnie)* apartment—you were crying, going, "I'm scared. I don't want to go on strike." Everyone went, "We know. We feel the same way."

CARLA: You try to tell somebody, "This is a big part of me."

DIANE: They can't understand what it means.

ALICE: You'd wake up and your mind'd already be going a million miles an hour.

DIANE: Every day'd be like that, for weeks and weeks.

CARLA: It was the longest six weeks of my life.

BONNIE: I don't even know why we kept picketing.

ALICE: We brought lawn chairs and sat on the lawn with our signs.

EVELYN: It was a stalemate.

DIANE: She knew she was done for.

EVELYN: But she was vindictive.

CARLA: She put that sign on the door—"Gone to Lac Philippe."

ALICE: I forgot about that.

CARLA: She wanted people to think Valley was still operating.

BONNIE: If anyone was going to Lac Philippe, we'd say, "Please keep an eye out for our kids."

DIANE: Then we had to move—twice.

ALICE: Then she gave up.

EVELYN: She didn't give up. She lost her lease.

CARLA: She finally gave up.

BONNIE: We won.

DIANE: We won.

CARLA: We couldn't believe we won.

ALICE: We were so happy.

EVELYN: Then we tried to set up the co-op.

DIANE: That was sad.

CARLA: It's still sad.

EVELYN: We operated under the City of Nepean for a year.

ALICE: We even got incorporated. We had the papers with the seals.

CARLA: Southview Park Co-op.

EVELYN: There were two years when we thought a co-op might happen.

CARLA: Then they said, "The Regional Municipality is taking you over."

ALICE: And we were exhausted and—

BONNIE: Everybody just—

ALICE: ... everybody got comfortable, the energy dissipated. There was that big meeting and they all went, "No way."

BONNIE: Nobody came right out exactly.

ALICE: It was more like, "Well, we get our supplies regularly now, and—"

CARLA: "We have security."

BONNIE: "Everything is going well."

EVELYN: "We're getting our pay cheques."

CARLA: "Why rock the boat?"

ALICE: We cried. We sat there and we said, "Don't do this, don't do this." And they talked about how they get supplies regularly and—

DIANE: "Screw you."

ALICE: "Yeah, screw you. We're supervisors now and we're not going to give it up."

BONNIE: If they were asked, they'd probably say the strike was an unqualified success.

DIANE: And we hired them.

EVELYN: We better go over that.

DIANE: We hired them to work in the Alternate Care.

BONNIE: While we were on the picket line. We thought, "When the strike's over, we'll get our jobs back."

DIANE: Then the Region took over the Alternate Care and these teachers all of a sudden had more seniority than us.

BONNIE: Because the Region considered the work in the Alternate Care for seniority, but not the time at Valley.

CARLA: We had that meeting with people from CUPE five-o-three. One of them said, "You don't want to be in five-o-three. It's too big. You'll get lost."

ALICE: And they told us, "The Region is a shitty employer. You'll lose your seniority."

EVELYN: We were talking about profit day care. Nepean and the Region just wanted to get Irene Logan.

CARLA: Our strike button said, "Profit Day Care Hurts Kids," and it was a big part of the issue for us.

EVELYN: It was more than revenge for us. We didn't want to work for a profit centre, and we never even thought we'd end up working for the Region. We wanted—

CARLA: We wanted a co-operative day care.

ALICE: For two years, we tried.

EVELYN: And then five-o-three took our seniority away.

DIANE: Right. We became a Regional centre, so we automatically became members of CUPE five-o-three.

EVELYN: Instead of twenty-two-o-four.

DIANE: And it was according to five-o-three's regulations that we lost our seniority.

ALICE: At Valley we had better holidays—we had four weeks—

CARLA: Four weeks from day one.

ALICE: At the Region they got four weeks after nine years. Carla and I remember them saying that our seniority would be recognized.

CARLA: I called them—I said, "I'm in my tenth year, I should be getting four weeks." They said, "No agreement was made." I said, "There was an agreement." They said, "No agreement was made."

BONNIE: They just wanted to forget that we were ever different from anybody else.

CARLA: And I just dropped it.

DIANE: You shouldn't have.

CARLA: I was too tired.

DIANE: It opened up my eyes to so many things.

ALICE: There's us and then there's them. Them are the ones that were happy the Region took over.

EVELYN: Still kissing ass.

CARLA: It was so horrible. It was like we fought for so long and then it all ended up—

BONNIE: Then Samantha was made supervisor.

DIANE: It was such a mess.

ALICE: Sam went to Evelyn and asked her to write that newsletter for the parents.

EVELYN: She told me to—

ALICE: Sam couldn't spell.

EVELYN: I wrote that if parents had any problems, to talk to their children's teachers. It was sent to the Region to be typed, and it came back, "Talk to the supervisor." I signed it "the staff." It came back, "Samantha Broughton."

BONNIE: We knew those kids better than she did and we were always, even at Valley, we were treated with respect. But the other teachers went, "That's okay."

ALICE: "We don't mind."

BONNIE: That policy came down about—"You can't use the TV anymore." Once a week the children'd watch a half hour of Sesame Street while we changed the sheets. Sam comes to us says we're not allowed anymore, and everybody else goes, "Okay," and we go, "Why?"

EVELYN: She'd come out of a meeting and I'd ask, "What happened?" She'd say, "Don't worry about it."

ALICE: She thought we should just say, "Yes, Boss," and we didn't know how to do that anymore.

CARLA: She was my best friend. She was the very first person I called after Nathan was born and I can hardly say her name—we were looking through a photograph album and my husband said, "Who's that holding Nathan?" "Never mind. Turn the page."

ALICE: I hated working there.

BONNIE: So we quit.

ALICE: Not all at once.

BONNIE: *(to Alice)* You left first.

CARLA: I left first.

BONNIE: I mean after that.

DIANE: I left first. I was sick.

CARLA: But you came back.

(Evelyn notices Carla is near tears.)

EVELYN: Carla.

CARLA: I shouldn't have left.

DIANE: It doesn't—

CARLA: If I hadn't left—

EVELYN: It would have happened anyway.

CARLA: I was supervisor and I left.

DIANE: You were having a baby. You couldn't afford to keep working.

CARLA: If I hadn't left, Sam would never have been made supervisor.

DIANE: You didn't have a choice.

CARLA: I had one in day care and one with a babysitter—I couldn't afford it. It would have cost me money to work.

DIANE: We know that.

CARLA: But I shouldn't—

BONNIE: Carla.

CARLA: I didn't want to leave.

BONNIE: We know.

CARLA: I wish I ...

(Bonnie comforts Carla.)

EVELYN: Then Alice left.

ALICE: Then you (Evelyn) and then Diane.

BONNIE: I was the only one left.

EVELYN: For three years we tried to make it work.

ALICE: It changed me permanently. The whole experienced changed me permanently. For some of us it was a turning point—it changed our lives and we see everything through that experience. For other people, it was an episode—it was like watching TV—and sometimes maybe they remember and go, "Oh, yeah."

BONNIE: It changed my life five hundred percent.

ALICE: Even though—well, I'm not involved in much, now. My husband and I talk about getting involved in the environment. But I left in defeat. I'm still recovering.

EVELYN: A lot of times I miss it. I really miss it.

DIANE: I was working with another profit day care, they wanted a union—

ALICE: Yeah, you're still active.

DIANE: It's become a way of life but—it's weird now. I haven't been to a union meeting in four months. Matthew is the most important thing in my life, but sometimes I go, "Is this all I do all day?"

ALICE: There's an adjustment.

DIANE: I'm not doing anything and I'm used to doing all these things.

EVELYN: *(moves off the paper)* I think we're done.

BONNIE: I tried to stay involved in CUPE five-o-three but it's this enormous union, there were all these truck drivers with their cigarettes at the meeting. I just felt like—

ALICE: You don't have a voice.

BONNIE: I went to a union meeting a few weeks ago and the old feeling came back. I thought, "I could do this again if I just had people where I work now." I shouldn't need anybody. I should just do it but it takes so much time. We have two kids. There just isn't the time.

CARLA: It gets harder.

DIANE: It does.

BONNIE: After the strike, I just wanted to have a normal job. Go in and work. Go home.

ALICE: I still look back to those days before the strike and I think, "God. Remember all the fun ..."

CARLA: We had some really good—

ALICE: *(to Carla)* The day you and Evelyn painted yourselves green for St Patrick's Day.

BONNIE: Saying you were leprechauns.

DIANE: With those big green sunglasses.

ALICE: I thought I was going to be sick.

BONNIE: That was at my wedding shower. I have pictures.

ALICE: Oh, God.

DIANE: I keep thinking about our strike bulletins and how much we laughed.

BONNIE: And our breakfasts on the picket line. We had parades and—

ALICE: The songs.

CARLA: Dressing up as clowns.

ALICE: *(sings)* "The parents are behind us, we shall not—"

BONNIE: The big rally.

DIANE: Right.

ALICE: *(sings)* "The union is behind us, we shall not—"

CARLA: And those newsletters were funny.

BONNIE: Oh, yeah. They were good.

DIANE: We had about five ongoing jokes that we always updated in the newsletter.

ALL: *(sing)* "Just like a tree that's standing by the water, we shall not be moved."

(Evelyn moves Alice off the paper.)

EVELYN: We have to get everything off the paper. We have to take the tape off.

(Everyone begins to move the paints, etc., aside. Alice mistakenly starts to remove tape between the sheets of paper.)

CARLA: That rally downtown for paid maternity leave when I was pregnant.

ALICE: They just zoomed in on you.

CARLA: My father saw me on the news. "Was that you dear? What were you doing there?"

EVELYN: *(to Alice)* The tape at the edges. ... Alice—

ALICE: What?

EVELYN: Not that tape.

ALICE: How am I supposed to know?

CARLA: Do we have to wear these? *(the overalls)*

(They remove the overalls.)

BONNIE: Evelyn ...

EVELYN: What?

BONNIE: It's a bit depressing—the story, I mean.

EVELYN: A bit.

BONNIE: Well, if we're making this video to ...

ALICE: I don't think it is. It is a bit, but—I'm not sad about it. I don't regret it all. It was great. It's the best thing that ever happened to me.

BONNIE: I don't either, but—

ALICE: I'm proud of it.

BONNIE: I am, too, but—

CARLA: Anyway, it's what happened.

(Evelyn organizes some of the others to raise the backdrop.)

ALICE: I'd work in daycare again. A permanent substitute position. Or a part-time job like before I had my baby.

CARLA: I'd never work for the Region again.

ALICE: No, in a co-op.

DIANE: Bonnie's going to get the feeling we're all down on Regional centres.

ALICE: They're better than profit centres.

BONNIE: They are—at least they start out to provide quality care for children. There's some problems with the way they deliver it.

ALICE: Some of them.

(The backdrop is raised.)

It's beautiful.

(Five chairs are arranged. Evelyn sets up the camera.)

CARLA: I don't think I'd go back to day care.

EVELYN: I'm going to get my teacher's certificate.

DIANE: Too bad. You look great behind a camera.

BONNIE: I feel guilty sometimes that I'm still in a Regional centre, but I'm not brave enough to start over somewhere else—or to start a co-op.

ALICE: We're not active enough.

CARLA: We got burned out. We got really burned out.

BONNIE: You get to this point where you think there's this fight waiting for me to get into and you just—

ALICE: I guess that's why I'm not active. I'm just not—

DIANE: You'd have to start the whole process.

ALICE: But I'd do it if—if we were still together.

(Evelyn turns on the camera and joins the others in the chairs.)

EVELYN: We're ready.

(pause)

ALICE: I'll start.

(The End.)

About the Author

Arthur Milner is a playwright, theatre director and journalist, and has worked in professional theatre since 1976. He has a long relationship with Ottawa's Great Canadian Theatre Company (GCTC), where he was Resident Playwright and then Artistic Director. His most recent plays are *Facts*, a murder mystery set in the Palestinian West Bank (which opened at GCTC and has been produced in Palestine in Arabic, Istanbul in Turkish, and London); and *Getting to Room Temperature* ("a hard-hitting, sentimental and funny one-person play about dying"). He has taught at universities and worked as a dramaturge across Canada; and is a featured columnist with *Inroads, the Canadian Journal of Opinion*. He lives with his wife, theatre director Jennifer Brewin, in Val-des-Monts, Québec; Toronto, Ontario; or Calgary, Alberta.